CW00556632

STEEL TOWN CRICKETERS

150-odd Years of Motherwell Cricket Club

STEEL TOWN CRICKETERS

150-odd Years of Motherwell Cricket Club

Steve Young
and Graham Robertson

Troubador Publishing Ltd
Unit E2 Airfield Business Park,
Harrison Road, Market Harborough,
Leicestershire. LE16 7UL
Tel: 0116 2792299
Email: books@troubador.co.uk
Web: www.troubador.co.uk/matador

ISBN 978 1805141 211

British Library Cataloguing in Publication Data.
A catalogue record for this book is available from the British Library.

Printed and bound by CPI Group (UK) Ltd, Croydon, CR0 4YY
Typeset in 11pt Minion Pro by Troubador Publishing Ltd, Leicester, UK

Matador is an imprint of Troubador Publishing Ltd

To all those who played for the club, took office, umpired, scored the book, made the teas, drank in the bar or were carried out on a table, totally inebriated …. this book is dedicated to you.

FOREWORD

It began with a phone call from my brother, Grant.

"Stevie's thinking about writing a book to celebrate the club's 150th anniversary."

More than a year later, after copious exchanges of emails and messages, countless hours of research, and drafting and redrafting stories, the book has been written. A book that started life as a 50-page brochure akin to our centenary publication has grown into a hardback tome of over 300 pages! That's inflation for you.

The seeds were planted in The New Century Bar in Motherwell when a group of old cricketers got together to work out the best way of celebrating the occasion. Once upon a time (over 50 years ago!), they were labelled the 'Young Lions' and they would all go on to play an important part in the story of Motherwell Cricket Club.

They're not so young now. More Mufasa than Simba. Let me make the introductions – Steve Young, Grant and Graham Robertson, Jim Bill, Gavin (Speary) Shaw and Jack Kelly.

Over a few beers (well, several) some ideas were floated but, most importantly, everyone was on board. Having established that we couldn't write the book by committee, Steve asked if I would help with the writing.

"No problem! I've a fair idea of what's involved," before realising I had no idea whatsoever. I dread to think of the amount of material that failed the editor's cut and is swirling somewhere up there in 'the cloud'.

The meetings continued every month or so, and quickly our respective roles fell into place. Grant, Jim, Gavin and Jack helped out by undertaking some of the research, providing old photographs and historical records, suggesting ideas for the book and contributing tales of their own cricketing lives. Steve and I, as lead authors, would write up the stories and send them out to the group for approval.

We had a simple but effective system. Steve was in charge of the early historical stuff, sourcing material from the British Newspaper archive, and I would write stand-alone stories and send them to Steve, thinking, *They're really good, he'll enjoy reading them.* And he did, but while I had the knack of writing a good story, Steve was able to embellish it and make it even better.

I've known Steve virtually all of my life but had never regarded him as a wordsmith. Then again, neither had Steve. If you can laugh together, you can work together, and that was the secret ingredient that made us such a good team. It's been great fun.

A big shout out goes to staff at the Heritage Centre in Motherwell – the kindness and assistance shown to our research team over the last year has been second to none. Thanks also to the Motherwell Times, Wishaw Press and Hamilton Advertiser for their permission to use their newspaper content. And to the publishers at Matador for helping to keep a couple of novice writers on the right track.

Our gratitude goes to our much sought-after snapper, Craig

Young. Whether taking photographs or making old photographs look presentable, the quality of all the images in this book look a whole lot better, thanks to Craig.

There you have it – a brief summary of how our book was conceived and delivered. I hope you get as much pleasure out of reading it as we have had writing it.

Graham Robertson

Gavin Shaw, Steve Young, Jack Kelly, Graham Robertson and Grant Robertson (inset: Jim Bill)

This book has been written on a not-for-profit basis. Any donations or monies raised will be used for the benefit of the game of cricket in Motherwell.

Introduction

If you were to stop someone in the street and ask them about cricket in Motherwell, chances are you'd get a raised eyebrow, a quizzical expression, a shake of the head. The idea of a cricket club being based in a town more associated with iron and steel and football – well, for many people, it's just incongruous.

Motherwell Cricket Club, it doesn't fit the mould. And that's what makes our story, our survival against the odds, so interesting. Here we are, 150 years old, one of the town's oldest institutions.

Formed bang in the middle of Queen Victoria's reign, we've seen off two World Wars, two pavilion fires, Spanish flu and coronavirus, and lots more in between, and we're still here. A century and a half of ups and downs, uninterrupted, sometimes thriving and popular, other times anonymous and barely alive.

There have been several occasions when the life support machine might have been switched off, but there's a dogged determination about Motherwell's cricketing fraternity. Our survival instincts have seen us through some dark times. When other clubs have passed away, we've pulled through – 150 not out.

There have also been some great times. When you read about our heroic victories over some of Scotland's biggest clubs, you might get the idea that we scaled these heights year in, year out. Such thoughts would be misleading. We've conveniently glossed over all the drubbings we suffered along the way, defeats that only served to make our occasional successes all the more sweet.

And that's the wonder of Motherwell Cricket Club. We're not a big name, our trophy cabinet is not bulging with silverware, we don't grab many headlines – and yet the club has given years of pleasure and joy to the thousands of players lucky enough to have donned the whites, and countless others who have followed our fortunes or attended our dinners.

Our story is told in three parts, in 50-year chunks, followed by reminiscences that bring back the great times, and the wonderful characters we played with.

Reaching Our First 50: There's the history of our formation in the 1870s, borrowing heavily from early editions of The Hamilton Advertiser and The Motherwell Times. We learn of Victorian promenades at the cricket field, of the move to Lord Hamilton's Dalzell estate, of police controlling thousands of rival fans, and of the club's struggles during the Great War.

Approaching Our Century: Those were the halcyon days of our cricket club, beginning with the title-winning teams of the '20s and ending with the title-winning teams of the '60s. Our 1973 centenary brochure contained first-hand accounts from legendary figures like Bill Jardine, Professor William Barclay and R K Hinshalwood Jnr, and we hear their voices once more to build a picture of Motherwell's glory years.

Pushing On To 150: From those who have worn the club colours over the past 50 years, we hear their highlights and lowlights and magical memories on and off the field. During this period, the club had to rise, not once but twice, from clubhouse ashes at Home Park. Determination prevailed over despair as we followed a nomadic trail, which would ultimately lead to Dalziel Park. Yes, from Dalzell to Dalziel!

The Young Lions: A bunch of promising junior cricketers started their love affair with Motherwell Cricket Club over 50 years ago, and now they've decided to write a commemorative book. Their qualifications to do so? None, only that they're still alive. We dig deeper into their stories – they're a strange lot.

Extras: Finally, we throw in a miscellany of out-takes that the editor couldn't handle, cuts that should have remained on the director's floor. Think of the sketches at the end of *Toy Story* or *Shrek* but not as funny, or Dennis Norden with *It'll Be Alright on the Night* but not as clever, and you'll get the drift. In truth, these memoires tell you more about Motherwell Cricket Club than any scorecards or statistics.

The cast of our story over 150 years are too numerous to mention, and we can only apologise for unconscious omissions. Equally, if we have offended anyone or any club on the bumpy ride through our history, please take it as a badge of honour and a token of affection. You have helped to add colour and humour to our turbulent tale to make the club what it is.

Scoring Our First 50

Getting off the mark is often the most difficult run to score, and that's how it was with Motherwell Cricket Club. It was an uncertain beginning and before getting our innings established we lost our way in the teens, but survived, benefiting from a sympathetic umpiring decision. After that, we were in full flow until the Great War intervened. These were hard times, but we persevered and reached our half century. But why did no-one applaud?

Our 150th!!!

The centenary year of 1973 – we remember it well.

Boundary boards were produced – 1873 to 1973 – and the players had centenary badges sewn onto their sweaters in club colours, maroon and sky blue. A centenary tie was commissioned, with 1873 printed below our MCC logo. We played a commemorative game, when Brian Adair brought his Bats team through from Edinburgh to play at Home Park, a side that included Ronnie Chisholm, George Goddard and Hamish More, the great and the good of Scottish cricket.

We were all very proud of Motherwell Cricket Club, a club who played its cricket under the radar, scoring its very own century. The provost even laid on a civic reception for us, and there was a free bar – we remember that, vaguely.

And a centenary brochure was printed and distributed to … well, anyone who was interested. It was a great success. It had a tribute from a former prime minister, Sir Alex Douglas Home, who had played against Motherwell in his youth, and an article written by Professor William Barclay, an academic theologian who was a regular on the television in those days – he had played with Motherwell in the 1920s.

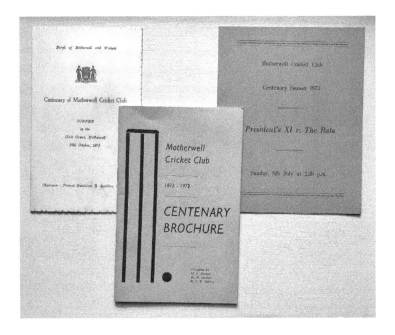

Famous games and great names of the previous 100 years were remembered in the brochure, and there was a potted history of the club, with photographs of Motherwell teams winning trophies. Many of the old stagers in 1973 could tell stories of playing cricket after the Great War and so, piecing it all together, we could build a wonderful picture of the club through the years.

Historical Records

Going further back, detail was a bit patchy and, of course, photographs were scarce. The authors had done well to spot the origins of the club in 1873, the earliest mention they could find of a cricket club in the town. The centenary brochure pointed to a listing that appeared in the Motherwell Almanac of 1874, along with local businesses, organisations and sporting clubs. As the book was printed the year before, logic had it that Motherwell Cricket Club must have been around in 1873.

The club listed in the Almanac was actually Motherwell Britannia, but that was ok. Local press cuttings confirm some name changes over the first couple of decades until the club adopted the simpler Motherwell Cricket Club in 1892. Same club, same players. The brochure had established the lineage, so they could say with confidence that Motherwell had an uninterrupted history dating back to 1873.

Job done! And now, 50 years after the publication of our centenary brochure, we celebrate the 150th anniversary of our foundation.

Or maybe not!

Back in 1973, the authors of the centenary brochure didn't have access to the internet or digital newspaper archives with search engines. Because, if they had, they'd have spotted that cricket was being played in Motherwell in the 1860s!

So where does that leave us? Months of research and deduction now allows us to show our evidence trail and paint a more accurate picture of the early days when our club was formed, and from this, we can conclude that in 2023, Motherwell Cricket Club is … 150-odd years old.

So what do we do? Wait for the 200-year celebration? Will the club still be going strong? Well, *we* certainly won't! After a bit of head-scratching, we reached a positive conclusion: if our club is even more historic than we thought it was, then that's even more worthy of celebration!

The Formative Years

The first mention of cricket in Motherwell was in June 1864, when The Motherwell Iron Works Victoria Cricket Club travelled to take on the might of Holytown Alexandra. The Hamilton Advertiser reported that the 'weather was all that the keenest cricketer could desire'. Motherwell 77 all out, and Holytown 79 for 9, a one wicket defeat.

Not bad for your first ever game. You wonder if there were games played prior to this encounter that went unreported, but regardless, cricket in Motherwell was off and running. The names of Lowe, Evans and the Jarvis brothers featured prominently in that Holytown game, and would continue to do so for several years to come.

Motherwell Victoria

By 1865, the name was shortened, thankfully, to Motherwell Victoria, and we have scorecards for two more games, and two more defeats – to Hamilton (54 runs v 27 runs) and to Wishaw (85 v 48). But Victoria turned the tables on Holytown (51 v 33) and travelled to Airdrie and won (48 v 35), but it was reported that 'the supporters were so unruly during the evening that the game had to be stopped more than once to clear the ground for the players'. This is more like it!

Who else did they play against? There were a number of teams in Coatbridge, Carfin, Newmains, Carluke and Hamilton. They also played some teams in the east end of Glasgow and sides made up of soldiers stationed in camps, usually at Hamilton Palace Grounds.

Victoria wasn't the only team playing in Motherwell in the late 1860s. Motherwell Albert, probably attached to the Albert Box, Nut and Rivet Works in Park Street, flourished for a couple of years. Craigneuk Glencairn was also a thriving club in Shieldmuir. Cricket was the fashionable sport in town and it had lots of players and followers.

Looking at the scores in those early games, it might strike you that the batting wasn't very good, and maybe it wasn't, but we have to consider the playing surface in those years. The game was commonly played on a farmer's field or on any sort of parkland that was relatively flat, so the batsmen of the 1860s had a decent excuse.

A more recent parallel would be the surfaces used for schools cricket in the 1970s. If you ever had the misfortune of facing Wishaw High's lethal fast bowler, Amjad Hassan, on the school's infamous coconut mat, you'll have an understanding of the challenges faced by Motherwell's early cricketers.

Over the next 5 or 6 years, Motherwell Victoria went from strength to strength, fielding two teams, playing and beating Glasgow sides and travelling to Edinburgh to take on Royal High at Holyrood.

Motherwell Britannia

With the advent of the '70s, things changed and a new name appeared on the schedule of cricket fixtures. In 1872, we

find a report on the Annual General Meeting of a club called
Motherwell Britannia – and, with the election of President,
Secretary, Treasurer and an Executive Committee, as well as
Captain and Vice-Captain, it looks like a properly established
club. It's interesting to note that these office-bearers are *re-
elected*, suggesting the club's existence in 1871.

> *Cricket Club – The annual general meeting of the
> Motherwell "Britannia" Cricket Club was held in the
> Volunteer Inn on Saturday last, when the following office-
> bearers were re-elected for the ensuing year:– Captain,
> John Evans; Vice-Captain Wm Davies; Treasurer John
> Downs; Secretary George Pettigrew with three of a
> committee, Messrs J Morton, B Morton, and D Stevenson.*
> Hamilton Advertiser, March 1872

And, sure enough, we find a result listed in 1871 when
Motherwell Britannia lost to The Crown, a Hamilton team.

> *Cricket – Britannia (Motherwell) v Crown (1st Eleven)
> – This match was played on the ground of The Crown on
> Saturday last, and the result was in favour of The Crown.
> Scores:– Britannia 24; Crown 33.*
> Hamilton Advertiser, July 1871

But their fortunes improved and, unlike the other cricket teams
in Motherwell, Britannia was here to stay. As Britannia's star
began to rise, Victoria's began to fade. The games reported in
1872 suggest a changing of the guard – Motherwell Albert was
long gone, and by 1873 we hear nothing more of Motherwell
Victoria.

In piecing together the history and timeline of our club,
it's plain sailing after 1872. Motherwell Britannia would drop

'Britannia' to become Motherwell CC in 1875, only to add 'Trinity' in 1887 and then drop it again in 1892. We are directly descended from these clubs – the only change to Motherwell CC was the suffix, which ultimately disappeared.

But now the big question: can we claim our history from Motherwell Victoria as well, thus giving Motherwell Cricket Club a foundation date of 1864?

There's no doubt that as one name faded, the other rose to prominence. We can also identify the transfer of players and officials from one club to another. In the list of Britannia office-bearers from the 1872 AGM, the names Evans and Downs had also appeared for Victoria in the 1860s. And Britannia ended up playing at the Victoria ground at Milton Street.

But is it the same club? Did Victoria become Britannia? It all comes to a head in 1872, and from that year, we have a list of cricket results. Here is an extract.

MOTHERWELL VICTORIA v SPRINGBURN, GLASGOW – Played at Motherwell, but owing to unpropitious weather, was drawn. Motherwell went 1st to bat and scored 63 for the loss of seven wickets. W Evans contributed 23 – not out.

MOTHERWELL BRITANNIA v DELLBURN CC – A match between these clubs took place in the field of the latter on Saturday, when Dellburn were victorious by 3 runs and 3 wickets to fall.
Hamilton Advertiser, July 1872

From this, it's clear that Motherwell Victoria and Motherwell Britannia (and Motherwell Dellburn, for that matter) co-existed and are different teams, local rivals vying for supremacy in the town. We also know from the 1874 Motherwell Almanac that

Britannia were still playing at Low Motherwell Farm in 1873, not Milton Street.

We now have a better understanding of our origins. Victoria folded after the summer of 1872, and several of their players joined Britannia, who moved to Victoria's former Milton Street ground a couple of years later. We can therefore conclude that, although cricket in Motherwell can be traced back to 1864, our club was formed in 1871, when Motherwell Britannia took the field against a pub team in Hamilton, and got beat.

It looks like, in 2023, we're actually 152 years old ... and that's even better than 150!

Our Founding Fathers

When we look at Motherwell in the 19th century, the town grew from a population of less than 1,000 (mostly farm workers and weavers) to around 15,000 by 1880, driven mostly by the influx of iron workers and coal miners from England, Ireland and Wales, as well as from other parts of Scotland. The vast majority of people in Motherwell were incomers – imagine the smorgasbord of accents you would hear around Motherwell Cross!

The rapid population growth had been triggered by the arrival of the railway and the growth of heavy industry. The ironworks were the largest in Scotland, and growing. Motherwell was a boom town, a bit like the Yukon without the gold.

We know that cricket first took root in the town in the 1860s. How did the sport become established, and who were the men who first played cricket in Motherwell? We are now able to identify the pioneers who introduced this new sport to the town and made it even more popular than quoiting.

The first clue lies with the 1864 team, Motherwell Iron Works Victoria Cricket Club. Unsurprisingly it was a works team based in the Milton Street area of town, and their cricket field was in a park adjacent to the works. The president and office bearers of the club came from the management and the players from the workforce.

But it's Motherwell Britannia that most interests us, and reports in the Hamilton Advertiser help us to identify the key individuals from some of the AGMs of the early 1870s.

1872 – Captain John Evans, Vice-Captain William Davies
1874 – Captain Sam Downs, Vice-Captain John Evans
1875 – Captain Benjamin Evans, Vice-Captain Edward Downs

Two surnames feature large in these Britannia elections – Downs and Evans. It seems likely that they came from the same families and, if we can look into the lives they led, we can get a better understanding of the players who first picked up a bat in the name of Motherwell Cricket Club.

Downs Family

Samuel Downs and, later in the decade, his brother Edward Downs, were Motherwell Britannia captains in the 1870s, and John Downs was treasurer for a time. From the census taken around that time, we discover that John was the father and Edward and Samuel the eldest sons of the family. All three were steelworkers, described as 'iron rollers'.

John Downs came from St Martin, Shropshire, and married Mary Harris in Wrexham, Wales, where Edward and Samuel were born. The growing Downs family then followed a circuitous route looking for work, spending time in Belfast and Bothwell until they eventually found what they were looking for in Motherwell in 1860. They settled in the steel town, and descendants of the Downs family continue to live in the area to this day.

John Downs had 7 children with Mary, and when she died in 1863, he married Ann Cullan and had a further 5 children. They were housed in 204 Milton Street, and it's fair to say that conditions would have been rather cramped in a small home built to accommodate the iron workers.

Their home was very close to the Victoria Iron Works and cricket field, and sure enough, the brothers played for Victoria in the 1860s, with Samuel winning the Best Batter award and Edward winning the cricket ball throwing competition on the day of the promenade. Of greater significance in the history of Motherwell Cricket Club, the Downs family made the leap to Motherwell Britannia in 1871 and were founder members.

Evans Family

The 1871 census shows the Evans family were living in East Milton Street and were also employed in the iron works. Parents John and Ann were in their 40s, Benjamin was 24, John 19 and William 16.

They had 3 rooms, a bigger home than most, reflecting John Evans' status as a Forge Manager. The census also shows that most of the family were born in England and further investigation tells us that they came from Shropshire – Dawley, to be precise.

They moved up to Scotland in the mid-1850s and spent time in Glasgow, where young William was born (at last, a Scotsman!), before finding work in Motherwell. It sounds very similar to the path travelled by the Downs family.

The Evans boys featured for Motherwell Victoria in the 1860s. Benjamin won the Best Bowling prize and was runner-up to Edward Downs in the cricket ball throwing contest. Young William also gets a mention, top scoring for the team. John and Benjamin would go on to captain the Motherwell Britannia side in the 1870s.

It's tempting to suggest that the Downs and Evans families might have known each other before their cricketing days. The fact that the fathers, John Downs and John Evans, started their lives in the same English county and ended their lives in the same Lanarkshire town adds credence to the suggestion, but their beginnings in Shropshire were far apart. (They didn't have Google maps in those days, but if they did, they would have known it was an 11-hour walk from St Martin to Dawley.)

Were there any indigenous Scots in the early Motherwell teams? The vast majority of the population were incomers, and if we look again at the 1871 census above, we can see that most of the Evans family's neighbours were occupied by English-born iron-workers. Sure enough, newspapers of the time refer to the Milton Street area as the 'English colony'.

In press cuttings of the mid-1870s, a few cricketers in the Motherwell team get a regular mention beyond the brothers Evans and Downs. Oliver Summers was born in Staffordshire; Benjamin Morton was born in Motherwell but to English parents; and finally we find George Pettigrew, born in Glasgow to Glaswegian parents.

Even if we wind the clock forward a decade to the 1880s, we find William Roebuck from Yorkshire and David Griffiths from Birmingham – both played for Dalziel Star before joining Motherwell. So it does look like the early years of our club were dominated by English and Welsh workers with a passion for cricket.

So there's little doubt about the founding fathers of our cricket club. Like the Downs and Evans families, many workers in the 1860s and 1870s were recruited from the Shropshire and Staffordshire iron works to bring their skills to Motherwell, and it's no surprise that they would bring with them their enthusiasm for the game of cricket.

Growing Pains

From the mid-1860s to the mid-1870s, cricket was the 'in thing', the new fad. Club memberships grew year on year, and the people of the town were keen to learn about the festivities around the cricket clubs.

Work teams were formed, men wanting to try their hand at this fashionable new sport, fuelled by an influx of workers from England and Wales arriving in Motherwell to gain employment in the town's burgeoning iron and steel industry. Some would already have had cricket in their blood.

The Social Scene

Annual General Meetings were always accompanied by dinner and entertainment, usually in The Volunteer Inn, The Masonic or The Railway Tavern. One report in the Hamilton Advertiser talked of a *'conversazione and assembly ... where a select and fashionable company of cricketers and their friends met to spend the evening ... The Quadrille Band played and dancing was kept up till the early hours'*.

It sounds a cracking night out.

They would organise gala concerts to raise funds and entertain the citizens of the town, and of course, there was the Grand Match and promenade to open the cricket season. Gentlemen were charged sixpence and there was no charge for the ladies. They would put on their best frock and head for the cricket ground, a bit like a Motherwell version of the debutante ball. It attracted hundreds – more music, more dancing, more late nights!

MOTHERWELL CRICKET CLUB
THE ANNUAL GRAND MATCH and PROMENADE
of the above club will take place on their field, off Muir Street, on Saturday, 1st July. Wickets to be pitched at One o' Clock, promenade at Four.
The Cleland Brass Band, in Highland Costume, will be in attendance.
Admission – Gentlemen 6d; Ladies Free.
Hamilton Advertiser, 1876

This advert states 'off Muir Street' here, but in other press cuttings, the location of the ground is shown as Milton Street. Both are still in existence today, so we can position the cricket field fairly accurately somewhere near the junction of the two streets.

The idea of music and dancing and ladies in their finery paints an idyllic picture of life in Victorian Motherwell, until we remember that this part of Motherwell was where the iron works was situated. So the promenade would take place against a background of smoke belching out of the industrial chimneys, noxious smells polluting the air and the noise emanating from neighbouring factories. But still…

Then, after the fanfare that greeted the arrival of cricket in Motherwell, the noise began to fade.

Changing Fashions

Most of the clubs that sprang up during the 1860s disappeared, leaving Motherwell Britannia, our legacy club, to carry the torch. Motherwell Dellburn and Craigneuk Glencairn kept going for a few more years, and some new names get a mention in the local papers, like Dalziel Star, Motherwell Thistle and Cleekhiminn Calderside, but their existence was fleeting.

For the next decade or so, the coverage dried up. Motherwell Cricket Club was still going – we see an occasional fixture list, an odd result or some office bearers voted in at an AGM – but gone were the halcyon days when cricket was the beating heart of the town's sport. A report of the club's AGM in 1884 stated that, although they had had a successful season in terms of victories, they had only played 7 games and there was a shortage of players.

There was a new kid in town. Football!

In 1872, the first Scotland v England game was played in Glasgow, ironically on a cricket pitch in Partick. Later in the decade, we find football being played in Motherwell, with two teams featuring prominently. Glencairn was founded in 1877 and Alpha in 1881, clubs that would ultimately merge to form Motherwell FC in 1886.

The football club moved to their Fir Park home in 1895, but before then, Alpha played at 'the splendid cricket field at The Meadows'. These footballers had not only stolen the headlines, they had also taken over our cricket pitch. You can imagine the competing forces facing off across the park, but there was only one winner, and they had a bigger ball!

Football was more accessible for kids in the steel town, and you see the rise in its popularity all over Scotland. Queen's Park had been going since 1867, Rangers formed in 1872, Hearts and Hamilton Accies in 1874 and, just after Motherwell, Celtic in

1887. For a wee boy growing up around these parts, a cricket bat would not have been top of his Christmas list. Motherwell's cricketers had to try harder to compete with football.

Getting A Better Press

The townsfolk had more papers to read. The Hamilton Advertiser had been going since the 1850s, the Wishaw Press opened its doors in the 1870s, and now the Motherwell Times hit the newspaper stands in the 1880s. To get cricket coverage in these papers was (and still is) a two-way process: the club needed to submit content, and the paper may or may not have been able to find space for it.

There was one letter to the Motherwell Times in 1884 that was quite telling. The writer was pleased to read the report of a local cricket match, but was surprised to find that Motherwell Cricket Club was still in existence. He thought it had gone the way of many before, and was disappointed that no-one had taken the trouble of informing him.

You can't help but feel that the bloke should have found out for himself, but the inference was that Motherwell Cricket Club had stopped promoting the game, given up on trying to compete with Alpha and Glencairn. The letter seems to have had an effect as, soon after, we start to find full scorecards appearing regularly in the Motherwell Times.

Here's the very first scorecard published by the Motherwell Times in 1884. It was an early season game against Dalziel Star, which Motherwell won comfortably in the end due to a last wicket stand. The Dalziel Star name didn't last long after the 1884 season but some of their players (Roebuck, Cameron, Walker and Dolphin) would become a fixture in the Motherwell teams for years to come. Indeed, Neil Cameron was Motherwell Club Captain for several years and Isaac Dolphin was still

MOTHERWELL C.C.		
J. Smith, c Brown, b Griffith,	...	8
T. Fieldhouse, c sub, b Cameron,	...	2
S. Swift, b Cameron, ...	...	0
T. Smith, not out,	...	28
H. Binner, c Knight, b Griffith,	...	6
F. Wilson, b Griffith,	...	6
J. Atheron, b Cameron,		0
J. Binner, c Cameron, b Griffith,		1
R. Cutler, l.b.w., b Cameron,		1
J. Binner, b Cameron, ...		0
W. Mash, b Cameron, ...	...	16
Bye, ...	...	1
		—69

DALZIEL STAR C.C.		
J. Brown, b Fieldhouse,	...	1
W. Roebuck, b H. Binner,	...	2
J. Bottomly, b Binner,	...	1
N. Cameron, b Fieldhouse,	...	9
J. Griffith, b Binner,	...	1
D. Griffith, c T. Smith, b Fieldhouse,	0
G. Walker, not out, ...	11
W. Smith, b T. Smith,	2
I. Dolphin, c T. Smith, b Fieldhouse,	0
T. Pettigrew, b Wilson,	0
M. Knight, c Atheron, b Binner,	0
Byes, ...	4
	—31

associated with the club beyond the Great War.

The Motherwell team in that 1884 match had three Binners in the line-up, and they would be influential in keeping the club going during these difficult times.

Our centenary brochure talked of a fourth Binner. In his younger days, George Binner (pictured) had played for Halifax and Yorkshire. He can't be found in a playing capacity at Motherwell, but he took on a coaching role in the late 1880s and became president soon after.

Talking of cricketing families, there's no mention in the 1884 team of any of our pioneers who were starring for the team less than a decade before. Where were the brothers Evans and Downs? In Victorian times, life was harder and, sadly, shorter. Benjamin Evans had died 2 years before, aged 36, and his brothers John

and William would die in their early 40s. Samuel and Edward Downs lived to the ripe old ages of 48 and 52 respectively. Clearly, cricket was a young man's game!

Road To Recovery

Before things got better, they got worse. In early 1886, we find a most worrying article …

> MOTHERWELL CRICKET CLUB – *We regret to learn that the state of this once flourishing club, notwithstanding their admirable facilities for playing and the almost nominal sum charged for membership, is in anything but a healthy condition. … It is often difficult to raise a team. … The treasurer's report is equally unsatisfactory. Funds are needed, and members, honorary members and intending members should take action at once. The annual general meeting of the club takes place on Friday next.*
> Motherwell Times, January 1886

How had it come to this? The club was teetering on the brink of extinction. Would this rallying cry help to turn things around?

The membership crisis seems to have been averted by the influx of players from Dalziel Star. There is no further mention of Dalziel Star after 1885. The clubs may have agreed to merge and play under the Motherwell name at the Motherwell cricket field, The Meadows. Either way, the town wasn't big enough for the both of them.

The next step was to re-brand as Motherwell Trinity CC. The Trinity name came from the church where many of the cricketers (maybe the Dalziel Star men) worshipped, having moved from England and Wales to Motherwell and joined the Episcopal Church. They had decided that, to save the local cricket club, it needed reinvigoration. This notice planted in the local paper a couple of years later tells us a lot.

MOTHERWELL CRICKET CLUB CONCERT
Since the institution of the Motherwell Cricket Club in 1887 as the Trinity CC, there has been visible in the conduct of all its affairs a higher strata of intelligence and tact than it is customary to find embodied in the management of similar institutions. This admirable trait was again apparent in the arrangements for the concert given under the club's auspices on the evening of Monday last. The company of artistes …
Motherwell Times, 1889

The words used in the press report are fulsome in praise for the Trinity boys and rather derogatory towards their predecessors, but we have to remember who wrote the article – those who had just taken over the running of the club. Self-esteem was not an issue!

It's difficult to say how this change was received by the 'pre-Trinity' Motherwell players. It sounds like a cricketing coup d'état, but it worked. The club survived, and it had a new name, a new direction and certainly a renewed confidence.

If we push the spin to one side, it had the desired effect. The club was saved.

There is a different version of events from Isaac Dolphin, one of the Dalziel Star players who joined Motherwell. Isaac had a long playing career with Motherwell, often captaining the 2nd XI, and in a speech at the 1912 club smoker, he toasted 'our 25th anniversary'. It is clear that he regarded the date of birth of the cricket club as 1887 when the Trinity name was attached!

Granted, Motherwell had been going through a rough patch in 1886, and without the intervention of Isaac and the other Dalziel Star lads, the club may well have folded. But there's continuity in terms of players (like all the Binner boys) and the ground (at The Meadow) and even club captaincy (James Binner was captain both before and after 1887), which shows there was no interruption to the history of Motherwell Cricket Club.

As it happened, the Trinity name would be dropped within 5 years, and by that time, the Duke of Hamilton had invited the cricketers to play on his estate. From there, the club would go from strength to strength.

In 1889, we played a few games at Adders Gill (near the Muirhouse end of the estate) but, by the start of the 1890 season, a new cricket ground had been prepared on a field adjacent to Home Farm.

A rocky road, for sure, but we made it. All of a sudden, cricket was fashionable again – a new Motherwell elite wanted to visit the Duke's lands, walk through the Knowetop gate in their whites, play cricket … and see their name in the Motherwell Times.

The Trinity Years

The name only lasted for 5 years but Motherwell Trinity deserves a special place in the history of the club. They rescued a team that was drifting through the 1880s and managed the successful transition from The Meadows to a new ground in Dalzell Policies in 1890.

We are also indebted to them for their weekly reports in The Motherwell Times during the summer months. It would actually be possible to list the team's full schedule of results over these 5 years, but we won't do that. What we can do is extract the detail to paint a picture of our early days at Home Park.

We adopted the Trinity name in 1887 and, by then, we were the only cricket club playing regularly in Motherwell. The teams may have disappeared, but many of their players kept playing. Motherwell Trinity hoovered up the best talent from other teams.

Our Opponents

There was no league structure, all the games being friendlies arranged by club secretaries. Motherwell Trinity had a loyal band of opponents that they would play home and away every year.

They included Newmains, Cambuslang, Arthur & Co (Glasgow), Civil Service (Govan), Vulcanite and St Andrews (both Edinburgh), St Mirren (Paisley) and several Coatbridge sides. It's evident that Trinity had good relations with Edinburgh club St Andrews, who were invited to play the opening fixture at Home Park on 3 May 1890. It was a closely fought match, with the visitors winning by 6 runs. And we have the scorecard …

MOTHERWELL TRINITY.

J. M'Lellan, b John Bull,	0
N. Cameron, do,	16
T. Ferguson, b Robertson,	1
D. Hardie, run out,	4
E. Dabbs, b J. Bull,	0
G. Walker, do.,	2
W. Ferguson, b J. Stirling,	8
J. Thompson, b J. Bull,	0
E. Coultish, c Henderson, b J. Stirling,	3
W. Roebuck, not out,	15
J. Linner, c Robertson, b Longmuir,	9
Extras,	10
Total,	68

ST ANDREW'S.

R. Henderson, c Cameron, b M'Lellan,	7
J. Farquharson, b Cameron,	2
G. Hannaford, c Cameron, b W. Ferguson,	18
J. Stirling, b Cameron,	5
J. Bull, b Roebuck,	15
J. Robertson, run out,	2
J. Longmuir, b Cameron,	5
W. Amos, b M'Lellan,	0
R. Stirling, do.,	0
D. Ferguson, not out,	2
D. Inglis, b Cameron,	11
Extras,	7
Total,	74

Other interesting opponents were the army teams. The Hamilton Garrison usually gave them a good game and Major Aikman's Ross Ramblers were regular adversaries. Their scorecard gave full military titles, with Sergeant Bugler Frost being a bit of a star. He scored 64 against Motherwell Trinity in August 1890 and, later that month, we see him pulled into the Trinity team for a visit to Edinburgh to play St Andrews at Raeburn Place. He scored 79 not out before the rains came with Trinity on 140 for 4. Maybe the bugler was our first 'ringer'.

Major Aikman became president of Motherwell Cricket Club. Educated at Eton and Oxford, he was a fine sportsman and included curling, riding and cricket among his many talents. In the grounds of his home at Ross House, he had a curling pond and a cricket pitch, where his Ramblers would play. And here he is, looking every inch the Victorian gentleman.

Travel difficulties of the day didn't seem to be an obstacle. Games in Glasgow were commonplace, and there were occasional matches in Edinburgh. But then we read of a touring party selected to travel across the border to Yorkshire. The Binner family hailed from Yorkshire – maybe that was the link.

We lost to Halifax Kings Cross 57 to 38, and the game against Farsley United was washed out. But it shows that Motherwell Trinity were a team with ambitions.

There were also 'celebrity matches'. Back at The Meadows, they were challenged by their footballing friends to play '18 of Motherwell Football Club'. The headline was that the cricketers lost, but it was an evening match and it took so long for all 18 of the footballers to get a bat that it was dark by the time Trinity batted. Officially, the score was 46 to 26 to the footballers.

A couple of years later, the staff at Dalzell House played a Home Park XI, and the House team included Hon G Hamilton, Hon L Hamilton and Hon J Hamilton. Dalzell House won by 69 to 67 and after the game, which spanned two evenings, the Duke invited everyone back to the 'big house' for supper, songs and dancing, and pledged his continuing support to the club. Sounds like a game worth losing!

Following the first season at Home Park, a Smoker was held at The Railway Tavern to award prizes to the best Trinity cricketers of 1890. There must have been a keen scorer preparing statistics for the team, in much the same way as the wonderful Peter Forbes would do almost a century later. Amazingly, we have the averages for the season, and we have a photograph of Mr Ferguson who topped the batting that year.

BATTING.

	No. of Matches	Times not out	Most in an in'gs	Total runs	Aver.
W. Ferguson,	14	1	36	171	13·3
G. Walker,	14	1	28	167	12·11
W. Whitefield,	4	2	16	26	12·2
N. Cameron,	12	1	31	114	10·4
J. Binner,	11	1	15	74	7·4
T. Ferguson,	12	1	24A	74	6·8
W. Roebuck,	13	1	20	77	6·5
G. Cameron,	9	1	23A	53	6·5
W. Goodwin,	2	0	12	13	6·1
D. Hardie,	9	1	9	34	4·2
E. Dabbs,	11	4	9	26	3·2
J. Thomson,	9	1	11	25	3·1
J. M'Lellan,	11	0	4	21	1·10

The following played one innings :—Major Aikman, 42A ; Sergt.-Bugler Frost, 79A ; J. H. Tremayne, 9 ; Hon. L. Hamilton, 6 ; Hon. G. Hamilton, 1 : E. Coultish, 3 ; A. Ferguson, 5.

A Not out.

BOWLING.

	Overs	Maidens	Runs	Wickets	Aver.
J. M'Lellan,	112·4	17	182	43	4·10
G. Cameron,	54·2	14	85	17	5·0
N. Cameron,	115	21	210	33	6·10
W. Roebuck	59	0	122	16	7.10

A Different Game

Cricket has evolved markedly over our 150 years. In modern times, we've witnessed a lot of changes to the way cricket is played, and back around 1900 it was a very different sport.

A specified amount of time (not overs) was set aside for the match. The team batting first would bat for as long as they were able. Usually, this allowed both sides a full innings, but not always. Motherwell Trinity scored 104 against a side called Temperance Athletic, leaving them only 15 minutes to bat. That's just not on – it could have turned the Temperance guys to drink.

A similarly high-scoring match tells us a lot about the bowling of the era. Trinity scored a massive 200 against Edinburgh side Vulcanite, who were then timed out at 9 for 3. During the Trinity innings, Vulcanite had no joy with their 'round arm' bowling, but their underarm bowler took 4 wickets. In another game, Motherwell Trinity prevailed because the opposition couldn't handle 'Ferguson's slow twisters'.

Another thing that seems strange to us today is that the side batting second didn't walk off the park after victory had been secured by passing their opponent's total. No, they would bat on until every member of their team had batted. The fielding side, even though the game was long gone, had to keep bowling until they dismissed all the batsmen, or until time was up.

There was no pavilion, of course. At home, whether at The Meadows or at Home Park, a tent would be erected. Away matches would be reached by train or tram (or the 'brake'), usually meeting at Motherwell station at 2.30. It may seem a late start, but most players would be working on Saturday mornings and, with scores usually around 40-70 runs per innings, the games wouldn't last as long our present-day games.

Such low scores brought into play that rarest of results – a tie. In September 1891, Motherwell Trinity recorded no fewer than 3 ties in successive games! After a 36-36 tie with Coatbridge Wesley, there was a 33-33 tie with Newmains and a 66-66 tie with Ross Ramblers. Surely this must have been some sort of record. The scorer would have been doing cartwheels!

Goodbyes

As for Trinity, that was just about it. They had a going away party at The Motherwell Inn for W Goodwin, who was leaving for Japan; they held a successful Grand Concert at the Town Hall; and, in November 1892, the president George Binner called a Special General Meeting to change the name of the club. Why? Maybe the Episcopalians who took over the running of the club in 1887 were now outnumbered by players who didn't relate to the Trinity name. Who knows?

Regardless, ever since then, it's just been good old Motherwell Cricket Club. Nothing too fancy.

The New Century

As the 1890s became the 1900s, things were changing. Queen Victoria's long reign came to an end, the Labour Party was formed and the first 'googly' was bowled by Bernard Bosanquet when Middlesex played Leicestershire. There were quite a few developments at Motherwell Cricket Club too.

Changes Afoot

In 1893, the first club professional was employed. Geordie Robertson (yes, yet another G Robertson!) was paid to help coach the Motherwell players, but he was also a pretty good all-rounder. Against Hamilton CC, he took 8 for 6 as we bowled out our opponents for 9. Geordie stayed for a few years before moving across to Hamilton (who obviously didn't want to face him again), but returned to play the odd game for Motherwell before the end of the century. When he left, he was given an engraved Albert watch and chain and a bag of sovereigns!

The ground at Home Park was enlarged, and a groundsman employed to look after the square and outfield. It was described in the local press as '*a scene of quiet and gentle beauty, an oasis in a desert of iron works and coal pits'*. It also made the Glasgow Evening News, who felt Motherwell to be *"an unlovely place, but the beautiful surroundings of its cricket ground may be unrivalled".*

You can understand why the people of Motherwell would visit the Duke of Hamilton's estate, whether to watch or play cricket. And they came in large numbers – by 1902, the club was fielding three senior teams and a junior XI. They had also helped Dalziel High School to start a team. The school had its own ground on Coursington Farm and from match scorecards, it is evident that several Dalziel pupils went on to become Motherwell cricketers.

The popularity of cricket in the town was not confined to Home Park. New teams sprang up like Motherwell Etna and, just to complicate things, Motherwell Britannia, who played at Enfield Park, Ladywell. There was no link to our legacy club and, in any case, their life was short-lived. When they folded in 1906, many of their players found their way to Home Park.

League cricket replaced the series of friendly matches and, in consequence, there were more games of cricket played. Initially Motherwell Cricket Club were put in Division 3 of the Lanarkshire Leagues, but we thought we should have been in Division 2. Suffice to say we failed to overturn the decision … and finished the season in the lower half of Division 3.

Behind The Scenes

Progress was being made though, and when we read the Committee Reports or the President's summary at Annual General Meetings of the time, it's all eerily familiar. Some of the items debated were:

- Should we continue with a pro? Could we afford it?
- Why did the 1st XI players not turn up for practice? Their fielding needed to improve.

- Everyone should turn up on time for matches, even if it was raining.
- An appeal would be made to the League to award Motherwell a win over Wishaw CC who, with 8 wickets down, walked off the pitch in light rain when the wicket was perfectly playable.
- League reconstruction was proposed. Should we support the new model?
- Some matches had been lost due to 'umpiring of indifferent character'.
- Mid-June and some subscriptions hadn't yet been paid.
- Players were calling off when the football season started.

Even today, around 125 years later, cricket club committees all round the country will be wrestling with the same sorts of issues.

In 1898, the committee also had to distance themselves from two articles that had been placed in the Motherwell Times. Under the name of 'A. Follower', the writer bemoaned the 2nd team selection and the lack of bowling changes.

The secretary wrote to the paper to say this was not a view shared by the club, and it might not have taken them too long to work out that Mr A Follower was someone who was rarely picked for the 2nd team and, when he was, he didn't get a bowl.

Financial Worries

An item that dominated the headlines in 1902 was the ill-fated Grand Miscellaneous Concert, which only a few of the Motherwell populace attended. Maybe a more snappy title would have helped, but regardless, it was a financial disaster.

The club appealed to the Town Hall to waive their booking fee, but a council sub-committee rejected their appeal. The

Cricket Club finances recovered after they played two benefit matches to raise funds, and the concert 'impressario' paid back £15 to the club out of the profits from his next event. Happy days!

One of the benefit matches was played against Uddingston's 1sts, who were one of the top clubs in the west of Scotland. The match was well attended; Motherwell raised some cash but were predictably well beaten. But one thing catches the eye. Three players in the Uddingston line-up were J Downs, A Downs and W Downs. Is it possible that they were the next generation of the Downs family who helped to form Motherwell Britannia back in 1871?

On The Park

There were some notable achievements in this era.

Motherwell's best player was William Steele, a wicketkeeper/batsman who travelled from Coatbridge to play for the club. He opened the batting in aggressive style and often ended up scoring most of the team's runs. After more than 10 years with the club, he trialled with Drumpellier against Grange at Raeburn Place, and that was the last of William Steele in Motherwell colours.

The first Motherwell century was scored in 1901 by another long-serving player.

SCOTSTOUN.

G. Roy, b Marshall,	6
C. M'Callum, b Hamilton	11
J. W. Birch, run out	1
M. Wilson, c and b Hamilton	0
A. Andrews, run out	7
W. Arthur, c Clapperton b Marshall	18
H. Adams, st Steel b Marshall	14
J. Adams, lbw., b Dolphin,	0
J. Haley, not out,	7
J. Martin, b Dolphin,	0
C. M'Quarry, b Dolphin	0
Extras,	9
Total,	73

MOTHERWELL

W. Steel, b Birch,	32
T. Marshall, c H. Adams b Birch	110
J. Hamilton, c and b Birch	3
W. Cartright, c Roy b M'Callum	1
J. Nixon, c Martin b M'Callum	1
G. Clapperton, b H. Adams	1
I. Dolphin, b Birch	25
J. Knox, c and b Birch	2
W. Wilson, not out,	8
J. Martin, } To bat.	
T. Plum, }	
Extras,	8
Total,	191

Thomas Marshall scored 110 (including 16 boundaries) against Scotstoun, and we have the scorecard. J. Martin was the captain – he was quite a celebrity in the town, a poet and author.

Some years before, against a Motherwell XI, Mr H Amory scored 109 out of a total of 133, playing in the annual Dalzell House game, featuring players from the Duke's family and staff. You do wonder if the competition was of its usual intensity, but it's Mr Amory who gets his name in the record books as the man who scored the first century at Home Park.

Joe Rhodes, a fast bowler from Yorkshire, had been employed in 1902, earning 35 shillings (£1.75) per week. He held daily coaching sessions for juniors after school at 4.00. He was quite a success with the ball, taking 81 wickets at an average of 3.8 runs per wicket in his first season.

But another thing changed in 1902 that stops you in your tracks. Conventional teas (sandwiches and tea) replaced pies, beer and lemonade!

So, for the past 30 years, Motherwell's cricketers had been knocking back the pints at the tea interval. Maybe the sanitation problems and poor water quality in Victorian times had influenced the menu, but it makes you wonder if Motherwell's poor standard of fielding wasn't purely down to lack of practice!

Crowds and Conflicts

The Edwardian era began with the coronation of the sport-loving Edward VII in 1902, and upon his death in 1910, George V acceded to the throne. In between, we had the crowning of Motherwell Cricket Club as Lanarkshire League champions.

Here's the oldest team photograph we possess of a Motherwell side. It hung in the pavilion for many years.

Back row: J H Duncan (scorer), J Grieve, I Dolphin, E T Evans, A Blacklock (pro), J Koop (umpire).
Front row: D Simpson, T Marshall, W H Cartwright (capt), J Young, J Lyle and J Baillie.

What do we know about them?

It is the 1906 1st XI, and we know that the photo was taken at Home Park just before the rain washed out their game against a Drumpellier XI. Sure enough, they don't look too happy.

It was a good season for Motherwell. They finished runners-up in the League to Wishaw, and won most of their friendly matches.

The chap with loud blazer is Andrew Blacklock, the professional, who came from Selkirk and played for Scotland. Although he only played for one season, Andrew was popular with all at the club. On the occasion of his marriage later that year, the players clubbed together to buy him a "handsome marble timepiece".

Other notable players were the opening bowlers Jamie Young and E T Evans. Evans is the bloke with attitude in the back row – he just had to be a fast bowler – and Young was from Northern Ireland. He arranged cricket tours across the water later in the decade.

Tom Marshall has the distinction of being Motherwell's first centurion, and the captain William Cartwright (in the polo neck) had a long career with the club, still playing in the 1920s. He was a decent batsman and was renowned for his catching in the 'long field'.

John Baillie had played since the early '90s and occasionally bowled his underhand lobs to buy wickets. John Lyle has the pads on, ready to keep wicket.

Isaac Dolphin had been one of the Dalziel Star team who joined Motherwell in 1886. He was always the first to propose a toast at AGM, and start the singing at the end of season Smoker.

Amazingly, some old fixture cards still exist from the Edwardian era, the earliest being 1902. Here it is, with Robert F McMurray's name and address.

It was a successful decade for Motherwell Cricket Club. The sport grew massively in popularity, there was now a league structure to local cricket and we developed some good cricketers over the Edwardian years. And, at last, plans were submitted for a pavilion to be built at Home Park.

New Pavilion

Club facilities were rather primitive. A tent was erected on match days to allow cricketers to change into their whites, and for teas to be served. On windy days, this was impractical so the farmer at Home Farm allowed them to use his barn. But in 1906, Lord Hamilton gave the go-ahead for a cricket pavilion to be built. A golf clubhouse would also be erected in the estate a few years later.

Our pavilion was completed a year later, ready for the start of the season. Arrangements were made to open the new pavilion with a garden party followed by an attractive fixture with Uddingston, champions of the Western Union.

The pavilion had been decorated with flags, and old photographs were hung on the walls. The ladies had supplied wonderful teas and the Boys Brigade Band was lined up to provide the music … and then it rained so heavily that the party and the cricket had to be abandoned. Still, everyone enjoyed the teas.

Remarkably the structure stood for 70 years, looking much the same in the 1970s as when it was first built.

Lanarkshire League Cricket

The intensity of matches really stepped up a gear with league cricket. It was the Motherwell president James Burns who put up the trophy, and competition was keen, sometimes more than keen. Local rivals like Bellshill, Wishaw, Coatbridge Victoria and Newmains were regularly battling at the top of the league with Motherwell, and would carry large bands of supporters to away matches.

For a while, this was great news for Motherwell, especially financially. They gathered 3d (just over 1p in decimal currency) at the Knowetop gate to Dalzell Estate for every match and this added up to a princely sum over the season. It allowed us to hire a professional who would prepare the ground, coach the kids, and bat and bowl to good effect.

How many turned up? The Motherwell Times wrote of 2,000 and 3,000 attending derby games against Newmains and Bellshill, who brought their own supporters with them.

There's a report that paints a picture of scenic beauty, when over 1,000 attended new professional Jack Schofield's benefit match in 1908, sitting around the boundary, enjoying their picnics in the delightful surroundings of the estate. But the crowds were not always so well behaved. There was an edge to proceedings when local derbies took place.

In one game against Newmains, their followers took to pelting the Motherwell players with stones. In another match against Coatbridge Victoria, their captain led his team off the park and refused to play on after the Motherwell umpire turned down an appeal – this almost caused a riot. When the game was replayed, police were in attendance to control the crowd.

Fauldhouse also had a good following, and a fine team. Their top batsman F Brown had scored 108 in the previous game against Motherwell, the first cricketer to score a century against us in a competitive match. For the return fixture, Fauldhouse brought a large support to Home Park, some of whom 'were intoxicated'. The local reporter was horrified by 'the foul language, the worst ever heard on the cricket field'.

Trouble at Home

Unruly drunks, foul language and baying crowds being controlled by police in Dalzell Estate – this was not what Lord Hamilton had signed up for when he allowed Motherwell Cricket Club to play in his grounds.

It was decided that, due to 'damage to foliage', the public would not be allowed to enter the estate unless they were members of the club. This effectively drained the finances of the club – we relied on gate receipts to survive.

We partially got round the problem by selling season tickets at the start of the season for a half crown (12.5p), and granted the season ticket holders the status of honorary members. These members were able to attend all Home Park matches, but the large crowds previously attending were no more. The one exception was the Pro's benefit, when the public were able to come and pay their 3d to thank Jack Schofield for his work. And they came in huge numbers.

But relations with Dalzell House were strained. A lamb had to be put down, and the estate manager said it had injured itself on cricket equipment. Next, he accused the club of allowing casual cricket followers (non-members) into the estate, which broke the agreement. It turned out there had been a march organised by the Temperance movement, which ended up in the estate. The marchers had deserted the speakers in the neighbouring field to watch the cricket.

The club, perhaps unwisely, decided to print the exchange of letters in the Motherwell Times, pleading our innocence and anger at the accusations. It didn't help. Later, we turned up for a match and found the wicket destroyed by horses galloping over the square.

There's no sign of the annual match between Dalzell House and a Motherwell XI taking place that year, nor the sumptuous entertainment usually laid on by his lordship. Had we not just built our new pavilion, it is probable that we would have looked for another ground, but thankfully, tensions relaxed, everyone calmed down and cricket continued at Home Park.

Motherwell had had enough of the Lanarkshire League. It had done a lot to promote the sport, and the club had been successful in winning the title in 1907. We had beaten Carfin on the last day of the season to secure the title, but match reports suggest that games were often clouded by controversy.

The lack of neutral umpires, or when the neutral umpires failed to turn up, was a problem. Local club umpires were often accused of bias, and the large crowds behaved in a way similar to a football crowd if they disagreed with a refereeing decision. It just wasn't cricket.

Motherwell resigned from the League and put together a more attractive schedule of friendly matches for the following season.

The Works Cup

All of this aggro didn't detract from a brilliant initiative by the club to run a competition for all the various iron, steel and engineering companies in the town. Motherwell had quite a transient population, and you can see names appearing and disappearing on their match scorecards over just a few seasons.

With so many continuing to arrive in town from England and Wales, and with the increasing popularity of the sport among the locals, there were many workers who wanted to play cricket.

Motherwell Cricket Club launched the Works Cup and the response was immense. Over 20 teams entered, including Nelson Hurst (with 4 teams), Colvilles, Clydesdale Works and the Tramcar Company. One company – Potts, Cassels and Williamson – were so enthused with the idea that they started up their own cricket team on their own ground.

It was a colossal amount of work for the organisers at the cricket club. A huge number of games had to be arranged and they had to find grounds, sort out umpires and scorebooks and re-schedule rain-affected matches. With no phones or other means of communication, much of the organisation was intimated through the Motherwell Times. The paper published the scorecards for every match, so that cricket scores took up almost a page of the broadsheet every week.

The most successful side was the Mill Floor team at Colvilles. The grounds used were mainly football pitches, including Fir Park and the Motherwell Athletic ground off Hamilton Road, with mats laid for the wicket. The final was played at Home Park.

Motherwell president James Burns (pictured) liked a trophy and, sure enough, he put up the Works Cup. His day job was Town Clerk and he was always keen to promote sport in the town.

Though it was hard work running the show, Motherwell Cricket Club benefited, picking a number of decent players from the Works teams. As for PR, it was the talk of the town with so many people and businesses engaged in the project.

The Irish Tours

One of the Motherwell veterans was Jamie Young, an Ulsterman who had played for the club since the early 1890s. He planned a tour to Northern Ireland in 1907 when a Lanarkshire select played 5 games during the July Fair holidays. It was so successful that the tour was repeated in subsequent years, sometimes with a Motherwell party and other times with guests from Wishaw and Newmains supporting us.

We based ourselves in Strabane and played games against the likes of Enniskillen, Dungannon, Sion Mills, Omagh and Fermanagh. The teams were evenly matched and a lot of good cricket was played, but there was a social side that may account for the great popularity of the trip. An extract from the Motherwell Times says that the last game before their departure was called off …

… allowing the cricketers time to bid goodbye to their many friends, especially those of the fair sex. Where each went is unknown but they arrived at Londonderry Pier quite disconsolate at their departure.
Present indications are that a similar tour will take place next year. Failing that, some of the players will be eager to get back on their own account to get in touch with their prospective mothers-in-law.

Sounds like quite a tour!

A Model Pro

After the employment of Geordie Robertson in the 1890s and Joe Rhodes in the early years of the new century, Andrew Blacklock was signed up in 1906. He only lasted a year at Home Park but he was a popular man, and when he died just a few years later, aged 39, two of the Motherwell team travelled to Selkirk for his funeral.

In 1907, the club engaged Jack Schofield as their professional. He came from Kirkheaton in Yorkshire and had been pro for Melrose the year before. An opening bat and left arm spin bowler, he was a more than useful addition to a good Motherwell squad.

He remained at Home Park for many years and, after the Great War, played as an amateur until his playing days ended. In his debut season he helped Motherwell to win the league, and the following year, he took 102 wickets. The year after, he scored an unbeaten 128 against Milngavie and Bearsden and then took 7 wickets for 20 runs.

Here's the man himself. Although he dominated several games, it was by no means a one-man team. Motherwell had good bowlers to back up the pro - the aforementioned Jamie Young with his 'swervers' and the pacy Jimmy Reoch who 'made batsmen step away'.

Batsmen came and went over the decade but special mention must be made of Marshall (who scored the first century for Motherwell), Gillespie (wicketkeeper/ batsman), Cartwright, Thomson, Fitzmaurice and Graham, who all scored consistently well.

It's fair to say that the Edwardian years had been an exciting adventure for Motherwell Cricket Club. The sport of cricket and the health of the club had progressed massively by 1910, and when King Edward died, all cricket games were cancelled as a mark of respect.

For King and Country

At Motherwell Cricket Club's Annual General Meeting in November 1914, president Arthur Low read a special message for those who had joined up to fight the Kaiser. Five players were already heading for the front, and many more would follow.

Among the five was Jimmy Reoch, who had signed up with the Gordon Highlanders. A Brechin lad, he had made quite an impact since his arrival at Home Park.

Reoch was a fast bowler and he was something of a hero among the Motherwell fans. In 1912, he had taken 8 wickets against Mount Florida and in 1914, around the time of Archduke Franz Ferdinand's assassination, he went one better with the remarkable analysis of 9 wickets for 2 runs as they bowled Golfhill all out for 29. Frustratingly, Jack Schofield took the final wicket in a low-scoring match to deprive Reoch of a full house.

A New League

Motherwell had put together a decent team before the war. With Reoch's pace and Schofield's left arm spin, they formed a potent bowling attack. Alex Gillespie was a fine wicketkeeper who rarely gave away byes and picked up regular stumpings off Schofield's bowling. The batting was less consistent but Wattie Graham, Tom Stewart, 'Bunt' Walker and George Hamilton all made decent contributions alongside Schofield and Gillespie, who scored a century against Caldervale in 1912.

In fact, 1912 was their 'glory year', when Motherwell topped the newly established West of Scotland Cricket Union. They won their first 9 matches to have the league wrapped up by mid-August. In a year of many highlights, their best performance was against Cathcart – they bowled them all out for just 7 runs. It was Schofield's turn to cash in this time, taking 8 wickets for 2 runs. Here's the scorecard.

Motherwell.	
J. Schofield, b Smith	1
W. Graham, lbw., b Smith	5
T. Scott, c and b Stewart	3
W. Cartwright, b Smith	4
A. Gillespie, b Smith	47
G. Hamilton, b Axford	27
A. Reoch, c Axford, b Stewart	1
J. Reoch, b Smith	0
D. Simpson, not out	1
Extras	5
Total (for eight wickets)	**90**

(Innings closed.)
J. Baillie and D. Nicol did not bat.

Cathcart.	
J. M. Muir, b Schofield	0
J. N. Dewar, c Simpson, b Schofield	2
W. Axford, b Schofield	0
W. Bissett, b Schofield	1
A. Ferguson, b Schofield	1
A. Smith, b Schofield	1
J. Stewart, b Reoch	1
A. Campbell, not out	0
M. Mitchell, b Schofield	1
J. Stewart, c Nicol, b Schofield	0
Extras	1
Total	**7**

A tricky question had to be answered at the start of the 1912 season. The rules of the new West of Scotland league didn't allow paid players, and Jack Schofield had been a fixture as Motherwell pro for 5 years. There was no question of him leaving – he had settled in the town and had a proper job outside of his cricketing role – so he played as an amateur.

The title-winning game was at Home Park, when Motherwell defeated Vale of Leven by 4 runs (102 v 98) in a closely fought encounter. With Vale closing in on the target, Jimmy Reoch clean bowled the last batsman to claim his sixth wicket and give Motherwell the 2 points they needed to be crowned champions. The crowd invaded the park, and Jimmy was carried shoulder high back to the pavilion.

The town celebrated, and badges were given to all of the players who had played a part in the success. The captain of the club that year was Alex Gillespie and, just over 60 years later in 1973, he contributed to Motherwell Cricket Club's centenary brochure. Among some wonderful memories, the 90-year-old talked of the victorious 1912 team and how he still treasured his winner's badge.

Cricket Crowds

Relations with Lord Hamilton and the estate managers at Dalziel House had improved markedly. With Jack Schofield stepping down as pro, there was no benefit game, so his Lordship allowed Motherwell to nominate two matches each year when the general public would be given entry into Dalzell Estate.

We could charge 6d for admission at the Knowetop gate and, of course, the club could retain the monies. Understandably we picked the derby matches that would generate most cash, so again we had over 2,000 fans at the Newmains and Bellshill games.

Some neighbouring clubs weren't enjoying the same success. Wishaw were forced to withdraw from the league when they lost their cricket field to industrial development, and Hamilton also folded. The only silver lining for Motherwell was when Hamilton gave them their seating, which was repositioned around the Home Park boundary.

Motherwell had enjoyed local rivalries with both clubs for many years. After the war, we hosted a veterans' match at Home Park between the old Wishaw players and the old Motherwell players, an annual fixture that continued until the 1930s.

In November 1912, when the various reports were delivered at the AGM, the club's finances were unsurprisingly healthy, and the president was triumphant as he declared the season the best ever for Motherwell Cricket Club.

We couldn't retain the title (Dumbarton won in 1913 and Babcock & Wilcox in 1914), and sadly, just two years after their title-winning exploits, a very different tone was required at the AGM. The proceeds of the August benefit match had been donated to the Red Cross, as some of the cricketers marched off to war.

To Play Or Not To Play

Arthur Low's presidential address grew more sombre by the year. The club secretary J Cottar spoke clearly about the main issues of the day in 1915 …

> *In the history of cricket, there never was a season commenced under such uncertainties. The nation was in close deadly struggle with Germany, and many felt that it was sheer folly that cricket should go on under such conditions. There were others who felt that those who were still at home, by force of circumstance, would enjoy*

a brief spell away from the making of shells and other
munitions of war. Judging by the attendances at Home
Park, the latter view was proved right. We commenced
our season scarcely knowing our program. True, we had
a full fixture card, but not a full team. We would have
been in a sorry plight but for the fact that outsiders,
whose clubs had disbanded, came to play with us.
Motherwell Times, November 1915

Among the 'outsiders' who had joined Motherwell was a certain
R K Hinshalwood, who would assume legendary status at the
club in years to come.

Keeping Going

The league had been suspended but Motherwell kept playing.
We dispensed with the groundsman and fielded only a 1st XI,
with an occasional Home Park select playing local works teams.
The friendly fixtures that had been scheduled were frequently
cancelled but the club invariably found someone to play at short
notice, sometimes from the army camps stationed nearby. Like
football, cricket was regarded as a means of raising spirits across
the town, giving spectators a welcome distraction from the
horrors of war.

Lord and Lady Hamilton did their bit too. Dalzell House
became a hospital for wounded soldiers who, if they were able,
would watch the cricket matches at Home Park. They also
opened up the estate for ventures like The Grand Country Fair,
which featured the brass band of the Royal Fusiliers, mock
bull-fighting with Spanish mules, fortune tellers, dancing
displays and an ice cream lorry … and a cricket match between
Motherwell and the Argyll and Sutherland Highlanders.
Around 2,500 attended.

Beyond this highlight, nothing much of note happened on the cricket field during the war years. Motherwell had 18 players doing their bit for King and Country, so the teams turning out at Home Park were not the strongest, and other clubs were similarly affected. There was no league, or competition of any sort, it was just a case of survival.

During this time, we find another Motherwell centurion, Tom Aitcheson, who scored 101 against Stewarts & Lloyds. It must have been the most unheralded 100 in history (there was no room for celebration in 1917) but, as Motherwell's opponents were bolstered by Bellshill and Drumpellier players, it's only right that Tom gets a mention.

In the summer of 1918, the club was given equal billing in the Motherwell Times to a tank that had been parked at the town hall. Under the heading 'Two places worth visiting on Saturday', both attractions were fund-raising initiatives with the proceeds going to the Dalzell House Hospital. The cricketing attraction was a match between Motherwell and Colonel Aikman's Ross Ramblers.

It's good to see Colonel Aikman still to the fore, and he certainly hadn't lost his pulling power when it came to getting a cricket team on the field. In the Ramblers line-up was none other than Herbert Sutcliffe, one of England's best batsmen of all time. With Jack Hobbs, he formed perhaps the greatest opening pair in history, making 26 opening partnerships of 100 or more.

You had to feel for Motherwell. With the majority of their team serving abroad, it was a much weakened team that took on Ross Ramblers.

It wasn't just Sutcliffe who caught the eye, scoring a stylish 55 – there was another first-class cricketer from South Africa called Shurrie, who top scored with 80. Inevitably the locals were well beaten, but there's no doubt that Motherwell's Simpson would have talked for many years about the day he took the wicket of the great Herbert Sutcliffe.

As the 1918 season went on, the mood was lifting a little. The end was in sight, and in October the president even hosted an end-of-season social in his workshop to thank everyone associated with the club, from the players who turned out through the war years to the men who tended the ground and the ladies who prepared the teas.

Of the 18 players who went to war, G McCracken and G Taylor didn't return, killed in action, as was a patron of the club, the Hon Leslie Hamilton. Tributes were paid to the fallen when the team got together for the first time at the start of the 1919 season.

It was good to see the old names back at Home Park and, although we were only playing friendly matches, we had a fine season under captain David Littlejohn, winning almost all of our matches. The bowling unit of Reoch, Hinshalwood and Schofield clicked straight away, and in Bob Morris we had found a batsman capable of scoring regular runs.

The one team we couldn't beat that season was Fauldhouse, who defeated Motherwell home and away. Still, the trip to Fauldhouse was an enjoyable one, as the team made the journey on Bob Mack's motor bus. Somehow it felt like a new era was about to begin.

And that's how we reached our first 50, except nobody celebrated … because nobody knew. Nowadays, there are quite a few of us alive today who played in the 1970s and who remember our centenary 50 years ago, but back in the early 1920s, lives (and cricket careers) were shorter. No-one had spanned the previous 50 years. Our oldest member, Isaac Dolphin, had died in 1919, and he had always preached that the club had been

formed in 1887 when our name changed to Motherwell Trinity. It's probable that the cricketers who played with Isaac before the war and were still playing in the early 1920s followed his version of the truth.
Only now, with the benefit of a digital newspaper archive, can we tell the story as it really happened.

Presidents and Captains (1871–1920)

We've found most of the individuals who ran the club in the first 50 years, but those in charge in the early days are difficult to confirm with certainty, hence the missing years.

The election of club president at the time involved the appointment of a senior businessman in the town. There's very little press coverage of Motherwell Cricket Club for the six or seven years before the launch of the Motherwell Times in 1883, but after that we're on safer ground.

It's probable that J R Cassells was president for some years either side of 1874 and 1875. From Robert Duncan's book, *Steelopolis*, we see that old JR was a partner in the Glasgow Iron and Steel Coy. He also sat on the town council after Motherwell was awarded Burgh status. It makes sense that he would have a longer tenure, but we have no confirmation to support our hunch.

Year	President	Club Captain	Year	President	Club Captain
1871		J Evans	1899	J Binner	T Rae
1872		J Evans	1900	G Fraser	J Baillie
1873			1901	G Fraser	J Martin
1874	J R Cassells	S Downs	1902	W H Hobbin	J Baillie
1875	J R Cassells	B Evans	1903	W H Hobbin	J Baillie
			1904	J Burns	T Marshall
1876–1883			1905	J Burns	W Cartwright
			1906	J Burns	W Cartwright
1884		J Binner	1907	J Burns	J Baillie
1885		J Binner	1908	J Burns	J Baillie
1886		N Cameron	1909	J Burns	J Hamilton
1887		N Cameron	1910	Clr. Ford	J Hamilton
1888		G Walker	1911	A Low	A Gillespie
1889	Col. Aikman	N Cameron	1912	A Low	J Baillie
1890	Col. Aikman	J Binner	1913	A Low	J Baillie
1891	J T Brassington	J Binner	1914	A Low	J Schofield
1892	G Binner	J McLellan	1915	A Low	J Schofield
1893	G Binner	G Walker	1916	A Low	T Stewart
1894	G Binner	J McLeland	1917	A Low	T Stewart
1895	J Binner	T Ferguson	1918	A Low	D Littlejohn
1896	D Hardie	D Cameron	1919	A Low	D Littlejohn
1897	D Hardie	G Baker	1920	A Low	R K Hinshalwood Snr
1898	J Binner	W Steele			

Reaching Our Century

After reaching our 50, there was no stopping us. Our eye was in and we played some wonderful cricket. The 2nd World War halted momentum but we emerged stronger and we accelerated towards our century. There were no nervous nineties until, on the cusp of our maiden 100, we didn't seem so self-assured. But we got there, and the celebrations were bounteous.

W B Jardine, Legend

*There's really only one way to kick off the next 50 years,
and that's to look at the life of one whose contribution to
Motherwell Cricket Club spanned the entire half-century and
beyond. To many in the town, W B Jardine was Mr Cricket.*

The word 'legend' is widely used nowadays but rarely deserved.
That couldn't possibly be said about Motherwell Cricket Club's
own legend.

W B Jardine, known to everyone as Bill or Old Willie (well,
he always looked old to us), began his lifelong love affair with
Motherwell in 1921 and faithfully served the Club until the day
he died in 2000, aged 92. That's almost 80 years.

During this time, he played for over 30 years, ran his very
own select side, acted as match secretary for over 50 years,
sat on committees for just about every cricketing body in the
west of Scotland, organised competitions, performed at the
annual cricket dinner, became something of a celebrity at the
Scarborough Cricket Festival, and was a wonderful ambassador
for the club and the game.

Long after his playing days had come to an end, he'd still

turn up. Saturdays, Sundays, evening cup ties, even practice nights, summer after summer, sunshine or rain, Bill Jardine would be there.

After all these years, it's still possible to picture him emerging from the trees at the Muirhouse end with his flask of tea and sandwiches, carrying his transistor radio so he could listen to Test Match Special while watching his Motherwell team in action. He would make his way to the clubhouse, order a glass of stout and find his favourite seat, happy as Larry.

If a game was interrupted by rain and the teams were looking less than positive about the prospects of returning to the field, Bill Jardine would always find a 'blue patch' somewhere in the leaden grey skies. Ever the optimist.

Playing Days

In the centenary brochure, Bill Jardine remembered his first year at Home Park, 1921. There were some other notable names among the lads he played with – Eddie Houston, Archie and Duncan Black, Tom Findlay and Bill Barclay. It was a fine summer and he played cricket with his pals every single night.

When they entered through the gates at Knowetop, it was like entering another world. The estate was strictly private and the boys felt privileged to gain entry. With a playing membership of 124 (!), it was hard to get a game, so the practice was always very competitive and enjoyable, whether selected or not.

Bill Jardine made his debut for the 1st XI five years later, pulled into the team as a late substitute. Motherwell had bowled Bridge of Weir out for 99, but were 9 wickets down for 90 runs when Bill made his way to the crease, last man in, to partner Laidlaw Byers. His forward defensive kept the bowlers out, and it took 9 overs to get the 10 runs required for victory when Bill's leg glance won the game.

The story was to repeat itself many years later during the war, when playing resources were stretched but teams did their best to keep cricket going. It was 1942 at Hamilton Crescent where West of Scotland hosted Motherwell. Tom Findlay bowled beautifully, taking 7 wickets for 31 runs, as West were bowled out for 84.

With the best of Motherwell's batsmen dismissed cheaply, the game was all but lost at 42 for 9. Bill Jardine joined Tom Findlay at the crease and held an end up as his partner laid about the West attack. Bill scored the winning single with 2 balls to spare to give Motherwell a famous victory over a top team.

When the two heroes of the day reached the dressing room, they found it pretty much deserted. Most of the team reckoned that it had been a lost cause and had gone for an early train home. How could they have doubted the swashbuckling Findlay and the obdurate Jardine?

There was also his story of a game at Cambuslang against a good Clyde Valley side. It was a time game (5 hours) and Clyde Valley batted 3 hours for their 112, leaving a weakened Motherwell team 2 hours to get the runs.

When they collapsed to 10 for 5, Bill Jardine and Tom Sneddon decided to shut up shop and batted out time to finish 23 for 5, much to the consternation of the bowlers. Here's the scorecard of the Motherwell innings. Bill's contribution was 8

CLYDE VALLEY v. M.C.C. 2nd XI.

Motherwell 2nd XI. travelled to Cambuslang on Saturday and held the home team to a draw in a game which was held up for an hour owing to rain.

Clyde Valley.

J. G. Boag, ct. Donnelly, b Muir	24
R. Weir, ct. Hamilton, b Muir	16
J. S. Shearer, ct. M'Farlane, b Muir	16
D. Donald, b Parker	7
C. Sherriffs, b Muir	12
J. Fullerton, ct. Muir, b Hamilton	23
T. Hill, not out	11
W. Willis, b Hamilton	1
R. Smeaton, not out	0
Extras	2
Total (for 7 declared)	112

G. Potts, T. T. Wood did not bat.

Motherwell 2nd XI.

W. B. Jardine, not out	8
T. Donnelly, b Sherriffs	0
G. M'Farlane, b Sherriffs	3
R. K. Parker, b Boag	1
I. Muir, ct. Sherriffs, b Boag	1
G. S. Hamilton, lbw., b Boag	0
T. A. Sneddon, not out	8
Extras	2
Total (for 5)	23

A. A. Miller, R. F. Gardiner, Dr. Grieve and D. Cameron did not bat.

not out in almost 2 hours, but to him, it would have felt like a century. He loved a draw.

In another game, Bill opened the batting and was still not out at the end of the innings, when Motherwell declared at 134 for 9. Bill's contribution was an undefeated 22! You get the picture.

He was an ever-present before and after the war – and, when he was available, during the war. This photograph was taken prior to Motherwell's first game after the war in May 1946. They beat Milngavie and Bearsden by 3 wickets.

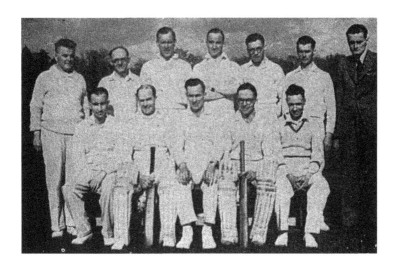

The line-up was …
Back Row: A Barr, R Tyrell, I Muir, T Donnelly, G S Hamilton, A Mitchell and V Crowley (scorer)
Front Row: W B Jardine, J Donnelly, R Russell (captain), F A Rooks and J Gibson

The W B Jardine XI

The stories of Bill's rearguard heroics tell you a lot about his battling qualities as a batsman, but not of his bowling. He was a decent off spin bowler, which became evident when touring with his very own select side.

Bill was a great advocate of Sunday cricket and after the war he captained a team known as the W B Jardine XI, consisting of players from various local Lanarkshire clubs. They'd play for their teams on a Saturday, and join Bill on the Sunday.

Bill recalled the excellent team spirit and some notable victories against senior sides like Ayr, Kilmarnock, Carlisle, Dumfries, Clackmannan and many others.

In 1955, they played a new club in Prestwick in a match that was remembered years later. It was 1980 and Alex Baird, Motherwell vice-president, was invited to propose the 'toast to Prestwick Cricket Club' at their 25th anniversary dinner. They made a point of thanking Motherwell, and in particular Bill Jardine, for encouraging the development of the Prestwick club. They reckoned that without the visits of the W B Jardine XI, it would have been a far greater struggle to become established.

Later in the '50s, in a game against Falkirk, the W B Jardine XI came up against Bobby Simpson, who would go on to become one of the great Australian captains. Bobby was playing as a professional in the north of England and had come up to Falkirk to visit his grandparents. Bill made such an impact on the young man that Bobby Simpson gave him one of his Australian 'baggy green' caps.

Bill's own high point was the day he brought himself on to bowl against Perthshire with both opening batsmen well set, approaching their 50s. The openers, Len Dudman and Tom Lodge, happened to be Scotland's opening pair as well. It took Bill Jardine just 2 overs to dismiss the pair.

The Jazzman

For many, the highlight of the Motherwell Cricket Club annual dinner came towards the end of the evening, when Bill Jardine stood up with his kazoo and performed a calypso to the rhythm of the twelve bar blues. Some were traditional songs like *The Old Bucket's Got A Hole In It*, while others had been written in honour of a guest speaker, like Hillhead's John McLean or Glasgow High's Andy Little. It was always the last act of the dinner – no-one could follow him!

In 1991, at Colville Park Golf Club, the Annual Dinner celebrated Bill's 70th year with the club. Even in his mid-80s, he stole the show with a unique performance, and here he is with other top table guests.

Back Row: Grant Robertson, Gavin Shaw, Paul Harding, Willie Miller
Front Row: Tommy Halpin (Prestwick), Douglas Dalgleish (vice-president, Scottish Golf Union), Steve Young, Bill Jardine, Andy Little (Glasgow High)

Bill's act was a throwback to his days as a trumpet player with the Four Aces, a touring jazz band of the 20s and 30s. Once billed as 'Scotland's Muggsy Spanier', Bill recalled a chance meeting with a cricketer called Major Street playing for the Army XI who was a "red-hot pianist" and had his own jazz band. He invited Bill to join the band for a concert together with drums, double bass and guitar – the 5-piece had a memorable jam session.

When he made his annual pilgrimage to the Scarborough Cricket Festival, lodging in the same digs every year, he'd get the kazoo out to entertain the locals of an evening – he was almost regarded as part of the festival!

He wrote music, and would send some of his songs off to favourite singers of the day, like Lena Martell, in the hope that they would record them. One song sticks in the memory – *The Girl In The Cafe* – which was played at his funeral.

During his travels, he managed to visit almost all of the English county grounds and met with some of the greatest cricketers of all time on a social basis, conversing with the likes of Don Bradman, Charlie McCartney, Frank Worrell, Wally Hammond and K R Ramadhin. You can imagine that they were just as interested in Bill Jardine as he was in them.

Match Secretary

Bill is also remembered for his many years as match secretary, laterally in tandem with Gavin Shaw. He was so well organised that he would turn up at the League AGM with Motherwell's fixtures and dates already written in tablets of stone, and other clubs knew to accept them. The only change year on year was that the promoted side would replace the relegated side. Simplicity itself.

Astonishingly, he didn't have a phone! It's unthinkable today but the league fixtures were already in place, and he arranged friendly fixtures from his council office in the Town Hall. He managed to get Sunday friendlies with some top clubs like Ayr, Stenhousemuir, Gala, Grange, Kilmarnock and the Edinburgh select side, The Bats – quite an achievement considering

Motherwell's place on the cricketing ladder.

Things didn't always go to plan though. There was one famous day when two different teams arrived at Home Park to play Motherwell! However, it just wasn't possible to get annoyed with Bill, as he quickly arranged for the two visiting teams to play each other while the Motherwell guys looked on, trying to appear happy with the situation!

Bill's love of the game never diminished. Even when his eyesight was failing, he'd still appear at Home Park, and his long-time friend Tom Findlay would give him a running commentary.

He was a true Motherwell legend, a constant reminder to every one of us why we love this great game. They just don't make them like WBJ anymore.

Home Park In The 1920s

The 1920s brought photographs, lots of them, as well as some names that have a familiar ring to them. It also brought its fair share of success. Although there was no league structure, the club had friendlies against the likes of Uddingston, Greenock, Drumpellier and Kilmarnock, and would compete well with them. We also reached the semi-final of the inaugural Rowan Cup, beating Glasgow Accies and Ayr along the way.

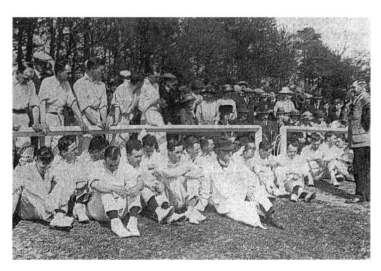

At the start of the decade, we erected the racecourse fencing, which was a feature of Home Park for many years. It was 'opened' with something of a fanfare with a fixture against Kilmarnock. A large crowd turned up to see Motherwell win with plenty of runs to spare. Motherwell 161 for 8; Kilmarnock 41 all out.

Playing Strength

The size of the club membership was incredible. The number of players reached a peak of 128, and there were weekly fixtures for three senior XIs, as well as Junior and Juvenile sides. Playing member subscription cost 10/6 (52p). There were over 250 non-playing members who would pay a fee of 3/- (15p), allowing them entry to Dalzell estate to watch the games. Interestingly, when the great depression began to bite during the '20s, the non-playing membership suffered but the number of people wanting to play cricket remained at well over 100.

Schools cricket was also strong, and scorecards of inter-school matches were published in the local papers. This enables us to follow the careers of players like Laidlaw Byers, Archie and Duncan Black, Tom Findlay and William Barclay, through from schools cricket to 2nd XI and then onto 1st XI cricket.

Looking back with the knowledge that Archie Black would become one of Motherwell's greatest ever players, it's pleasing to see him make his mark as a 17-year-old, starring for Dalziel High one week, and scoring 105 against Newmains 2nds the next.

Annual Holiday Match

A feature of the 1920s was a mid-summer trip for players, committee members, wives and girlfriends. The day would be built around a match in Moffat, or Bridge of Allan, or Selkirk or anywhere in a country setting, to get away from the smoke and grime of industrial Motherwell. Fresh air (and probably alcohol) was the key.

The day would start at 7am when two 30-seater charabancs deluxe drew up at the Knowetop gates to load up the excited travellers. The photo shows the type of vehicle but not, sadly, the Motherwell contingent!

For the Moffat trip, the charabancs would stop at a hotel in Peebles for breakfast, then drive along St Mary's Loch, stopping at Tibbie Shields' Inn for refreshments. The last leg of the journey would take them past the grey mare's tail and, on arrival at Moffat, a fine lunch would await them at the cricket ground.

Cricket would be played, usually against a team of English school-masters who taught at a local private school. With victory secured, teas taken, music played and songs sung, they would round up the party and head for Motherwell, back home by 10.30pm. On one occasion, it rained heavily on the way back – but, as the Motherwell Times reported, 'nothing could dampen the spirits of the happy party'.

The Great Depression

Of course, the 1920s saw some very difficult times, with high levels of unemployment bringing misery to many. Amidst a general strike and the Wall Street crash, the post-war years were challenging, and Motherwell Cricket Club struggled financially like everyone else. We needed more money.

A Grand Fete was held. Subscriptions were increased by 20%. Lord Hamilton allowed the club to charge an entry fee for members of the public to watch 1st XI matches. But the biggest successes by far were the biannual whist drives, which were consistently well attended and raised income for the club. Times were tough but they survived.

Celebrities

The year 1921 saw the visit of a future British prime minister, **Sir Alex Douglas Home**, playing for Colonel Aikman's Ross Ramblers. He was still a schoolboy at the time, and played under the title of Lord Dunglass. He gave a stand-out performance, scoring 41 out of a total of 87. That said, he was overshadowed by R K Hinshalwood Snr, who scored a fine undefeated 70 as Motherwell clocked up 136 for 6.

His lordship, circled in the photograph, had a decent cricket career. The following year, he played a match-winning innings at Lords for Eton against Harrow; after school, he played first-class cricket with Oxford University and Middlesex; and he toured Argentina with an MCC side led by Pelham Warner. And, of course, he became PM in 1963. So it looks like he managed to overcome the disappointment of defeat at Home Park.

Although not quite in the same vein as Lord Dunglass, Motherwell had their own celebrity player in the early '20s. **Jimmy Jackson** was a star footballer with Motherwell who, at the end of the football season, would discard the claret and amber for his cricket whites. Jimmy was a decent batsman who scored two 50s and would take spectacular catches – the press would always focus on his performance. Great things were predicted for Motherwell's footballing cricketer … but then he was transferred to Aberdeen!

Another famous name graced the Home Park turf – **I A R Peebles.** He played for Uddingston and Middlesex and had made his debut for England the previous year, going on to win 15 test caps. He played against Australia (dismissing Don Bradman for 14), New Zealand and South Africa … and Motherwell.

Ian Peebles was part of a Scottish XI playing against Motherwell to raise funds for the widow of Jack Schofield, the former professional and groundsman, who had spent over 20 years with the club. Jack had died suddenly, aged 55.

For a time, Motherwell scented a shock victory when they bowled their illustrious opponents out for 87, but when Peebles got hold of the ball their hopes were quickly dashed. In what is generally regarded as the best spell of bowling ever seen at Home Park, he took 9 wickets for 6 runs. He was unplayable.

A Happy Ending

After playing friendly matches for most of the decade, the West of Scotland Cricket Union was re established in 1928. The 1st team finished mid-table but you could see a decent side developing as the young players gained experience, and they still had old RKH, who could win matches with bat or ball or both.

The big success story that year belonged to the Motherwell 2nd XI who won the inaugural reserve league. They were awarded the league flag, and prior to the presentation a flagpole had to be hurriedly attached to the pavilion. The team (pictured) was:

Back Row: R Jack (scorer), J Aitchison, T Donnelly
Middle Row: T W Findlay, D Coats, C A L Robertson (president), C Cornes, R Baillie, A Murdoch
Front Row: J Alexander, S Anderson, J R Baillie, J Gibson, T Share Jnr

In 1929, the 2nds retained their title, and the 1sts were competing for the First Division title (Dawson Shield). Motherwell had won almost all of their matches, most of them convincingly, losing only one. But Cowlairs, a Springburn team, had only dropped points in a drawn match, having won all of the others ... and the sides were meeting in the final game of the season at Home Park. Cowlairs only needed to draw the final game to win the title; Motherwell had to win.

The weather wasn't good, and it rained on the Saturday morning. Cowlairs didn't want the game played – a postponement would suit them fine. They turned up an hour late, they wouldn't play on the prepared wicket (a new strip was hurriedly prepared), they'd forgotten their match ball, one player had forgotten his flannels – they tried all the delaying tactics under the sun. Eventually, with the skies brightening, they agreed to start the game.

Motherwell skipper Laidlaw Byers won the toss and, on a difficult wicket, the home side managed to post a reasonable score of 92, with Tom Findlay and Duncan Black top-scoring with 16 runs apiece. Their opponents felt the score beyond them and, after all, a draw would suffice. So they went into their collective shell and tried to bat out the two hours remaining. But R K Hinshalwood (6 for 7) and Tom Findlay (4 for 3) bowled superbly to skittle Cowlairs for 12 runs! Lord Hamilton was in attendance and joined in the celebrations.

It was a joyous Annual General Meeting in October (apart from the fact that we were still losing money!). Motherwell had done the double, winning the first and second divisions. The president Charlie Robertson declared it the most successful in the club's history, especially as we had achieved the feat with teams substantially made up of young home-grown cricketers.

And it wasn't only the league titles – there were a number of other talking points. R K Hinshalwood had scored 2 centuries that season, we'd beaten West of Scotland comprehensively in the Rowan Cup, and the whist drives had been the best yet!

A young man called Tom Findlay had a sensational debut season. He had taken 102 wickets.

1st XI OPPONENTS	Total Runs FoR	Total Runs Against	my score	Bowling	No. of Wickets	Runs Against	Average	2nd XI OPPONENTS	Total Runs FoR	Total Runs Against	My Score	Avrge	No. of Wickts	Runs Against
Kilmarnock	113	66	1	1	4	10	2·5	Johnstone						
Johnstone								Cowlairs						
Cowlairs		94						Fauldhouse	94	48	38	38	2	8
West of Scotland	113	69						Anchor	116	59	40	78	2	11
Fauldhouse	99	50						Drumpellier	57	52	44	92	3	10
Anchor	51	60						Newmains						
Newmains	108	78						Carslairs	70	13	0	46	4	4
Drumpellier	75	106	8	9	2	12	3·6	Stobcross	106	27	6	327	4	1
Edinburgh Indians	92	51	0	4·5				Hyndland FB	104	91				
Newmains	109	90	18	9	4	8	3·	Bellshill	72	69	12	27·5	3	29
Uddingston								Clydesdale W.	100	31	0	22·0	5	11
Bellshill	202	48						Caldercruix	77	223	9	199	3	52
Uddingston	26							Carslairs	84	80			6	25
Drumpellier								Fauldhouse	97	43	37	209	4	9
Fauldhouse	141	80						Caldervale	102	74	44	23·75	2	24
Tannochside	141	184						Tannochside	188	31	34	24	6	8
Bridge of Allan								Clydesdale W						
Johnstone	128	70						Johnstone	110	45	6	23·	8	104
Tannochside	107	84						Caldervale						
Hillhead FP	152	112	0	3	21	4		Tannochside	180	56				
Renfrew								Drumpellier	130	73				
Bellshill	130	23	22	9·4	3	3	3·4	Bellshill						
Cowlairs	92	12	16	10·5	4	3	2·25	Cowlairs						
East Stirlingshire	168	74	40	14·	5	25	3·28	Caldercruix	58	44				
Renfrew	87	89	0	12·4	5	98	3·5	Renfrew	49	39				

Amazingly, 21-year-old Tom Findlay kept a note of the results (and his own performance) in the pages of his membership card. It's in minuscule writing but all neatly tabulated, and shows Tom's own progression from 2nd XI to 1st XI mid-season. It helps us to gain an understanding of the fixture list and the pathway to success for both teams.

A Full House

In 1929, young Willie McGuire produced a bowling performance that, statistically speaking, will be hard to beat. He took 10 wickets for 1 run in a match against Hamilton Academy. How bad must Hamilton have been? Conversely, how good was Willie McGuire?

Willie's medium quick deliveries took many wickets and, although he never managed to repeat his exploits of 1929 (well, nobody could!), his name featured on Motherwell scorecards for almost 30 years, before he donned the umpire's white coat. And as an aside, he wasn't a bad footballer either!

He was presented with the match ball, suitably inscribed, at the Annual General Meeting, and it is still proudly displayed in the home of his grandson.

It was a nice way to end the decade.

Professor William Barclay

In the 1960s, William Barclay was a well-known TV personality. He was Professor of Divinity and Biblical Criticism at University of Glasgow, and his engaging presentation style made him a popular figure on our television screens.

His formative years lay in Motherwell, and as a young man, he played cricket at Home Park. For our centenary brochure in 1973, William Barclay recalled his cricketing days 50 years before. Now, hearing his voice once more as we re-publish his article word-for-word, it gives us a fascinating insight into our Club and its characters 100 years ago.

I am not quite sure, but I think it was in 1923 that I became a member of Motherwell Cricket Club, and after half a century, I still remember! The gates at Knowetop and the long walk up the Avenue, where even bicycles were barred; the odd never-to-be-forgotten times when you would arrive at the gates at the same time as one of the 1st XI and he would walk up the

avenue with you; the taste of water – no water like it – from the pump in the Home Farm yard.

I remember the players 50 years ago – R K Hinshalwood, the dashing cavalier dancing out to crack the ball to the boundary; C A L Robertson, with his short leg, leaping between wickets like a kangaroo; Bob Morris, the craftiest of batsmen and bowler; A Gillespie, the wicket keeper, dapper in every action; Jack Schofield, the professional, most cunning of slow bowlers; John Baillie, past playing but always ready to show the boys how to do it.

I remember my own contemporaries – Eddie Houston, cutting the ball on the offside like a fencing master; Duncan Black with an off-drive like a shell from a howitzer – if it connected; and Archie Black, slashing fast bowlers through the slips at a speed that would have taken the fingers off any man who tried to catch the ball.

But of all the games, one I remember specially. I cannot now remember what the occasion was, but it was a celebration of some kind. A special team had been assembled to play Motherwell and among them was Ian Peebles – his father had been a minister in Uddingston – then at the height of his Test Match career. Motherwell batted first and Peebles bowled unchanged.

We had heard that he was a medium to slow spin bowler – he looked only slightly slower than greased lightning! I don't think that Peebles would be exhausted by bowling through that innings unchanged – maybe I haven't got the figures quite right, but I think that Motherwell managed to get a total of 16 and Peebles took 9 wickets for 6 runs. You got the same kind of thrill in watching it as you might have got watching early Christians being thrown to the lions!

Those were the days. I was never a good cricketer, but I usually got into the team because I was one of those people specially created by heaven to be a secretary, and as a reward for my labour, they let me play.

Motherwell gave me a happy boyhood, and not the least of the happiness came from cricket. Blessings on Motherwell as they set out on their second century.

Professor William Barclay, 1973.

A Golden Generation

*Throughout the '20s and '30s, the financial reports at
the AGMs made for consistently grim reading. Times
were difficult in the town (and elsewhere, of course) with
the great depression and unemployment, and gone were
the days when hordes of fans would pay their sixpence
to come and watch the game. But on the field, it was a
different kettle of fish.*

In the 1930s, the names on the team sheets become even more familiar. When talking to Bill Jardine about the old days, he would reminisce about the great pre-war players. Bill himself was captain of the 2nd XI for much of the decade but would practice and play with the great names of the era.

Here's a photograph of Bill with his team, who won the West of Scotland Union Reserve League in 1934. They won 17 out of 23 games that year.

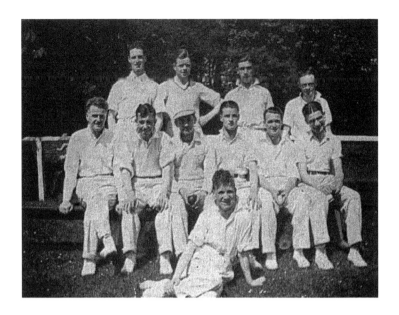

The full line up is:
Back row: G Paterson, T W Findlay, F S Crossley, R Tyrell
Seated: A Barr, P Danskin, W B Jardine (captain), G Nichols, W W Miller, G Hamilton
Front: J Walker

Several of Bill's team would go on to play a big part in Motherwell's history. Frank Crossley scored 4 centuries for the club; Bob Tyrell took many wickets; and Alan Barr became president in the early 1950s.

Tom Findlay, who would also take the president's chair in years to come, was described by some as the fastest bowler in Scotland. However, after a serious knee injury, he was recuperating in 2nd team cricket. Although his run-up was curtailed, he could still cause batsmen problems with his classic high-armed action and whip-crack deliveries. He wasn't bad with the bat either – he scored 101 not out against Lanark later that summer.

There were so many talented players, like Eddie Houston, Archie and Duncan Black, Tom Findlay, George Clark, Frank

Crossley and the star turn, R K Hinshalwood. So why didn't we win more trophies during this period? We won most of the games we played, yet the trophy cabinet wasn't exactly bulging.

The answer lies in the fact that Motherwell Cricket Club pulled out of the League. We apparently didn't want to spend our summers playing home and away against Bellshill, Newmains, Cowlairs (Springburn), Tannochside and Johnstone.

We had grander ambitions, and arranged friendlies against clubs like Uddingston, West of Scotland, Boroughmuir and Stirling County. It's clear that it wasn't just who we played but where we played, visiting pleasant pastures at Hillhead, Kelvinside Accies and Anchor.

The only competition we contested was the Rowan Cup when we were playing alongside the Western Union teams. We claimed quite a few scalps over the years, beating Clydesdale (when O T Wassell took 7 for 11), Uddingston, Drumpellier and West of Scotland, and reached the semi-finals on two occasions. But, despite these heroics, no finals, no silverware.

Whilst R K Hinshalwood Snr topped the averages year after year, the highlight performance of the decade belonged to Archie Black, who hammered an undefeated 148 against Singer CC. It was a record score for a Motherwell player, which stood for 50 years. Even today, it is the 2nd highest score by a Motherwell amateur.

A few were tempted to leave Home Park to see how they would fare in the Western Union. Some of the leading Motherwell players of the 30s, like Eddie Houston and Jack Lyle, joined Uddingston, and played well.

Motherwell Toffs?

We also get a better understanding of how the cricketers were perceived by the people of Motherwell. In his delightful booklet 'Motherwell at Leisure', Norman Moir remembered ...

*Without a doubt, in the 20s and 30s, cricket was a
sport indulged in by the "better-off" in Motherwell, and
I remember the cricketers of that era strolling down
Edward Street from the Knowetop gate of the estate on
summer evenings, after a match or practice, looking
resplendent in their … snow-white shirts and jerseys. It
was a pleasant sight in a somewhat grey background of
depression and unemployment.*

Motherwell At Leisure, Norman Moir

There are a few points raised which we can develop here …

Firstly, the Knowetop Gate was exactly that – a large
iron gate guarded by a gatehouse, with a formidable-looking
character checking if you were permitted to enter. Players
and members were waved through and, when spectators were
allowed, there would be an admission charge of sixpence
(2.5p).

Once through the gate, signs all the way down the path told
you not to walk on the grass. Before entering the lane leading to
the cricket ground, you would stop off at Home Farm to get a
drink of water from the pump.

On match days, a container of water was gathered from the
farm, and there was a boiler out the back of the pavilion to make
tea. Toilets were not installed until the early 1950s – you can fill
in the rest!

Secondly, were our cricketers among the better-off members
of Motherwell society? Whilst we don't know all of the players'
occupations, quite a few got a mention in the papers for
graduating from university.

We know that Duncan Black became a leading economist,
and that his brother Archie had a Classics degree, gaining prizes
for Greek! Although they had stopped playing by the '30s,
William Barclay was a theologian, and John Smellie Martin an

author and poet. And we had Dr Grieve and Dr White, both of whom started playing pre-war.

If we add in the fact that Motherwell had given up the rough and tumble of league cricket to play on nicer grounds against bigger clubs, maybe Norman Moir had a point.

He painted a vivid picture of a group of cricketers, still in their whites, wandering through the town after a match, and we'd have to say … what a bunch of posers!

Harking back to our Victorian roots, when the team was made up of immigrant iron workers from England and Wales, it's obvious that times had changed. You can't imagine our players of the '30s getting ready for the early shift down the mine or in the melting shop in the steelworks.

It's a generalisation, of course, but Motherwell's cricketers of the pre-war era probably were 'better off'.

Keeping the Club Afloat

There were repeated calls in the local papers for the Motherwell populace to turn out. In 1937, President Arthur Low hoped that "cricket would be more popular with the townsfolk than it had in the past". Arthur had been president before the First World War and had seen the massive crowds at Home Park, but these days would never return.

One of the contributing factors was the success of Motherwell Football Club – they won the League in 1932, contested cup finals and were a great team to watch. It was even noticeable within the cricket club that, when mid-August came along, they had problems getting two teams out.

One of the more innovative fund-raising initiatives took advantage of football's popularity and involved a cricket match against a Scottish Footballers XI. At the time, a number of players across the country played cricket in summer and football in winter, and this press cutting shows that some came to Home Park from afar …

The Footballers' XI will include J M Black (Kilmarnock and West of Scotland), S Renfrew (Queen of the South and Clydesdale), T G Smith (Queens Park), H Bremner (Motherwell), R Bennie (late Airdrie and Hearts), R Paton (late Third Lanark and Brentwood), J Harkness (Hearts), W Allan (Motherwell), J Crapnell (late Motherwell), A McClory (Motherwell), G Brown (Rangers) and T Bradshaw (Liverpool).
Motherwell Times, June 1935

The attendance was excellent, with a good number of football supporters turning out and paying their sixpence at the gate. The game ended in a draw, though the football fans were probably scratching their heads wondering how a match where one side scores 113 and the other 78 for 9, could be called a draw!

The cricket club also held grand fetes in the estate and ran raffles to generate income, but the whist drives were still the most popular events in town. They were followed by dancing, and on one occasion, the band playing was none other than Bill Jardine's Four Aces, fronted by a guest singer.

The club had a healthy playing membership, and the pipeline of talent was good. Dalziel High School had 5 teams playing cricket, with both Motherwell and Carfin Hall making their grounds available for school cricket.

One of the most pleasing items to find in a box of 'old cricket stuff' passed on to Jack Kelly following Ronnie Morrison's death was a collection of old membership cards. We have all the cards for the 1930s, some belonging to Eddie Houston, others to Tom Findlay, giving us the full fixture list for the decade.

But then the game of cricket and the raising of funds for the club were put into perspective.

It was a solemn message given to the assembled company of players and members at the 1939 AGM by Fred Rooks in his Secretary's Report …

> *"The club is making arrangements to carry on next summer in spite of the circumstances prevailing at present, and it is hoped that all members will assist in continuing the club's activities during a year which promises to prove extremely difficult."*

Keep Calm and Carry On

The 1940s were fraught years for everyone. Britain had entered the war in September 1939, and in January 1940, food rationing was introduced. An average weekly shop consisted of small portions of bacon, butter, sugar, cheese and meat, and if you were lucky, cooking fat and milk … how on earth were we supposed to prepare cricket teas for 22 players, 2 umpires and 2 scorers on that?

Of course, it was no laughing matter. Just 20 miles away, Clydebank was being bombed, air raids by the Luftwaffe were targeting the shipbuilding and munition-making industries, and it all felt very close to home. Would Motherwell's steel mills be next? These were worrying times.

Just like during the First World War, cricket and other sporting clubs provided a welcome distraction for the town. Most of Motherwell's cricketers were serving king and country, but the Home Park flag was kept flying by some of the old stagers and those who weren't able to join up.

If they had formed a Home Guard platoon, we can be sure that they would have ignored the words of Private Fraser – "We're doomed" – and adopted Lance Corporal Jones' catchphrase

– "Don't panic!" – a sentiment that reflects our approach to difficult times throughout our history.

The Motherwell Times summed things up well after the club had struggled through the 1940 season …

> *The club, while finding considerable difficulty in fielding a full team on occasion, due to so many of the members having been called up to the Forces, has nevertheless managed to keep its head above water during the past season and is able to record a balance of wins over defeats. We sincerely hope that, by next season, the names of the boys who are at present engaged in "other duties" may all have returned to their old accustomed places on the team sheet.*
> Motherwell Times, 1940

The "other duties" took priority for a few more years. Cricket was played but it was a low-key affair, reported in brief.

Wartime Cricket

We only fielded one team during the war years, and were restricted to matches with clubs nearby. Motherwell's cricketers got to know our neighbours extremely well, with Woodhall, Bellshill, Lanark and Carfin Hall featuring regularly, as did games against Army and RAF teams stationed locally. The games against the RAF became so regular that 5 fixtures took place each year, a series that was christened 'The Ashes'.

Tom Findlay and Bill Jardine shared the captaincy of the side. When players came home on leave, they would bolster the side. Occasional appearances from Frank Crossley, Jack Donnelly and Archie and Duncan Black would strengthen the batting, and R K Hinshalwood Snr reappeared towards the end of the war.

The rest of the Motherwell team was less familiar, and if short on numbers, we would co-opt some players from the Army or RAF teams, or from other clubs. In one game, there were 5 guests from Carfin Hall making up the numbers.

How did we do? Well, Tom Findlay and Bob Tyrell took lots of wickets, Frank Crossley scored a century, Archie Black scored four 50s in consecutive matches and, in 1945 when circumstances allowed a more extensive fixture list, we defeated Drumpellier, Uddingston and West of Scotland. But results were not celebrated; they didn't really matter.

Several initiatives were launched to help the war effort and to raise spirits in the town. With travel restricted for the townsfolk, we organised games for locals as part of a 'Holidays at Home' initiative. An effort was also made to re-start the works league.

In October 1945, the AGM was chaired by Allan Barr, who told the meeting that, with many members still to return from overseas, the club had little idea of our playing resources. The club proposed to run two XIs in 1946, so we needed to find new players and generate more income. For the first time in a while, a full list of office-bearers was voted in, and it started to feel like life was returning to normal once again.

Back Up And Running

The club made a remarkably quick recovery. We did indeed manage to field two teams and, after a couple of years, a 3rd XI was added to give everyone a game. As an added bonus, Bill Jardine took a Sunday XI made up of players from Motherwell and Carfin Hall to Dumfries to play Crichton Royal. Here's a photo of that very first W B Jardine XI.

The Scottish cricket captain, J M Fleming, brought a select side to Home Park. In front of several hundred fans, Motherwell

acquitted themselves well in a drawn match. Fleming was so impressed with Frank Crossley's performance that he took him on their tour of Wales, where he played every game, averaging 35.

Frank Crossley took over the captaincy of Motherwell Cricket Club in 1947 and promised to 'bring back former glories'. And he did – it was a memorable year for the club with Frank scoring two centuries, and a young man called R K Hinshalwood Jnr made a sensational impact with both bat and ball.

The highlight was Archie Black's 10 for 22 to beat Clydesdale at Titwood in the Rowan Cup. Archie bowled leg-spin but pushed them though at a decent pace. He was unplayable that night against one of the top Western Union sides, clean bowling 7 of his victims. Jack Donnelly's 37 not out allowed Motherwell to reach 75 for 7, as Archie dismissed Clydesdale for 52.

Here's a photo of the 1st XI in 1949 with a number of stalwarts pictured. Bill Jardine told the AGM that it was the best Motherwell team he had seen since the '20s.

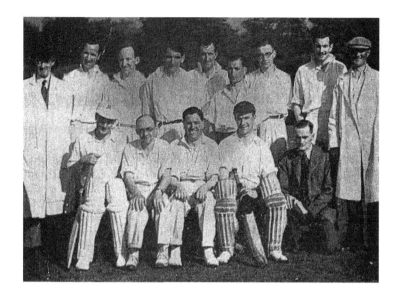

The club captain, George Clark, is absent but it's great to see the two umpires, Laidlaw Byers and R K Hinshalwood Snr, who had been such an important part of Motherwell Cricket Club during the 1920s and '30s.

Back Row: R K Hinshalwood Snr (umpire), A Black, N McNeice, P Pritchard, T Sharp, W Kay, G Hamilton, G McFarlane and J L Byers (umpire)

Front Row: R K Hinshalwood Jnr, R Tyrrell, W McGuire, J Donnelly and V Crowley (scorer)

Frank Crossley moved to Uddingston, but it didn't stop Motherwell Cricket Club's run of success. George Clark and Jack Donnelly scored runs consistently, and with spin-twins Johnny Gibson and young R K Hinshalwood, we won many more games than we lost.

There was also a strong Junior team. By the end of the decade, several young players were introduced to senior cricket, including Jim Logan, John Welsh and Bobby Steel, boys who would carry the torch for the next two decades.

The Hinshalwoods

When you hear the roll call of Motherwell's cricketing greats, one name stands out, and that is R K Hinshalwood. What makes it doubly impressive is that there were two of them, R K Hinshalwood Snr and R K Hinshalwood Jnr, and they're both deserving of top billing.

To be totally accurate, there were actually three of them. Back in the 1880s, there was an R K Hinshalwood playing for Newmains Cricket Club, one of Motherwell's local rivals, and he was always a thorn in our flesh, taking wickets, scoring runs, all the way through to the First World War.

It was during the Great War that his son, then known as R K Hinshalwood Jnr, first appeared for Motherwell, and it was obvious from the outset that the lad had bundles of talent. An all-rounder like his father, he featured impressively with both bat and ball for many years, still playing the odd game in the 1950s.

Just to confuse matters, he named his son R K Hinshalwood. So the bloke who used to be called R K Hinshalwood Jnr had to be re-christened R K Hinshalwood Snr, and the new kid in town became R K Hinshalwood Jnr.

The young lad inherited not just his father's (and grandfather's) name, but also the family cricketing genes. Both father and son were all rounders, and were the star players of their generations.

Their record stands up against any cricketers in our 150 year history. If we look at centuries scored by non-professionals, only Frank Crossley in the '30s and '40s, and Alaguraja Pichimatau (Raj!) in recent years can compare with the Hinshalwoods.

R K Hinshalwood Snr

'Old Bob' joined Motherwell in 1915 as a lad and, bizarrely, one of the first games he played was against Newmains, where his father was still a top player. Needless to say, he clean bowled his old man.

In an era when team totals were generally less than 150, he frequently passed 50 and scored five centuries …

- 129 v Cowlairs in 1921
- 111 v Hutcheson's FP in 1921
- 111 v Hillhead HSFP in 1925
- 106 v Bellshill in 1929
- 107 not out v Hillend in 1929

He was appointed captain in 1920 and led from the front. In his century against Cowlairs, he hit seven 6s, which gives us a good idea of how he batted!

Another highlight was the game against Colonel Aikman's XI which featured Lord Dunglass (who became Sir Alex Douglas Home) and other top players. 'Old Bob' scored 70 not out to win the match.

He must have enjoyed playing against Colonel Aikman's

teams. In 1923, R K Hinshalwood Snr became the first Motherwell player to take all 10 wickets … and we have the scorecard.

The Colonel had put together a decent team, with a few Western Union players in the line-up. Bob Morris and Alex Gillespie had managed to get Motherwell to a total of 105, and the result was always in the balance, but Hinshalwood's heroics secured a 19-run victory. He recorded bowling figures of 10 for 26, hitting the stumps no fewer than seven times.

ROSS RAMBLERS.

W. R. Aikman, c Gillespie, b Hinshalwood	14
J. Paterson, b Hinshalwood	2
Lieut. c Peacock, b Hinshalwood	6
Capt. Russell, c Smith, b Hinshalwood	9
Capt. Cavendish, b Hinshalwood	16
W. Bartelot, b Hinshalwood	0
Capt. Moran, b Hinshalwood	1
Lan. Corp. Cohen, b Hinshalwood	0
D. Grant, b Hinshalwood	0
J. Philipson, not out	24
J. Graham, b Hinshalwood	5
Extras	9
Total	86

There was also the famous benefit match in 1928 for the widow of Jack Schofield, a great servant of the club as professional, amateur and groundsman. We've heard of Ian Peebles' 9 wickets, but 'Old Bob' took 7 wickets for 34 runs that day, against a team featuring several Scottish internationalists. He was mixing it with the best of them.

That same year, he captained a West Scotland team and, the following year, he scored two centuries in successive weeks. R K Hinshalwood Snr headed the batting averages almost every year for the next decade, and frequently the bowling averages too.

He took on the club presidency in 1953, but donned his whites one more time to help Motherwell beat Carfin Hall by hitting two 6s to win the game. He must have been about 60 at the time – good on him!

R K Hinshalwood Jnr

After breaking records in school cricket playing for Dalziel High, 'Young Bob' made his first appearance for Motherwell in 1944, and over the next few years, his career took off stratospherically. It took a couple of years before he became a first team regular and after that, there was no stopping him.

In 1946, young Bob started the season with the 2nds and, after a series of big scores, was promoted to the top team. It was his breakthrough season, averaging 48 with the 2nd XI and 38 with the 1st XI.

In a match the following year, Golfhill witnessed his all-round talents as he scored 102 not out and followed it up with 7 for 20 with the ball. Just like his father had done in the '20s and '30s, young Bob dominated many games with bat or ball or both.

The pair turned out in the same Motherwell team on a few occasions after the war, and it must have been a proud day for the old man when father (29) and son (64 not out) opened the batting for the 1st team, putting on 70 for the first wicket in a victory over Bellshill. The baton was being passed from one generation to the next.

Against a West District X1, young Bob's leg breaks took 7 wickets for 4 runs, and he very soon found himself picked for the Western Cricket Association (effectively a trial for the national side).

There was a memorable performance against a British Army XI at Carlisle. Six of the Army side who played in that match turned out for the Forces team against the Scotland national team the following week. Young Bob excelled, taking 7 for 32, and the Army skipper couldn't believe that the Motherwell leg spinner hadn't been picked for the Scottish side.

He continued to bamboozle batsmen with his bowling, leading to another East v West trial, and he clocked up four centuries for Motherwell …

- 110 not out v Barr & Stroud in 1946
- 102 not out v Golfhill in 1947
- 105 v Babcock & Wilcox in 1950
- 106 not out v Weirs in 1951

In 1954, we find young Bob at Uddingston, joining a number of Home Park players trying their luck in the Western Union. His Motherwell career lasted less than a decade, but he achieved so much in that relatively short time. Those who played with him reckon he was the most naturally gifted cricketer ever to play for the club.

For a period of 40 years, the name of R K Hinshalwood dominated the Motherwell Cricket Club headlines, with 'Old Bob' starring for the club after the First World War and 'Young Bob' after the Second World War. Whether Snr or Jnr, it was a rare thing to pick up the Motherwell Times during the summer months without reading of the cricketing exploits of an RK Hinshalwood.
Quite a dynasty!

Riding The Waves

Things were so promising at the start of the 1950s. There was a post-war optimism about the club, and we were fielding three senior teams to give everyone a game. In addition, W B Jardine took his team of Lanarkshire cricketers on tours and there was an exciting crop of juniors taking their first steps in the 1st XI.

Wind the clock forward to 1960 and we find a banner headline in the Motherwell Times …

CRICKET CLUB'S LAST SEASON?

What on earth had gone wrong? In less than a decade, our optimism had been ripped up and tossed to the winds, replaced by a desperate cry for help: *the end is nigh!*

Triple Success

To find the answer, we need to walk through the 1950s to understand the peaks and troughs of our cricket club's fortunes, both on and off the field.

It all started so brightly. 1952 was one of the most successful years in the club's history. There was still no league to win, just friendlies, but of the 32 games played that year, we won 26. Several cups were up for grabs, and we pretty much cleaned up – three trophies were paraded at a celebratory dinner at The Crown in Wishaw.

The Wrangholm Cup was a knock-out competition for Lanarkshire clubs, and it was first to fall. Motherwell defeated Stewarts & Lloyds in the final.

In the Murray Cup (sometimes called the Drumpellier Cup), Motherwell fielded a 2nd XI but played against the 1st XIs of local teams. In the final, we defeated Woodhall's top team with Stan Solly 'hitting the ball with violence'. Remarkably, we had also won the Murray Cup in 1951, when Jim Logan's batting and Johnny Welsh's bowling proved too much for Carfin Hall.

The Western Cup win was the big one. We defeated Lennox, Cowlairs, Carfin Hall and Milngavie & Bearsden to reach the final, where we faced Clydesdale 2nds. It was a close-run thing but we got over the line with 8 wickets down. All the way through the competition, Bob Tyrell bowled superbly, along with his new opening partner Gordon Hallam.

We have more photos of the class of '52 than any other year. Everyone wanted their picture taken. Here's the 1st team squad, abounding with talent …

Back Row: J Ritchie, A Hamilton, G Hallam, L Jones (secretary), R Steel, J Logan, W Hardie
Front Row: J Donnelly, R Tyrell, R K Hinshalwood Jnr, G Macfarlane (captain), R K Hinshalwood Snr (president), G Clark, S Solly, N McNeice, A McCracken

This photograph was actually taken at the start of the 1953 season after 'old Bob' Hinshalwood had assumed the presidency, but here's another that was taken the previous year with George Clark in the president's chair. He decreed that the year had been a triumph for everyone associated with the club – players, officials and the ladies who had helped with the teas. They all got together at Home Park for a club photograph …

There were various other items of note that year. Gordon Hallam had taken 100 wickets (including 4 in 4 balls against Boroughmuir), and George Clark scored 600 runs and John Ritchie 400 runs.

John Ritchie was with us for only a few years but made his mark with many fine innings. Educated at Gordonstoun, he often opened the batting with Andrew Ross, a Fettesian! How posh were we?!?

Feeder Club?

Another trophy followed in 1953 with the Coronation Cup, by virtue of a win over Fauldhouse – we were on a roll! Around this time, several Motherwell players – Frank Crossley, John Ritchie, George Clark and R K Hinshalwood – took part in the West v East matches, regarded as trials for the national team.

What followed was predictable. If these players wanted to take the next step and play for Scotland, they had to play competitive games, week-in, week-out, in the Western Union. So Motherwell Cricket Club witnessed an incredible exodus of talent with Crossley, Clark, Hinshalwood and bowler Eric Clarke joining Uddingston. It was a path followed by Jim Logan and young Bobby Park a few years later.

How did Motherwell feel about it? They left with their 'best wishes', and in the Motherwell Times, the fortunes of the ex-Motherwell players were highlighted if they performed well for Uddingston. And they did, often. But there was a sub-text … *no matter how good you are, you'll struggle to get capped if you're playing for Motherwell.*

It was good to see Frank Crossley come back to Home Park for a couple of seasons before concentrating on his football refereeing and cricket umpiring, both at the top level. And, of course, Jim Logan returned to be part of the excellent Motherwell teams of the '60s.

A New Generation

The departure of so many top players left a gaping hole, but young talent was maturing and became the core of Motherwell's 1st team by the mid-50s.

Bobby Steel had been a promising junior and had also trialled for Motherwell Football Club. He became the mainstay of the team for years. His wickets and runs won many a match, and it was no surprise that success in the '60s coincided with Bobby's elevation to captaincy.

Another well-known name opened the bowling for most of the decade. After a comfortable victory, the local paper reported that the 'menacing figure of *John Welsh*' routed the Allan Glens batting. That must have been something to see!

Gavin Forbes was a fine wicketkeeper and middle order batsman. During the '50s and early '60s, he was a regular contributor with both bat and gloves, captaining the side for several years.

David Brady developed into one of the most destructive batsmen in the club's history, and was still scoring runs for Motherwell 20 years later. He formed legendary opening partnerships with *Baxter Rae* in the late '50s and *Archie Syme* in the '60s. And, of course, both David and Archie could bowl a bit.

Alastair Hamilton and *Ronnie Morrison* were batting technicians, and *Jim 'Peaky' Anderson* (father of David, a future Motherwell stalwart) and *Morton Mitchell* picked up wickets. This was a fine team in the making.

The most precocious of all the young cricketers was *Bobby Park*. As a 16-year-old, he was a 1st team regular, scoring runs – big runs – and taking wickets. When Motherwell won the Connell Cup in 1958, it was Park's innings that beat Lanark in the final. Inevitably, in 1959, he was playing for Uddingston, scoring a 50 on debut and picking up his first century the following year.

Looking at these young players, it's evident that many of those who debuted for Motherwell in the late '40s and early '50s – like Steel, Brady, Syme, Morrison, Hamilton and Welsh – were still going strong for Motherwell 20 years later.

... And Our Cricketing Doctors

Jim Logan was another. A true sporting all-rounder, as well as a doctor. He was awarded his 'blue' at Glasgow University for both football and cricket, and played cricket for Scottish universities and British universities. He also played golf for Lanark and tennis for Wishaw.

He was a classical batsman and tidy off spinner, and had a habit of dominating an innings. In his early days at Motherwell, he scored 35 not out when the 2nd XI was skittled for 38 by Ruchill. Later in his career, when the W B Jardine XI accumulated 160 against Ardeer, his contribution was an undefeated 130. Bill Jardine said it was one of the great innings by a Motherwell player.

On occasion, Jim Logan mixed cricket with his day job. At the very end of his career, he was famously dropped from the first team for scoring too slowly in a midweek cup match, and played for the 2nds on the Saturday. He was on call and was summoned to attend to a patient mid-innings, but returned later to complete his half century, and retired from cricket shortly thereafter.

Alex McCracken was a contemporary. Like Jim Logan, he also played for Glasgow University before starring with Motherwell in the mid-1950s. Although he contributed useful runs, it was as a fast bowler that he made his name, regularly picking up 6 or 7 wickets. His best return was 8 for 15 against Kelvinside Accies, before he gave up the glories of Home Park to continue his pathology career in Texas.

Jimmy White (The Doc) was a feisty cricketer and individual who captained both the 1st team and 2nd team, and became club president for the glory years of the 60s. His diminutive presence, complete with splendid moustache and hooped cricket cap, was a familiar image at the club. He was a splendid raconteur and a natural leader of men.

Kerr Grieve was a famous Motherwell medic who played either side of the war, and became president for the centenary celebrations. He was the consultant obstetrician at Motherwell Maternity and was known for his strict regime. With his dashing mop of hair and matching moustache, he was in his element at cricket dinners. After presiding over the event, he would end the evening bashing out songs on the piano.

Singh Alhuwalia was only with us for a few years, but made a huge impact on joining the club. He was an integral part of the late 1960s side that swept all before it. Resplendent in his turban, Alhuwalia would open the bowling with Bobby Steel and the pair would frequently share the wickets between them, as their opponents were stifled by the accuracy of their deliveries. He rarely bowled a bad ball.

The Glasgow League

At last, after season upon season of friendly cricket, the Glasgow and District League was formed in 1955. Needless to say, Bill Jardine was involved in the setting up of the league … in much the same way as he was involved in the organisation of the Western Cup, the Murray Cup, the Wrangholm Trophy and the Connell Cup, mostly as president. He was involved in everything cricket-related, and became a West District selector.

In any newspaper photo of a cricket team receiving a cup, there's Bill Jardine wearing his Motherwell jumper under his jacket, handing it over. There was even a report in the local paper when his 8-year-old daughter won a sandcastle building competition on Montrose beach – except it wasn't a sandcastle, it was a model of Montrose Cricket Club!

But with a league structure in place, Motherwell's talented cricketers had the opportunity to win something. The founder members were Anchor, Cartha, Golfhill, Glasgow Accies,

Glasgow High, Glasgow University, Helensburgh, Hillhead, Kelvinside Accies, Milngavie & Bearsden and Motherwell.

Changes at Dalzell Estate

Lord Hamilton, our Honorary President and owner of the estate, died in 1952. His successor decided to live in England and put the estate up for sale. By 1955, Dalzell House became Gresham School, and plans were presented for a college to be built and for housing to be developed in the Burngrange area near to the cricket club.

The biggest change for Motherwell Cricket Club was the removal of the gates to Dalzell Estate, which allowed the general public access to the grounds. Vandalism became a regular occurrence with damage to the pavilion and to the boundary fence. Break-ins were frequent – the mower motor was stolen, windows were broken, the pipes stripped and the crockery smashed.

After 70 years of peaceful existence at Home Park, it looked like there was no future. More pressingly, all the repairs and replacements cost hundreds of pounds, money that the club didn't have. When the Motherwell Times ran the story questioning the future of the club, you could sense the feeling of helplessness and despair. What had happened to our idyllic cricket ground?

Another factor added to the concerns. There were now only 18 senior members and 10 juniors, a far cry from the huge playing membership just a decade before. The good news was the large number of juveniles wanting to learn the game, but the club's needs were more urgent.

Looking back, this was the pivotal moment when life became an awful lot tougher for Motherwell Cricket Club, opening sores at Home Park that never really healed.

The old pavilion (miraculously!) lasted another 17 years, and we stayed at Home Park for 22 years after that ... but, just like the graffiti on the old clubhouse verandah, the writing was on the wall.

The Memory Man

Here's a question. Who featured in just about every 1st team photo from the early '60s through to the late '90s? An ever-present. Clue : he wouldn't be wearing whites, he would be his usual dapper self, standing at the end of the back row.

OK, it might have been Bill Jardine, who was never too shy when a photo was being taken, but this is another individual who was a club servant until the day he died. The answer, of course, is Peter Forbes, our scorer for longer than any of us can remember.

Some people aren't fully appreciated until they're not there. Peter was a bit like that. Due to his long-standing role as scorer and statistician, we took it for granted that Peter would attend every 1st team game, keep an immaculate scorebook, work out the averages and retain all the data for posterity. He loaded all the records onto computer, belying his traditional appearance and behaviour.

But then in 1999 he passed away, and there was no Peter Mark 2. How could there be? We thought he would go on forever. And it's only now, when we're pulling together club records to celebrate 150 years of Motherwell Cricket Club, that the truth is staring us in the face: up to 1999, Peter had laid the foundations to facilitate our research; 2000 and beyond, we are on our own!

50 Years of Service

Every club needs a Peter, and we are luckier than most to have had Peter Barrie Gibb Forbes as our companion for most of our cricketing lives. His middle names make him sound like a Bee Gees tribute act, but nothing could be further from the truth. Peter was a man who went about his business quietly and professionally, never looked for any praise or pats on the back, and we always found him the same way – neither up nor down.

He played for 10 years or so, initially for Uddingston and then for Motherwell, alongside his brothers Gavin and Scott, but only once did we find three Forbes in the same team when they played for the 2nd XI in the early '60s. Gavin was a very talented player, keeping wicket and scoring runs and captaining the club in the '50s. Peter didn't have the same skills but was no less passionate about the game.

With his love of statistics, it was a no-brainier that Peter would become club scorer when he finished his playing career. His meticulous attention to detail, his different coloured pens to highlight the various scoring shots, the amount of information contained in his book from partnerships to the time taken to score a 50 – and, of course, it all squared up – the runs and the extras would always tally with the aggregate of the bowlers' analyses.

As well as scoring, he would keep the scoreboard updated over by over, and he was a human encyclopaedia of cricket's rules – he knew them all. When some captains were struggling to make sense of it all, the answer was … ask Peter.

At one cricket dinner, Eddie Rose of Hillhead was a guest speaker, and he emphasised how lucky we were as a club to have living legends like Bill Jardine and Peter Forbes. Eddie would always make a point of appreciating Peter's scorebook and, if ever there was any discrepancy with the other scorer, everyone knew that Peter's book would be the correct one.

There was a memorable incident when Motherwell participated in a cricket quiz in Glasgow against other cricket clubs and, of course, Peter was part of our team. A question was asked about an English player who had scored over 400 runs in an innings in a county match, to which the expected answer was Graham Hick.

The quiz had to be temporarily paused when Peter pointed out that Archie McLaren had been the first Englishman to do so – for Lancashire v Somerset in 1895, when he scored 424. And no-one dared to dispute the fact.

In an early round of the Western Cup in the '80s, after Robertson and Bill had done the hard work, Steve Young cleaned up the tail by taking the last two wickets in consecutive balls. About three weeks later, in the next round, Steve was brought on to bowl mid-innings and took a wicket with his first ball. No-one thought much about the dismissal until Peter ran down from the pavilion to the boundary edge shouting, "It's a Western Cup hat-trick."

This was lost on everyone, including Steve, but Peter had it all in his head – same competition, three wickets in three consecutive balls, spanning three weeks! Hat-tricks aren't actually defined within the laws of the game, but Peter reckoned it was something worth celebrating, something which would have been overlooked without his attention to detail and passion for the game.

Peter's Travels

He was also a member of Durham County Cricket Club, and he would travel to Chester-Le-Street a couple of times each year. Chester-Le-Street isn't the easiest of places to get to and, when you don't drive, it's even more of a challenge. But not to Peter. He had all the bus timetables memorised and the connections he'd have to make, everything stored away. We know this because he told us. In every detail.

It wasn't the most scintillating conversation, but Peter couldn't be happier – his travels had all gone swimmingly due to his meticulous planning. Of course, when he got to Durham to watch the cricket, what did he do? Keep a scorecard of the day's play!

He also attended the cricket festival at Scarborough, and twice went on tours organised by the MCC (not Motherwell, the other one!) to Australia to watch the Ashes. Again we heard all about his travels, the players he met, the games he watched. When he wasn't present in person to watch the cricket down under, he would set the alarm for some ungodly hour to tune in to Test Match Special for the commentary.

His Legacy

Peter was a unique individual. Never in all of his 50 years' association with the club did anyone hear him complain. He was always immaculately dressed and punctual to the second, traits drilled into him from his days in National Service with the navy.

Scoring the book was a chore for some, but not Peter – he loved what he did and being part of something that mattered to him. That something was Motherwell Cricket Club. He had been researching and writing up the 1st XI results for many years, going through old newspapers in the library, and completed this work just prior to his death. The scores were collated neatly in several ring binders, and over the past year, those statistics have been of great help as we tried to piece together the historical elements of our book.

Throughout the years, many club photographs have been taken, some of winning teams, some at our annual dinners and some just for fun. Peter was the constant, the man who was always there and appeared in almost every team photo. Here, with the 1961 league-winning team, Peter is pictured far left wearing the dark suit, with his brother Gavin in the middle of the same back row.

The full line-up is…

Standing: P Forbes (scorer), R A Morrison, G Smith, A R Syme, J R Logan, G Forbes, J Thewliss, K Ridley, W B Jardine (match secretary) and R Findlay

Seated: T A Sneddon (vice-president), R S Steel, J H White (president), and D A Brady

(J Anderson and A Hamilton were absent)

Will our club ever have another Peter? We doubt that very much. Thank you, Peter, for your 50 years of dedicated service to our club.

Table Toppers

It seemed like someone had flicked a switch. The 1950s became the 1960s and everything changed. Music, fashions, television, colours and even the permissive society, but in Motherwell, people were stopped in their tracks by the front page headline: *Motherwell's Cricketers Win League.*

We weren't used to winning things. Our club produced some great players, we always played an entertaining brand of cricket, we turned over the best of teams (only to lose to inferior teams) and finished a respectable mid-table. It had been a long while since we had won a league title – since 1929 to be exact. But that's what happened, and not just once.

Our Golden Decade: Year by Year

1960 was our warm-up, but it was clear that something was afoot. After a dodgy start, Motherwell won ten games in a row, some in the cups, some in the league. We enjoyed the winning feeling, and finished a creditable 3rd while again securing the Connell Cup. Something was brewing.

Baxter Rae and David Brady were a potent opening pair

and, in a cup tie against Fauldhouse, they had the 100 up in the eleventh over. It's a feat quite commonplace nowadays in T20 cricket but, back then, such an exhibition of big-hitting was awe-inspiring.

In **1961**, it all came together and the league was wrapped up by early August. In the Motherwell Times, Bill Jardine was quoted as saying it was 'the greatest achievement for the Club'.

The newly appointed captain was Bobby Steel, an all-rounder who seemed to take wickets every week. He didn't disappoint. He took 7 wickets against Hillhead, and it was fitting that, in the league-winning match against Milngavie and Bearsden, he scored a 50 and took 4 wickets.

Gavin Forbes excelled as a wicketkeeper-batsman, Johnny Welsh and John Anderson took wickets as opening bowlers, and David Brady and Alastair Hamilton chipped in with useful runs. But the key piece of the jigsaw that had fallen into place was the return of Jim Logan from Uddingston. He declared his intent with 98 against Kelvinside Accies, and picked up regular wickets with his off-spin throughout the season.

He was also a secret weapon in evening matches. The Home Park wickets ran east to west and, as the sun slid lower in the western sky, Jim Logan was brought on to bowl. He flighted his spinners up into the glare of the sun, which reflected off his baldy pate, blinding the batsmen.

Endless arguments ensued, with some teams demanding we bowl all our overs from the east, and others insisting that the baldy bowler wear a cap. Needless to say, we pointed out that the late evening sunshine was a natural phenomenon to be enjoyed, and that Jim Logan couldn't do much about his lack of hair.

There was one particularly notable game in 1961 when Motherwell bowled Cartha out for 4 runs, including a bowling change! John Anderson took a couple of early wickets but, with dark clouds gathering above, there was concern that rain might save Cartha and the game declared null and void.

Bobby Steel reckoned that John's run-up was too long and that his overs were eating up too much time. John was sent to field at short fine leg while Jim Logan's spinners cleaned up the Cartha tail. The bowling analyses: Steel 5 wickets for 2 runs, Logan 3 for 2 and Anderson 2 for 0.

We were runners-up in **1962** with more sterling efforts from Logan, Steel and Forbes, but a new name featured amongst the wickets: Robin Findlay. Son of the legendary Tom Findlay, he made a name for himself in his own right with medium pace bowling and stalwart fielding.

1963 was another glorious year, champions once more. The league records show Played 10, Won 8, Lost 1 and Drawn 1. Having also reached the final of the Western Cup, there was a whole lot of winning going on.

Steel and Logan were again among the wickets but it was Robin Findlay who caught the eye, including 8 for 18 against Golfhill. With the bat, Jim Logan had an undefeated 96, again against Golfhill, and David Brady scored 101 against Collins. Motherwell had a well-balanced side, strong in every department.

We retained the title in **1964** in a canter. The league was as good as won by the end of July with Motherwell well out in front on 100%. We were used to bowling teams out cheaply and we were now posting big scores with the bat. Steel, Syme, Forbes and Findlay all contributed, but it was David Brady who was the star performer, including 109 against Golfhill.

Motherwell failed to make it three titles in a row, finishing 3rd behind Glasgow High in **1965**. But we didn't have to wait long to get back to the top of the tree.

Although Robin Findlay had left for Canada, there was

another new face at Home Park in **1966** – R S Ahluwalia, an opening bowler who immediately formed a fine opening partnership with Bobby Steel. The pair often bowled throughout the innings and shared the wickets, with Gavin Forbes taking numerous catches behind the stumps. The swinging sixties!

Hyndland must have been fed up with the sight of the Motherwell bowlers. They recovered from 10 for 7 to post 39 all out, with Steel taking 6 wickets and Ahluwalia 4. A month later, Hyndland managed to reach 50 as Ahluwalia took 5 wickets and Steel 4 in the game that won the league for Motherwell.

Archie Syme was the top batsman in '66, forming an opening partnership with David Brady that would continue for years to come. He scored his maiden century with 110 against Strathclyde University, while Logan, Brady and Steel all scored well throughout the season. But the opportunities for big scores were limited when Steel and Ahluwalia were dismissing the opposition for less than 50!

It came as some surprise when Motherwell lost a couple of early matches in **1967** and, as a result, were always chasing the leaders. The batsmen were full of runs with Brady (97 and 91), Logan (88), Steel (108 v Clydebank) and a young Bobby Kerr (100 v Bishopbriggs) all scoring well.

They also had big wins against Gala and Edinburgh select side The Bats, but defeat in the last game of the season to Prestwick robbed us of another title – we finished 2nd.

In **1968**, we really were robbed – well, that's how we felt. Motherwell's cricketers celebrated a closely contested league victory in September, only for the league committee to uphold an appeal against Hillhead for fielding an ineligible player. How did this affect Motherwell? Games against Hillhead were declared void, and a recalculation of percentages left us as runners-up.

It had been another memorable season. Bobby Park had

returned from Uddingston, where he had been one of the best batsmen in the Western Union for a number of years, but it was the old firm of Logan and Steel who featured most in Motherwell's run of victories.

Two 19-year-old lads from Wishaw also made their mark. Bobby Kerr kicked on from his maiden century, securing a place in Motherwell's top order, and with Gavin Forbes leaving for America, Allan Johnston took over the wicket-keeping duties. He reflected in later years that it was the easiest job in the world, such was the metronomic consistency of Bobby Steel and Ahluwalia. "Shelling peas!"

The young wicketkeeper had been given a suspension the previous year under the strict captaincy of Jim Logan. It had been absolutely bucketing down in Wishaw and, as it had been pouring all week, the ground conditions made cricket impossible. Allan was an 18-year-old student and skint, and didn't want to waste money on his bus fare to Motherwell. He was called before the committee on the Monday, reprimanded and barred from the ground for two weeks ... for not turning up to a match where not a ball was bowled!

The Motherwell team in 1968 is shown opposite.

In **1969**, Motherwell finished 3rd, remarkably their lowest league position of the '60s. If there was one feature that summed up the season – perhaps the decade – it was Bobby Steel's bowling.

His returns during '69 included 5 for 23 v Hillhead, 5 for 8 v Milngavie & Bearsden, 6 for 11 v Fauldhouse, 5 for 24 v Greenock and 4 for 8 v Hillhead.

Motherwell also experienced another Western Cup final defeat. David Brady and Bobby Kerr were both run out when going well, losing to Irvine after good wins against Fauldhouse and Greenock.

Standing: J L Sommerville, R A Morrison, T S Haroon, J Anderson, R S Steel, H Brady
Seated: R G Kerr, A J Johnston, D A Brady (captain), A R Syme and J R Logan
(*Absent*: R S Ahluwalia)

However, the club did end the '60s on a high note with Archie Syme and Ronnie Morrison establishing a record 3rd wicket stand of 133 against Dunlop. And, to top it all, the 2nd XI won the Reserve League. George Smith captained the side, which featured match-winning contributions from David McAllister, Jack Smith, Morton Mitchell and Willie Macfadyen.

The summary below shows the remarkable consistency of the 1st XI across the decade, without doubt the greatest period in the history of Motherwell Cricket Club.

1960 – 3rd
1961 – 1st
1962 – 2nd
1963 – 1st
1964 – 1st
1965 – 3rd
1966 – 1st
1967 – 2nd
1968 – 2nd
1969 – 3rd

And it happened at a time when there were strong competitors in the league - Glasgow High with Andy Little and Cameron MacIntyre, Fauldhouse with Charlie Singh and Alex Cruikshanks, Prestwick with John Leven and Johnny Hubbard, Hillhead with Harry Locke and John Maclean, and Macleod and Parker from Allan Glens.

Good players, good teams but, for most of the decade, Motherwell were more than a match for them, because we had some good players too.

A Familiar Refrain

Just like at the end of the '50s, there were more problems with vandalism. The pavilion was again broken into and trashed, the boundary seats destroyed. To make matters worse, there was concern over the tenure of Home Park as counsellors debated the future of Dalzell Estate. For the club to repair or even replace the pavilion, we needed certainty over our future at the ground. Although the signs were positive, it was taking an age to get confirmation.

The situation was progressed after the annual cricket dinner. It was a pincer attack by the eminent medics who were president and vice-president of Motherwell Cricket Club – Dr White, who had presided over the entire decade of success, and his successor, Dr Grieve.

They invited the Provost to deliver the final speech of the evening. The fact that every speaker before him had highlighted the difficulties of running the club amid such uncertainty left the poor Provost with little option but to promise to hurry things along. And he did.

And that was it, not just for the 60s, but for our 100 years of Motherwell Cricket Club. Well, not quite. The committee had established that 1873 was the year of our formation (wrongly, as we now know) and started to make plans for our centenary celebrations in 1973.

Presidents and Captains (1921–1970)

Year	President	Club Captain	Year	President	Club Captain
1921	H Reid	R K Hinshalwood Snr	1946	O T Wassell	R Russell
1922	H Reid	R K Hinshalwood Snr	1947	T W Findlay	F S Crossley
1923	H Reid	R Morris	1948	T W Findlay	P Pritchard
1924	H Reid	R Morris	1949	T W Findlay	G Clark
1925	J Baillie	C A L Robertson	1950	A Barr	G Clark
1926	J Baillie	C A L Robertson	1951	A Barr	G Clark
1927	J Baillie	C A L Robertson	1952		G McFarlane
1928	C A L Robertson	J L Byers	1953	R K Hinshalwood Snr	G McFarlane
1929	C A L Robertson	J L Byers	1954	T W Findlay	W Hardie
1930	A B McNair	J L Byers	1955	T W Findlay	G G Forbes
1931	A B McNair	A Marshall	1956	T W Findlay	G G Forbes
1932	A B McNair	A Marshall	1957	T W Findlay	G G Forbes
1933	A B McNair	O T Wassell	1958	J H White	A Hamilton
1934	J Baillie	A M Black	1959	J H White	R S Steel
1935	J Baillie	A M Black	1960	J H White	R S Steel
1936	A Low	A R Baillie	1961	J H White	R S Steel
1937	A Low	J M Donnelly	1962	J H White	R S Steel
1938	A Low	J M Donnelly	1963	J H White	R S Steel
1939	O T Wassell	A R Baillie	1964	J H White	R S Steel
1940	O T Wassell	T W Findlay	1965	J H White	J R Logan
1941	O T Wassell	T W Findlay	1966	J H White	J R Logan
1942	O T Wassell	T W Findlay	1967	J H White	D A Brady
1943	O T Wassell	T W Findlay	1968	J H White	D A Brady
1944	O T Wassell	T W Findlay	1969	J H White	R S Steel
1945	O T Wassell	T W Findlay	1970	J K F Grieve	A Syme

Pushing On To 150

*Rejuvenated after reaching our 100, we recovered
our form and settled into a rhythm, never too down
with failure, never too dizzy with success. There were
highlights, many of them, but also some scary moments
that stopped us in our tracks and almost brought our
innings to an end. But we re-took our guard, got back
into the groove and eventually runs flowed from the bat
like there was no tomorrow …*

*…. except, at Motherwell, there always seems to be a
tomorrow.*

Centenary Celebrations

Punching the air in celebration one year, head in your hands the next – that was the story of the '70s. Two relegations and a promotion, a burned-out pavilion and a shiny new clubhouse rising from the ashes. But there's only one place to start and that's 1973, our centenary year – or so we thought.

It was a peculiar year. Happy to be celebrating our 100 years, but sad about being demoted from the 1st Division for the first time since the league was formed in 1955. If only we knew then what we know now, we would have reached the milestone in 1971 without the dark cloud of relegation hanging over proceedings. Mid-table mediocrity and another Western Cup final defeat would have been a more fitting backdrop.

Regardless, we celebrated in style.

The Dinners

To mark the occasion, we did a lot of eating and drinking. In March we hosted our Centenary Dinner at The Garrion and in October, the Burgh of Motherwell and Wishaw granted us a Civic Reception to acknowledge our survival for 100 years. This was no mean achievement, especially for a cricket club in Motherwell.

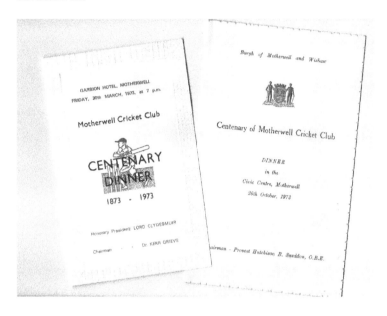

We held the Centenary Dinner pre-season, and it was a splendid night. It attracted cricketers old and young, many guests from other clubs, and a number of notable dignitaries. The organisers had tried to get Mike Denness to speak at the event, but the great Scottish cricketer happened to be captaining the English cricket team in India at the time, and sent us a telegram from Bombay to let us know that, with regret, he would be unable to attend. As excuses go ...

Thankfully, another cricketing legend, Ian Peebles, was able to come along, and he proposed the Toast to Motherwell Cricket Club. An Aberdonian, he had the distinction of playing for Scotland, MCC and England and had written several books on cricket. He was also cricket correspondent for the Sunday Times and, most importantly, had once played against Motherwell at Home Park.

If we were to wind the clock back another 40 odd years to the early 1930s, we'd find the same Ian Peebles dismantling the local team, taking 9 wickets for 6 runs with a brilliant display of spin bowling. And some of the Motherwell side that day were still around in 1973 to face him once again at the Centenary Dinner – but thankfully his words were kinder than his leg breaks.

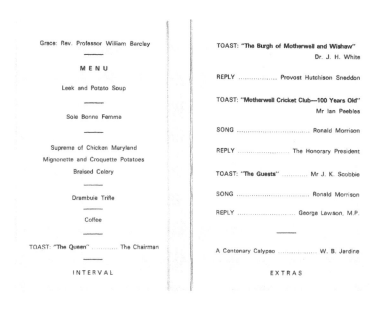

Grace: Rev. Professor William Barclay

M E N U

Leek and Potato Soup

Sole Bonne Femme

Suprème of Chicken Maryland
Mignonette and Croquette Potatoes
Braised Celery

Drambuie Trifle

Coffee

TOAST: "The Queen" .... The Chairman

I N T E R V A L

TOAST: "The Burgh of Motherwell and Wishaw"
Dr. J. H. White

REPLY .... Provost Hutchison Sneddon

TOAST: "Motherwell Cricket Club—100 Years Old"
Mr Ian Peebles

SONG .... Ronald Morrison

REPLY .... The Honorary President

TOAST: "The Guests" .... Mr J. K. Scobbie

SONG .... Ronald Morrison

REPLY .... George Lawson, M.P.

A Centenary Calypso .... W. B. Jardine

E X T R A S

The dinner was chaired by Dr Kerr Grieve, and the Rev. Professor William Barclay said grace. Lord Clydesmuir, our Honorary President, spoke on behalf of the club. Doc Whyte toasted the Burgh, J K Scobbie toasted the guests, and there were many other contributions, some impromptu, from the likes of W B Swan (Scottish Cricket Union president) and Willie Waddell (manager, Rangers FC, who were also celebrating their centenary). As top tables go, this was no lightweight affair.

There were some who didn't fancy the braised celery but that apart, a great time was had by all.

Post-season, we had another grand feed, this time at the Civic Centre, hosted by Provost Hutchison Sneddon. We knew it was a special occasion when the Toast List included qualifications and letters after the speakers' names. The provost had his OBE; Ian Livingstone had his BL; but it was difficult to get one over on the Motherwell president – J F Kerr Grieve, O St J, T D, B Sc, M B, Ch B. A fine way to conclude our celebrations.

It was a joyous occasion, with many of the old guard meeting up for the first time in years. Alex Gillespie, at 90 years old, could go further back than anyone – he kept wicket for the league-winning side of 1911. Allan Barr wasn't far behind him – he, like many of the cricketers of his generation, fought in the Great War, at Paschendale. But that night, the talk was all about cricket and the games they played all those years ago.

On-Field Celebrations

The centenary wasn't just celebrated at the dinner table. Badges were produced and sewn onto cricket jumpers, hoardings were erected around the ground showing 1873–1973, and an excellent centenary brochure was published, written by Maurice Bonnar and Robin Stirling, with input from Bill Jardine and others.

The old stagers played a veterans' match organised by Willie McGuire, who had turned out for the club in the '30s, '40s and '50s, and Peaky Anderson, who featured regularly in the post-war years. Motherwell's elder statesmen and guests from Woodhall and Carfin Hall turned back the years.

Bill Hardie top-scored and Kerr Grieve and R K Hinshalwood Jnr batted well. Bob Browning bowled his slow stuff and even Tom Findlay donned his whites, almost 50 years after his Motherwell debut. Noel McNeice deserves special mention, flying in from

Kuala Lumpur to participate in the match. It ended in a draw, which pleased everyone, especially Bill Jardine. He loved a draw.

The main event was a show game between Motherwell and The Bats, and a healthy crowd turned up to watch the game. The Bats were an Edinburgh Select side put together by Brian Adair, a Watsonian and a great friend to Motherwell Cricket Club. And he certainly did justice to the occasion by bringing some legendary names to Home Park.

Ronnie Chisholm, Hamish More and George Goddard, between them, could boast over 100 caps for Scotland. And the rest of the line-up wasn't bad either, including E J Mentiplay and Freddie MacLeod as well as Brian himself.

The Motherwell line-up was bolstered by some local guests of our own. Ronnie Lang (Uddingston), David Bean and Geoff Cook (Hillhead) and Alastair Forbes (Glasgow High) joined the Home Park team, along with Bobby Kerr.

Although Bobby had captained the Motherwell side in 1972, he had recently moved to London on business, so technically he represented Finchley CC.

A Thriller

The game itself was a close-run affair. Brian Adair opened with a fine 50 and, after The Bats collapsed to 107 for 7, George Goddard's undefeated 36 helped his side to post a total of 157. Jack Smith and Archie Syme were the pick of the Motherwell bowlers.

By some strange coincidence, the first four Motherwell batsmen all scored 18 runs and, when Alastair Forbes (39) and Archie Syme (21) put together a fine partnership, the game was set for an exciting finish. With Chisholm's 'loopy leggies' at one end and Goddard's off-spin at the other, Motherwell went for the win but finished just 5 runs shy of the target, George Goddard completing his 5-wicket haul.

The Motherwell XI was:
Standing: R Browning (umpire), R Lang, W Lindsay, A Forbes, A Syme, J Smith, R A Morrison, P Forbes (scorer)
Seated: D Bean, G Cooke, R G Kerr, G Smith, H Forbes (12th man), G J Shaw

A great game, enjoyed by 200 or so spectators, and a fitting way to celebrate Motherwell's 100 years.

A Changing Landscape

At the beginning of the 1970s, we felt a wee bit sorry for ourselves at Home Park. Times were changing and we faced challenges throughout the decade. But we weren't alone.

Arthur Scargill was fighting the good fight on behalf of the miners, there was crippling unemployment, inflation was spiralling, and a three-day week was imposed to save electricity during the miners' strike. Everyone seemed to be striking – postmen, dustmen, the lot.

Yes, times were tough for a lot of people, and to cap it all, the weather was so hot that there was a hosepipe ban. How on earth were you meant to water the wicket?

Exactly! Home Park! The tabloids made no mention of the dilemma happening in the steel town. Our club was about to enter one of the most challenging periods in its history. We were at a crossroads. A mini crisis was brewing.

One by one, the headliners from the '60s disappeared. It started with the retiral of Bobby Park and Jim Logan and the departure of Alhuwalia and Loudon Sommerville, followed by Bobby Steel and Bobby Kerr moving to England, and Archie Syme hanging up his boots.

We had no choice but to roll up our sleeves and get on with it. And what a rollercoaster journey the decade turned out to be.

It's impossible to over-emphasise how much we missed the presence of Logan and Steel, who had been scoring runs and taking wickets week after week for 20 years, and when the heir apparent Bobby Kerr left for north London, it was obvious to all that there would be difficult times ahead.

Davie and Hilton Brady, Ronnie Morrison and Allan Johnston were still around, and their presence was critical as a promising bunch of juniors were thrust into the void, but the days of fighting it out at the top of the 1st Division were over … for the time being anyway.

A Team In Transition

It's easy to paint the early '70s in a dark light with the older generation moving on, leaving those that were left to pick up the pieces. But the team didn't disintegrate overnight; the blows came one by one over a two- or three-year period.

We held our own in the first couple of years of the decade, mid-table finishes in the league being augmented by a couple of great runs in the Western Cup. Having lost in the finals of '63 and '68, we repeated the trick in successive years, being runners-up in 1971 and 1972.

Our failure to win the trophy was especially frustrating for players like Bobby Steel and David Brady, who had experienced cup final defeats four times in 10 years, but it must be remembered that we played a lot of good cricket to reach these finals.

The 2nd XI won the reserve league in 1970 with a healthy 88% record, with some of the juniors being given their first taste of senior cricket.

But just as we were preparing to celebrate our centenary, we were relegated at the end of the 1972 season. The loss of so many top players had taken its toll and, for the first time, we were playing 2nd division cricket in 1973.

The 1st XI looked very different...

Standing: Dr Kerr Grieve (president), Bill Jardine (match secretary), Ronnie Morrison, Jim Anderson, Willie Lindsay, Jim Dobbie, Billy Alexander, Bob McKenzie, Dr Jim White (past president), Jack Shaw (vice president)
Seated: Jack Smith, Allan Johnston, Bobby Kerr, Alastair Hamilton, Stevie Young
Absent: David Brady, Hilton Brady, Archie Syme

The photograph was taken in late 1972 for inclusion in the centenary brochure but by the start of the 1973 season, we had lost our captain and best player, Bobby Kerr. Allan Johnston took over the captaincy.

The Brady brothers really stepped up to the plate. David had been a top player for many years, and continued to score runs and take wickets, but Hilton emerged from his shadow to contribute some match-winning innings. Jack Smith was also in good form with the ball, and these senior cricketers helped us through a difficult couple of years.

But, year by year, the average age of the team grew younger as more of the junior cricketers were introduced to the senior teams. We emerged from the depression of our relegation, and there was an acknowledgement that the 2nd division was an easier environment in which this young Motherwell team could serve an apprenticeship.

Stevie Young, Grant Robertson, Jim Bill, Billy Alexander, Ian Wilson ('Big Yanny' to all!), Gavin Shaw and Jack Kelly all became regulars in the 1st and 2nd teams. An even younger Hamish Forbes also made his debut, and another young cricketer, Adrian Gibb, joined the club from Drumpellier soon after.

They were christened the 'young lions', so called because they were young and … well, they didn't really know where the lion bit came in, though it could justifiably have related to their voluminous mullets. The name stuck and several of them would go on to play an important part in the history of Motherwell Cricket Club right through the '70s, '80s and '90s, and some even longer.

After a couple of middling seasons, the team was ready to make a push for promotion. We recovered from a poor start to the 1975 campaign to go into the final fixture against Hyndland, knowing that a win would take us back to the big time (well… as big as it was going to get for Motherwell Cricket Club!).

Glory In The Gloom

It was a grey day at Scotstoun Showground, long before it became home to Glasgow Warriors Rugby. Late summer felt like early autumn and the cricketing gods weren't smiling. Nor were the Hyndland team. They had nothing to play for and would rather be spending their Saturday evening in a warm hostelry somewhere in Glasgow's west end. In all honesty, we would have felt much the same in their shoes, but we had a league to win.

How did we get to such a thrilling denouement? We can follow the fortunes of the team through the ups and downs of our 1975 league campaign as we made our bid for promotion.

Thornliebank v Motherwell: Rained off.

Motherwell 133 for 9; Milngavie & Bearsden 134 for 8. Despite David Brady and Alastair Hamilton putting on 78 for the first wicket, we couldn't build a winning total. A close run thing but match lost, 0 points: **0%**

Motherwell 106; Old Grammarians 73. Gavin Shaw was the chief contributor with the bat scoring an unbeaten 36, with Johnny Welsh taking 5 wickets for 6 runs with the ball. Match won, 6 points: **50%**

Motherwell 142 all out; Hyndland 50 for 6. An opening partnership of 74 by David Brady and Alastair Hamilton got Motherwell off to a fine start, but our bowling failed to dismiss a dogged Hyndland side. Match drawn, 4 points: **56%**

Motherwell 90; Babcock & Wilcox 91 for 2. Poor performance all round with Gavin Shaw's 32 the only meaningful contribution.

We slipped back into the lower half of the league. Match lost, 0 points: **42%**

Motherwell 149 for 9; Bishopbriggs 88 for 9. Adrian Gibb scored a fine 78 allowing Motherwell to post their best score of the season, but our opponents held out for a draw. This was chiefly down to Bishopbriggs batsman Jones – an injury required him to get treatment at Law Hospital but he returned to frustrate the Motherwell bowlers. Match drawn, 4 points: **47%**

Thornliebank 94; Motherwell 95 for 4. David Brady and Adrian Gibb both performed well with the ball, and Motherwell cruised to an easy victory. Match won, 6 points: **56%**

Babcock & Wilcox 140; Motherwell 141 for 6. Jack Smith starred with the ball taking 7 wickets, but Motherwell had to fight back from 54 for 6 to win. Allan Johnston (46) and Grant Robertson (50) put together an undefeated partnership of 87 to get us over the line. A pivotal result! Match won, 6 points: **62%**

Motherwell 79; Dunlop 74. Sitting in 3rd place, Motherwell overcame the leaders in a tight contest. Grant Robertson was the hero with 6 wickets. Match won, 6 points: **67%**

Old Grammarians 156 for 9; Motherwell 138 for 9. After Jack Smith's 6 wickets, Motherwell's batting began well with good knocks from David Brady and Adrian Gibb, but a mid-innings collapse in the run chase led to Jack Kelly and Jack Smith having to bat out the last 8 overs for a draw. Draw, 2 points: **63%**

Motherwell v Milngavie & Bearsden. Rained off (while Old Grammarians won their match, forging ahead at the top of the league): Motherwell still **63%**

Dunlop v Motherwell abandoned. A thunderstorm brought an end to a low-scoring game that could have gone either way. There is a memory of Adrian Gibb in red Y-fronts splashing his way out to the middle to rescue the stumps as lightning lit up the flooded playing field. Game abandoned, but news came through of defeat for Old Grammarians: Motherwell **63%**

Bishopbriggs 116; Motherwell 119 for 5. A routine win that put Motherwell right back in the hunt. Allan Johnston scored 27 not out, and had 3 stumpings off David Brady's bowling. Match won, 6 points: **67%**

Hyndland v Motherwell. And that led us to Scotstoun knowing that a win would put us in an unassailable position, regardless of how Old Grammarians or Dunlop fared. Victory and 6 points were a must!

Hyndland were put into bat, and compiled a solid 124 for 7, Grant Robertson taking 4 wickets. The Motherwell response was stop-start in nature, with rain interruptions and several batsmen getting a start but failing to register a match-winning innings. David Brady (31), Adrian Gibb (20), Ronnie Morrison (31) and Allan Johnston (21) batted well enough to get the team within range but, with 8 wickets down, we were still short of their target.

The leaden skies grew greyer still in the evening gloom and light rain began to fall. Thankfully, the neutral umpires decided that, with a potential promotion at stake, the game should be played to a conclusion. With no sight screens, batting was difficult and the batsmen in the middle, Jim Bill and Hilton Brady, had difficulty picking up the flight of the ball.

The Hyndland fielders weren't helping. Between each delivery, they would insist on drying the ball thoroughly with a rag – this was fair enough, but it was taking an eternity, and the light grew appreciably worse with each passing over. It prompted a suggestion from the clutch of Motherwell players in the pavilion that the batsmen might want a copy of *War and Peace* to pass the time between balls.

Eventually, the ball strayed onto Jim Bill's pads, and a perfect leg glance sent it racing to the fine leg boundary to pass the Hyndland total. Match won, 6 points: **70%**

With victory in the bag, promotion was secured, and it was a happy Motherwell contingent that sped home to the Steel Town to reach the Dalziel Arms before last orders were called.

The pleasing thing about our success was that it had been a team effort with everyone contributing. 20-year-old Grant Robertson burst onto the scene – as well as scoring his maiden 50, he took a barrowload of wickets, including a hat-trick against Hillhead in a friendly match.

Adrian Gibb, Allan Johnston and David Brady topped the batting averages, while Jack Smith and David Brady bowled well. The fielding was first class with Steve Young, Adrian Gibb and Jack Kelly outstanding.

Some might say that, after winning several 1st Division titles in the 1960s, a 2nd Division title shouldn't warrant as much attention, but for those that played in the 1975 season, the success was every bit as sweet – especially for the youngsters who had only recently emerged from the junior ranks. This was their first league title, and they would all go on to serve the club massively for decades to come.

Here's the squad (well, most of them) with the Macfarlane Trophy:

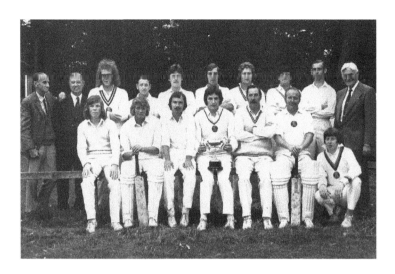

Back Row: Bill Jardine (match secretary), Peter Forbes (scorer), Gavin Shaw, George Smith, Grant Robertson, Steve Young, Jim Bill, Hilton Brady, Douglas Burke, Kerr Grieve (president)
Front Row: Hamish Forbes, David Brady, Jack Kelly, Allan Johnston, Jack Smith, Ronnie Morrison, Joe Gillick
(*Absent from the photo were Adrian Gibb, Alastair Hamilton and Johnny Welsh*)

The Day We Played An Aussie Legend

To introduce the man who would go on to captain Australia, we have to wind the clock forward a few years.

1981 will forever be remembered as Botham's Ashes. Ian Botham was the England captain going into the series, but stepped down after the 2nd Test after a lapse in form. Mike Brearley took over, but Botham was like a man re-born, his 149 at Headingley the stuff of legend, and England went on to win the series 3-1.

So much for the English captaincy, but who was the Australian captain?

Kim Hughes led the side, batting at 3 or 4 throughout the series in a side that included cricketing greats Dennis Lillee, Allan Border and Rodney Marsh. Hughes had made his debut for Australia in 1977, and had become a fixture in the side, scoring a wonderful century in the Lords Centenary Test in 1980, which earned him a Man of the Match Award.

Yet in 1976, just before his entry onto the international stage, he played at Home Park! Motherwell Cricket Club had an annual Sunday fixture against an Edinburgh select side called The Bats, led by Watsonian Brian Adair, and it was always a day of great anticipation.

Kim Hughes had taken Scottish cricket by storm, scoring 100s in each of the three games leading up to the match, and would go on to score a remarkable 1700 runs during the summer of 1976. Such was the excitement around his appearance that a decent crowd turned up at Home Park to watch the brightest star on the Scottish scene.

He arrived at the crease second wicket down and despatched Jack Smith's first ball straight down the ground for four – no effort expended, pure timing. When another boundary followed, the Motherwell lads looked to be in for a long afternoon in the field. Local skipper Steve Young decided a change of pace was required and introduced left arm spin in the shape of Uddingston's John Gillies, guesting for the day.

Hughes looked to cut a good length ball, which grew on him, inducing a false stroke that ended up in the safe hands of Grant Robertson at gully. The Aussie star was back in the pavilion for 11 runs. It was difficult to know whether this was a cause for celebration or not – the crowd was deprived of seeing the Australian in full flow, but it gave Motherwell a great chance of a rare victory against The Bats.

John Gillies bowled beautifully and went on to claim 7 wickets and, with the fielders backing up the bowlers with some stunning catches, Motherwell restricted the visitors to the modest total of 126. But if we thought we had seen the last of Kim Hughes, we were mistaken. After Hamish Forbes and Adrian Gibb had given Motherwell a solid start, Hughes was brought on to bowl and ended up with 6 wickets, 4 of them to LBW decisions!

Looking at his career statistics, Kim Hughes never bowled in Test cricket but has 3 first class wickets to his name. Certainly, his medium-fast deliveries were good enough to win the game for The Bats, albeit helped by some umpiring decisions that some felt were over-generous. Motherwell were dismissed for 78.

In truth, the result of a Sunday friendly didn't matter a great deal. It had been a thrill to play against a player who would become one of Wisden's global cricketers of the year.

A keenly contested game was followed by a memorable evening. Players chatted over a few beers, perched on the verandah of the old timber pavilion as the sun inched lower in the skies over Home Park. Kim Hughes was the centre of attention, mixing with the Motherwell lads.

The conversations are lost in the mists of time, but you can imagine that John Gillies would be talking Kim through his 7 wickets, and Steve Young and Jim Bill would be debating the LBW decisions that cost them their wickets. Whatever the chat, it was a perfect way to end a memorable day.

In an interview after the end of his playing days, Kim Hughes said that his 6 months in Scotland in the summer of 1976 were perhaps the most enjoyable of his career. It's nice to think that Motherwell Cricket Club may have played a small part.

Ups and Downs / Downs and Ups

Back to league business, and a triennial pattern began to develop. Having spent three years in the 2nd division before our 1975 promotion, we competed in the top tier for three years before being relegated in 1978, and it would be a further three years before we returned.

There was a lot of good cricket played during our yo-yo period. The scores from this era show that we had a strong bowling attack – Grant Robertson and Jim Bill were the opening bowlers who took a hatful of wickets, Steve Young and Dougie Burke were change bowlers, and spinners David Brady and Adrian Gibb.

Notable performances with the ball included Robertson's 7 for 26 against Irvine and 6 for 22 against Renfrew; Bill's 6 for 27 against Kilmarnock, 6 for 48 against Anchor and 7 for 23 against Kelvinside Accies; Young's 6 for 17 against Alva; Burke's 4 for 0 against Irvine.

More bowling options appeared.

Dr Gulam Moorad came from the townships of South Africa and was given a post at Motherwell Maternity under the tutelage of Kerr Grieve. Gulam's shifts were always organised to enable him to play weekend and midweek matches. He was quick, and after Motherwell had defeated a very good Prestwick team, the legendary Johnny Hubbard quipped in his Afrikaner accent, "When I saw the South African fella step out of the car, I knew we were in trouble."

Bill Lowden arrived from Huntly, and was a great servant to the club, defying his advancing years to play on into his '60s. And we had another Robertson, off-spinner Graham, who followed brother Grant into the 1st team.

Batting was more of a challenge. Adrian Gibb, David Brady and Gavin Shaw were the mainstays, and there were useful knocks from Ronnie Morrison, Allan Johnston and the all-rounders, Robertson, Bill and Young. The highlight was a record opening stand of 152 by David Brady (75) and young Hamish Forbes (56) against Anchor.

After a promising 3rd place finish in '76 in the 1st Division, we dropped off the pace the following year and fell back into Division 2 in '78. The captaincy had passed from Allan Johnston to Douglas Burke, then to Steve Young, and in our first season in the 2nd tier we finished runners-up, which augured well for the future as we looked forward to the '80s.

Another thing excited us. The next swathe of junior cricketers had arrived! Ian Sharp, Grant Alexander, Ian McDonald, Andrew Barrie and Steven McGill all performed admirably in beating many of their junior contemporaries, including Uddingston, Fauldhouse and Helensburgh, and were now making their mark in senior cricket.

Rising From the Ashes

Perhaps the biggest story of the decade was the destruction of our 70-year-old pavilion by fire in 1977. In some respects it was a wonder that the old wooden structure had survived so long. It was the culmination of 20 years of mindless vandalism, ever since Dalzell Estate had opened up to the public in the late '50s.

It was a sorry sight. As well as the building itself being a total loss, a new mower was burned out, kit was destroyed and old photographs lost. It was a sad day, but it gave us the impetus to make plans for a new pavilion. It was long overdue ... all that was needed was money!

There was a very modest insurance settlement, and our 'centenary club' weekly draw brought in a few pounds, but we needed significant funds from somewhere to raise the cash.

We were very fortunate in two respects – our president Tom Barrie was a driving force, leaving no stone unturned to reach our financial target; and a generous bequest was left to the club by Catherine Black, the sister of legendary Motherwell players, Archie and Duncan Black.

With grants from The Sports Council, awards from other organisations, and monies from individual donations, we got there. The new pavilion was completed in 1978 and officially opened in 1979.

During the construction, we had been allowed to use the stables at 'the big hoose' (Dalzell House as was) as dressing rooms and as a place to lay out the teas. Initially it was actually quite exciting, but the completion of the new pavilion gave us all a huge boost, not just on the field, but socially as well. Within our new clubhouse was our very own Motherwell Cricket Club bar!

We started the '70s with a crisis and ended the decade with a much more positive outlook, voicing Nina Simone's great anthem ...

"It's a new dawn, it's a new day, it's a new life ...
feeling good."

The Black Legacies

The survival of Motherwell Cricket Club is due in no small measure to brother and sister, Duncan and Catherine Black. Their legacies have sustained the club through difficult times, and laid the foundations for a financially secure future.

Dr Duncan Black was a Motherwell-born economist whose academic career spanned a number of British and American universities. Amongst his many achievements was his influential work on voting theory and social choice theory. Most importantly, he played cricket for Motherwell!

Back in the 1920s and '30s, Duncan and his brother Archie were regulars in the Motherwell 1st XI. Archie was one of the Motherwell greats, an all-rounder whose performances still feature in club records, but Duncan's on-field contribution should not be under-estimated – he was a fine batsman. These were great days at Home Park, one of the most beautiful grounds in Scotland, surrounded by a white racecourse fence, nestling in the private grounds of Lord Hamilton's Dalzell Estate.

However, it was their sister Catherine Black who had the first say in the family's support for the club, leaving us £10,000 in her will along with some kind words: *"The happiest times of my life were those I spent at Home Park, helping to make teas for my two brothers as they played cricket."*

It was the mid-1970s and the donation triggered talk of building a new pavilion. The old wooden structure was on its last legs. It had served us well and, picturesque though it was, it lacked some fundamental services that we now take for granted. Toilets had been added in the 1950s, but there were still no washing or showering facilities for the players.

The wooden planks that constituted the pavilion floor were fraying at the edges so, when changing into their whites, players would get a good blast of cold air coming up through the gaps between the floorboards, and a few skelfs on their feet for good measure.

One visiting team, Allan Glens, referred to us as the Viet Cong, such was the primitive nature of our ramshackle abode nestling under the boughs of aged woodland.

It was late 1977 when the place was burned down, just two years after Catherine Black's bequest. All the talk of building a new pavilion very quickly became a reality.

A New Pavilion

Catherine Black's generosity provided the launching pad for raising funds, and under the expert guidance of Club President Tom Barrie, we started to raise the £24,000 needed for the replacement pavilion. The Sports Council provided an £8,000 grant on the back of Catherine Black's legacy, an essential component of any award, and the remainder was raised from donations, appeals and fund-raising efforts.

Our new clubhouse was opened in 1979 by none other than Ally MacLeod, not long returned from his adventures in Argentina.

It was quite a day. Several of the older statesmen of the club attended – Bill Jardine, Tom Finlay, RK Hinshalwood, Willie McGuire, Bob Browning, Tom Donnelly and Eddie Houston.

Ronnie Morrison read out telegrams of congratulations from cricketing royalty …

"Congratulations to Motherwell Cricket Club on a great effort in rebuilding your pavilion. Cricket will never die whilst there is such dedication to the game. Best wishes."
Freddie Trueman

"Just to wish you every success in 1979, make a lots of runs but, most of all, enjoy your cricket."
Mike Brearley

"What splendid news that you have finished your new clubhouse. It would be good to be with you but since I cannot, do let me send all good wishes for a grand opening day, a really good match and a fine party."
John Arlott

Duncan Black was the only surviving member of the Black family and, in retirement, was living in Paignton, Devon. An invitation was extended to him to attend the opening ceremony but was respectfully declined.

A cheque, however, was received to help with costs. The spark of his sister Catherine's legacy ignited a generous flame, and Duncan sent a very helpful financial contribution year after year.

Duncan's Visit

It was Alex Baird who regularly corresponded with Duncan. David Anderson would take photographs of the team playing at Home Park, and Alex would send them off to Duncan to remind him of the beautiful ground where he had played cricket many decades before.

Years passed, and we eventually met Duncan. But we very nearly didn't!

Alex lived near Home Park and on return from his work one evening, he was informed by his wife Doreen that an elderly gentleman had been sitting on a bench at the cricket club for several hours in the afternoon, taking photographs of the ground and the new pavilion.

Puzzled, he wondered if it might be Duncan Black. If so, he

wanted to take the opportunity to thank him in person for his financial support.

Motherwell boasted only one hotel. On a whim, Alex telephoned The Garrion and asked if he might speak with a Dr Duncan Black. To his delight, the receptionist confirmed that she would put him through and, for the first time, he was able to speak to our great benefactor. Alex suggested they meet for dinner while he was in town. Although he was returning home to Devon the next day, he was available that evening.

No time to lose! Alex called Steve Young and Grant Robertson and asked if they could come along for the meal and both were happy to do so. They arranged to pick up Bill Jardine and Tom Findlay, both of whom had played cricket pre-war alongside Duncan.

A table was reserved at the Cartland Bridge Hotel, and it was a memorable moment when Duncan entered the dining room with Alex to find the waiting party of Bill, Tom, Steve and Grant. A wonderful evening followed, with much reminiscing of the times they had shared together at Home Park – stories of games in the '20s and '30s, the feats of Duncan's brother Archie, and memories of his sister Catherine.

Some years later, Duncan paid us another visit, and was presented with a Life Membership of the club. Here is the man himself with 1st XI captain Grant Robertson. They were joined by, *left to right,* Jack Shaw, Bill Jardine, Frank Crossley, Tom Barrie, Frank Bent and Tom Findlay.

But the story doesn't end there. Duncan died, aged 82, at his home in 1991. Some time later, Tom Barrie received a letter from a local lawyer. They had been contacted by a firm of Devon solicitors to advise that Duncan had remembered his beloved Motherwell Cricket Club in his will. He had left us his house in Paignton!

The will stated that the funds were to be used to '*encourage and foster the playing of cricket in Motherwell and Wishaw and surrounding district; to assist all young people who desire to play cricket in whatever way the Trustees may consider proper and expedient; etc*'.

The house was sold for around £80,000 and the funds invested, professionally managed by trustees chaired by Alex Baird. The trust has sustained the club ever since.

When vandals burned down the new pavilion in the late '90s, a significant capital sum was paid out to assist with our relocation from Home Park to Cleland Estate. To this day, Duncan's legacy allows the trustees to make an annual donation to the Club to meet its running costs.

It is a privilege to remember Catherine and Duncan Black in our celebration of Motherwell Cricket Club's 150 years. They, more than anyone, have helped us to achieve this milestone. Thank you.

The Lions Roar

The '80s were an exciting time to be around. Yuppies were upwardly mobile, MTV music channels were all the rage, clothes were a bit weird and VHS and Betamax videos allowed you to watch the best movies in your own living room.

We fought a war in the Falklands, Margaret Thatcher was Prime Minister and, closer to home, there were strikes at British Steel, with massive picket lines outside Ravenscraig.

Big hair and mullets were commonplace, as were spandex and leg warmers – and that was just the Motherwell players … you should have seen the opposition!

New wave music had also made its journey to Home Park and was being belted out in our shiny new pavilion. Discos, party nights and quiz nights were commonplace after a hard day's toil on the cricket field.

Back then, stag parties weren't weekends in Magaluf or Benidorm, they were one-night affairs in the bar after the game on a Saturday. Grant Robertson and his brother Graham can categorically say they have little recollection of the last hours of their own stags.

Others fell by the wayside too. Steve Young followed Jim

Bill and Gavin (Speary) Shaw. All had similarly messy stag experiences in the pavilion and were extremely grateful to their teammates for filling in the blanks at Monday night practice after a 'forgetful' weekend.

Arnie Schwarzenegger, 'The Terminator', had also burst on the scene, coining the phrase 'I'll be back', and that term was to play a part in our history throughout the '80s. Motherwell Cricket Club just wouldn't go away, nipping at the heels of the top teams in the league.

We had built the nucleus of a decent team during the '70s, and the starlets were now in their mid-20s, shining brightly. Big hair seemed to be *de rigeur*. Just to prove the point, here's a photo of the 1981 side.

Back: Ronnie Morrison, Grant Robertson, Allan Johnston, Ian Sharp, Maurice Bonnar, Bobby Buchanan
Front: Danny Donnelly, Frank Bent, Steve Young (captain), Steven McGill, Gavin Shaw

The 1980s brought some great performances from both 1st and 2nd XIs, and at last delivered some silverware.

New Kids on the Block

This was a glorious period for the club.

The youngsters who had kept the flag flying through the 70s had matured (well, maybe not … they had just got a bit older). Steve Young led the side at the start of the decade, Grant Robertson at the end, and with Jim Bill, Gavin Shaw and Graham Robertson, they formed the core of the 1st XI. A pride of 'young lions' with manes to match.

We also had some fine additions to the Motherwell ranks during the '80s. John Gillies, former captain of Uddingston, was a key recruit. Danny Donnelly and Bobby Buchanan joined us from Woodhall and another star player, Harry Tart, joined from Fauldhouse. All of them went on to have fine playing careers at Home Park.

Ian Sharp, David Anderson, Grant Alexander, Steven (Carrots) McGill and Alastair Jackson all graduated from the junior ranks. Roger Newton, Hughie McGinley and Frank Bent arrived on the scene to give us the healthiest playing resources we'd had for many a year. Both 1st and 2nd XIs were strong.

Having finished as runners-up in division 2 in 1979, we got that bit closer in 1980. Grant Robertson was on fine bowling form, taking 7 for 18 against Old Grammarians, and 7 for 31 against Hyndland, and Allan Johnston's 67 not out won a crucial game to take the promotion race to the very last game.

It was a winner-takes-all game, the only problem being that Kilmalcolm only needed a single point to get promotion. Elaborate plans were put in place to frustrate our opponents, but they fell apart when we lost a wicket in the first over, giving Kilmalcolm the bonus point they needed to win the league.

With everything sorted, they produced champagne and a spectacular tea in celebration. No-one can recall who actually won the game, but Motherwell were runners-up in the league yet again.

Champions!

In many ways, the 1981 season had been years in the making. 1979 and 1980 had been dress rehearsals and, at the third time of asking, Motherwell won the 2nd division title. It's a year that deserves closer examination.

Steve Young was captain, and behind any great man lies an even better woman – without an extremely understanding bride-to-be, Steve may well have missed part of the season. He persuaded Christine that late September would be a fine time to get hitched, and October perfect for a honeymoon, but the girl was under no illusions. She understood that a summer wedding may derail the club's season as most of the team would also be invited to the big day. Well played, Christine!

It all panned out rather well …

- *Kelvinside Accies 113 all out, Motherwell 117 for 3 (Jim Bill 6 for 30, Grant Robertson 4 for 38)*

- *North Kelvinside 86 all out, Motherwell 87 for 7 (Danny Donnelly 4 for 20, Steve Young 3 for 19)*

- *Anchor 40 all out, Motherwell 42 for no wicket (Jim Bill 6 for 12, Ian Sharp 33 not out)*

- *Ardeer 92 for 8, Motherwell 93 for 5 (Danny Donnelly 5 for 10)*

- *Motherwell 133 for 8, Woodhall 52 all out (Grant Robertson 6 for 18, Allan Johnston 43)*

- *Motherwell 120 all out, North Kelvinside 95 all out (Jim Bill 4 for 40. Allan Johnston 42, Steve Young 39)*

- Motherwell 102 all out, Dunlop 104 for 6 (Grant Robertson 4 for 45)

- Motherwell 142 all out, Woodhall 79 all out (Jim Bill 5 for 35, Steve Young 59, Grant Robertson 38)

- Motherwell 117 for 8, Old Grammarians 83 all out (Danny Donnelly 5 for 25, Danny Donnelly 40)

- Motherwell 129 all out, Anchor 73 all out (Grant Robertson 4 for 20, Jim Bill 4 for 21, Steven McGill 35)

- Motherwell 51 all out, Ardeer 52 for 2

- Dunlop 151 for 9, Motherwell 152 for 6 (Danny Donnelly 5 for 31, Alan Johnston 49, Hugh McGinley 44 not out)

The match results show the strength of the Motherwell seam attack. Grant Robertson and Jim Bill were arguably the most prolific opening bowling attack in the Glasgow and District League, with Steve Young and Danny Donnelly playing key roles as change bowlers. We didn't score huge totals with the bat, but we didn't have to – games were won in the field.

Holding Our Own

After such a great season in 1981, the 1st XI struggled to win matches in the top division. There were some great individual performances – Jim Bill, Grant Robertson and Danny Donnelly all enjoyed 5-wicket hauls and Grant closed out the season with 8 for 42 against Helensburgh. Ian Sharp and Jim Bill recorded an 85-run last wicket stand in a losing cause against Hillhead, and Steve Young's all-round performance saved the day at Irvine.

The fact that Hugh McGinley's 51 was the only half century of the season showed where the problem lay.

1983 followed the same pattern. Allan Johnston's 49 at Helensburgh and Steven McGill's 56 at East Kilbride won games, but Grant Robertson's undefeated 50 wasn't good enough to beat Irvine. An Aussie from Craigneuk, Gerry Whelan, returned to his roots that year and took a few wickets but the season was saved by Motherwell's batsmen digging in to secure draws.

The arrival of John Gillies in 1984 helped markedly, picking up 5 scores in the 60s, as well as securing 7 wickets against Kelvinside Accies with his left arm spin. This helped others to up their game with Alan Black, Steven McGill, Allan Johnston and Bobby Buchanan all scoring 50s. Predictably, Grant Robertson again finished off the season with 8 for 58 against Hillhead.

A comfortable mid-table finish promised much, and it wasn't just the 1st XI who had seen an upturn in fortunes. The extent and quality of our playing resources meant that the 2nd XI were strong, with Jim Anderson leading the side for most of the decade.

Bill Lowden was Mr Consistency, picking up six or seven wickets on frequent occasions, forming an effective opening attack with Douglas Burke. Later in the decade, Phil Andrews' pace and Graham Robertson's off-spin were potent weapons.

The 2nd's batting had depth – a line-up of Roger Newton, Jack Kelly, Hugh McGinley, Gavin Shaw, Frank Bent and David Anderson illustrates the strength and experience of the team, and explains why they were always in contention for honours.

The leading individual performance of the 80s was unquestionably Roger Newton's 138 against Babcock & Wilcox in 1987 as Motherwell 2nds posted a remarkable 217 for 1 wicket, before Colin Harrop's 6 wickets wrapped up a 180-run victory.

Band Aid or Sticking Plaster?

While Bob Geldof and Midge Ure were putting together their epic concert, Motherwell Cricket Club were agonising over the employment of a professional. Some teams had a pro, others didn't. Motherwell were more than a match for most teams, but a pro in the opposition ranks frequently tilted the odds in their favour.

Motherwell was not unique. Other clubs experienced the same difficulties, juggling with the desire to remain competitive against the consequent financial outlay. The truth was that if you didn't employ a pro during the '80s, you'd spend the season fighting relegation.

Motherwell's 1985 season had been looking very much like previous years, with 50s scored by Steve Young, John Gillies and Allan Johnston, and the odd victory in amongst some brave draws and heavy defeats. But it wasn't getting us anywhere fast. After an indifferent start, we bit the bullet mid-season and hired Nadeem Yousuf on a trial basis.

Scoring a century against Irvine wasn't a bad audition, and we promptly signed him up. Nadeem thus became Motherwell's first modern-day professional.

His CV was impressive, a highly rated all-rounder. He had previously been pro at Ferguslie and, back in Pakistan, Nadeem had a double hundred to his name when sharing a 10th wicket partnership of 196 runs, a score that would stand as a first-class record for almost 40 years.

He made a difference. There was more discipline about the club, our practice sessions were better organised and, importantly, we won more games. It wasn't just Nadeem's runs and wickets but his winning mentality – he hated to lose – that drove us on to greater things.

Another Nadeem century won the game against North

Kelvinside, and the season finished with a remarkable partnership of 144 at Hillhead between Steve Young (87) and Steven McGill (55 not out) after coming together when the score was 6 for 4. We approached the 1986 season with renewed confidence.

Annus Mirabilis

In the years after our centenary, we hadn't managed to replicate the league-winning feats of Motherwell teams of the 1960s. Still, we had survived, and had enjoyed ourselves immensely. To be fair, success had been building. The 'young lions' were in their prime, new recruits had strengthened the batting line-up, and now we had a professional.

The headline item of our glorious year was the winning of the Western Cup, a 20 overs-a-side knock-out tournament with no professionals allowed.

Motherwell had reached the final on several occasions, but hadn't won the thing since 1952. That changed in 1986, overcoming some good teams along the way. Here's the cup run!

First Round: Motherwell struggled to post a competitive total against Drumpellier 2nds, ending their innings with a below par 68 for 7. But the bowling and fielding were excellent, restricting Drumpellier to 49 for 9. Grant Robertson and Harry Tart shared the bowling honours with 4 and 3 wickets respectively.

Second Round: This one was a tight squeeze, just edging East Kilbride for a last ball win. Chasing EK's 84 for 5, Allan Johnston was the mainstay of the Motherwell innings with 36, but it took a heroic rescue act from David Anderson to take Motherwell to 85 for 6 with two boundaries in the final over.

Third Round: Uddingston 2nds batted first to score 76 for 5 with Jim Bill and Harry Tart taking the wickets. Harry Tart scored an unbeaten 29 and, with useful contributions from Allan Johnston and John Gillies, Motherwell reached 77 for 3 with time to spare.

Quarter Final: Motherwell recorded an impressive win against Ayr 2nds, scoring 103 for 4. Steven McGill top scored with 39 with John Ralston and Steve Young boosting the score beyond the ton. Ayr never threatened and were all out for 54, Grant Robertson taking 5 wickets.

Semi Final: Another nervous finish as Greenock 2nds fell short by 1 run. Motherwell posted a total of 101 for 2 with Steven McGill and Steve Young undefeated on 54 and 35 respectively. Greenock were always in the hunt and needed 4 off the last ball to win. There were no fielding restrictions in these days, so Motherwell were able put 9 men on the Glenpark boundary and restrict their opponents to two runs. Jim Bill took 3 wickets.

Final: A good crowd gathered at Hillhead to watch a close encounter with West of Scotland's 2nds. Tight bowling restricted Motherwell to 79 for 8. Steven McGill, Allan Johnston, Steve Young and Alastair Jackson all reached double figures without going on to make a match-winning contribution. Instead it was Jim Bill's bowling (5 for 29) and excellent fielding as West were dismissed for 62.

And here are the happy faces of those who played their part.

Back Row: Steven McGill, Alastair Black, Hugh McGinley, John Ralston, Alastair Jackson, Jim Bill, Allan Black, Peter Forbes (scorer), Gavin Shaw, David Anderson, Allan Johnston
Front Row: Harry Tart, Steve Young, Grant Robertson (captain), Jack Shaw (president), John Gillies, Nadeem Yousuf (professional, who didn't play in the Cup but was very much part of the team)

Something very noticeable in the cup tie summaries is the fairly miserly totals required to win games. Nowadays, with the advent of T20, such scores would be risible, but not in 1986, not in Motherwell. Slogging our way to 200 was not for us; we were more cultured in these days, playing proper cricket. Well, cultured? Maybe not.

It was tight bowling and our performance in the field that tipped the balance, helping us win close-run matches. When presenting the Western Cup, league president Albert Slack said he had never seen such a fine display of fielding.

If you think 1986 couldn't get any more exciting, you'd be wrong. Just after the Western Cup success, Motherwell's 2nd

XI took the field against Prestwick at Home Park to settle who would win the Reserve League. Motherwell were a few points ahead going into the game, so 2nd-placed Prestwick had to win.

Douglas Burke's side posted a competitive 141 for 8 with top scorers being Gavin Shaw (28), Hugh McGinley (22) and Frank Bent (30 not out). In response, Bill Lowden and Phil Andrews starred with the ball as Prestwick could only manage 102 for 9, and the draw was good enough to give Motherwell their first Reserve Division title for 15 years.

The team posed with the trophy afterwards ...

Back Row: Bill Lowden, Gavin Shaw, Peter Harding, Alastair Black, Willie Miller, Bill Jardine (match secretary)
Front Row: Roger Newton, Hugh McHinley, Douglas Burke (captain), Murray Learmonth, Frank Bent, David Anderson

Motherwell's 1st XI had also been in contention at the top of the league table all season with the bowling of Nadeem Yousuf and Grant Robertson and the batting of Steven McGill and

Harry Tart being consistent threats. We faltered in the latter stages to finish 3rd but, all in all, 1986 was a glorious year to be a Motherwell cricketer.

We had to say goodbye to Allan Johnston, who was moving away on business. He had been a stalwart for almost 20 years, captain for many of them. It was fitting that he left on a high.

The Nearly Men

The excitement around Home Park continued right through to the end of the decade as Motherwell maintained their form, battling it out at the top of the table. But the 1st division title proved elusive.

We have a recurring nightmare of the game when it slipped through our fingers. It was an end of season shoot-out between Irvine, North Kelvinside and Motherwell. If we won our last two games, we would win the League title.

The penultimate game took place at a dreich, drizzly Home Park against North Kelvinside. Not a day for cricket but, due to the importance of the fixture, the umpires agreed that the game should be played.

It had been a successful season. Grant Robertson was on great form with the ball, taking 5 wickets or more in five league matches. Nadeem, Harry Tart and Steve Young all weighed in with match-winning performances and a golden shot at the league title.

The Home Park wicket was damp, and North Kelvinside's bowlers were proving unplayable. We somehow managed to reach 50 all out, and all seemed lost when our opponents reached 26 for 1, halfway there. Then, in a wonderfully crazy spell, Motherwell captured 8 wickets in next to no time, leaving the Glasgow team on the brink of defeat at 39 for 9.

Surely! The last pair of batsmen trusted their luck and played shots that narrowly evaded the grasping clutches of Motherwell fielders, and somehow they found the 12 runs they required for victory.

Grant and Nadeem had bowled brilliantly but to no avail. Should we have changed the bowling to mix it up a bit? Should we have changed the fielding positions? It mattered not – the chance was gone – and it was a sad and frustrated home dressing room that night.

Ironically, neither Motherwell nor North Kelvinside won the league. On the final day of the season, while Motherwell were winning at Hillhead, Irvine overcame North Kelvinside to take the title.

We tried to take some consolation from our 1987 performances. We finished 2nd, our highest league finish since the '60s, we had qualified for the Scottish Cup, and John Gillies scored a century in the final match of the year, but all to no avail. The nightmare won't go away!

The next year followed a similar pattern, finishing in the top three (that means we finished third!) and going on decent cup runs without any more silverware. We reached the quarter final of the Rowan Cup, beating Uddingston's first team along the way, and in the Scottish Cup, Alastair Jackson's century helped Motherwell to a thrilling victory over Gala.

New Pro, Same Outcome

Nadeem Yousuf had played well in his three and a half years with us. Even in his last year, he scored six 50s and took his fair share of wickets, but to take us to the top of the league, we felt that a change of professional might do the trick.

Our 1988 campaign had been plagued with draws – five of them – and that's why we finished third rather than first. So the giant frame of Barkatullah Khan took Nadeem's place. As a fast bowler and Pakistan B player, some saw him as the natural successor to the great Imran Khan, and certainly with his height, physique and flowing locks, he looked the part.

Barkat was quick, even on the softer Scottish wickets. It made for an exciting season with stumps cartwheeling, and balls screaming towards the slip cordon.

His line was just outside off stump, swinging away, and although he had a lethal bouncer, he didn't bowl short to any batsman … except, bizarrely, Hillhead's Graham Locke. Graham was one of the nicest guys you could meet, a fine opening batsman, but he made the mistake of taking on Barkat's bowling with some rash shots, and the big bowler had to show him who was boss.

Later that season, on a hot summer's day at New Anniesland, Motherwell were playing a league match against Glasgow Accies. Barkat was enjoying the first hard and fast track he had encountered since his arrival in Scotland.

Wicketkeeper Steven McGill and his slips took more than a few steps back as Barkat got into his stride, bowling at a speed we hadn't seen before. Most batsmen couldn't lay a bat on his deliveries, but the Accies' pro Phil Cooper was good enough to get an edge to his outswinger.

Willie Miller had stepped into the team that day after a late call-off, and was expecting a quiet afternoon in the summer sun, standing at first slip. The ball seemed to gather pace off the edge of the bat. It was right down Willie's throat. But that was the problem.

Willie – crouched, bespectacled and motionless, more used to the gentler pace of 2nd XI cricket – was oblivious to the fact that this missile was flying in his direction at upwards of 80 mph. Without intervention, Willie's throat may well have been its next destination.

Keeper McGill had decided it was a slip catch, but mercifully, Grant Robertson, at 2nd slip, instinctively stuck out a left hand

and clutched the ball in front of Willie's face. The startled veteran could only stammer a few words ... "I think you just saved my life, Grant!"

Lifesaver or not, Willie was grateful to watch Barkat's next over from the safety of fine leg. But that wasn't the end of his day's work.

Ironically on a hard, fast track, it was Alastair Black's slow bowling that did most of the damage, taking 7 wickets. Grant Robertson scored a fine 70, but it was Willie who shared a last wicket stand with Gavin Shaw to see us over the line.

It had been another decent season. Barkat picked up a lot of wickets, as did Grant Robertson. Harry Tart, Mike Saunders and Steven McGill all batted well at the top of the order. The 1st XI were competitive in every match, and the 2nd XI won the McInnes Cup for the second consecutive year.

We were playing well, but where did all this leave us? Well, having changed professional after five drawn matches and a third place finish in 1988, we finished the 1989 season in third place, having drawn six matches.

Plus ça change, plus c'est la même chose!

Alex The First

The opposition didn't bat an eyelid as the last man approached the wicket. The batsman assuredly asked the umpire for 'middle stump', surveyed the fielders' positions and then calmly took guard to face the next ball. Only then was there a double take, a collective raising of eyebrows, quizzical expressions etched on faces.

History was being made at Home Park that Sunday in the summer of 1987. Alex Black was making her debut for Motherwell Cricket Club.

Historical Perspective

Looking back through the club's history, the ladies played a big part in Motherwell's happiest years. In Victorian times, they were the focus of attention at the Annual Grand Match and Promenade, where they would don their best frocks and dance the night away into the wee small hours.

At the opening of our first pavilion in Edwardian times, the wives and girlfriends of the players all got together and provided a wonderful selection of teas, which were so good that they got a mention in the local press. They organised garden fetes, musical concerts and whist drives to raise funds for the club.

They were unsung heroes, whose dedication and commitment helped to keep the club going through good times and bad. But never, for a single moment, did anyone ever think that a woman would actually take the field. Surely not – the very thought of it!

Well, that was about to change …

A Pioneering Journey

Rachael Heyhoe Flint made her mark on cricket throughout the '60s and '70s, captaining England and serving as a role model for women in sport. In the '80s and '90s, Motherwell Cricket Club had our very own pioneer. Alex Black was our modern-day version of the great lady, now a Baroness, and we were extremely proud to have her.

Alex was known to everyone at the club. She was the younger sister of the cricketing brothers Allan and Alastair, and made her first appearance at the club in the mid-'80s. She was taught to score the book by Peter Forbes, our club scorer, and subsequently undertook the role for the Sunday XI and later for the 2nd XI.

Motherwell has always been a diverse club – no obstacles are put in anyone's way. If you owned a white shirt, that was good enough for us. If you fancied a game, you had a chance of being selected … and that's how it all started for Alex.

It seems ridiculous now, but Alex actually had to get the committee's approval to play. We're not exactly sure why but anyway, approval was given and Alex began to attend training sessions on Monday evenings.

Alex at last donned her whites in 1987, the first lady ever to have played senior competitive cricket for our club. After that, there was no stopping her – most weekends for the next 7 or 8 years, she would would play for the 2nds on a Saturday and the next day for the Sunday XI.

In fact, she may well have been the first female to play competitive cricket in the Glasgow and District League … a fact we can't quite corroborate, but none of us can recall a female cricketer playing for an opposition team before Alex turned out for Motherwell.

In some respects, her story is reminiscent of the character in the film *Bend it Like Beckham*, a tale based on a girl who loves to play football but has to keep it a secret from her family. Except Alex turned that notion on its head – she didn't keep it a secret from anyone. She loved her cricket and she loved playing it.

She still recalls a humorous event while playing for the 2nd XI at East Kilbride. Motherwell had won the toss and put East Kilbride into bat. Alex took a tremendous catch at mid-off to great applause from her teammates. Later, when Motherwell came into bat, Alex took over the score book and noticed the East Kilbride scorer had noted her catch as being taken by 'A. Female'!

Alex was having none of that and immediately corrected the entry to 'A. Black'. How dare they?!

Bill's Letter

Bill Jardine would have been in his 80s when Alex first played for Motherwell. Some might think that an octogenarian would have taken a traditional or old-fashioned view of cricket being a gentleman's game, but not old Bill. He had always been an innovator, always pushed the boundaries, and he was delighted.

He presented Alex with a cap on the occasion of her first match, but not any old cap. From the note that accompanied it, it's evident that the baggy green cap was given to Bill by an opponent who played against the W B Jardine XI back in the 1950s. And that's how we found out that Motherwell Cricket Club had connections with another Australian captain.

We had been thrilled to play against Kim Hughes in the 1970s, and now we discover, through the story of Alex's cap, that Bill Jardine's team had played against Bobby Simpson, one of Australia's greatest.

Bobby was the son of Scottish immigrants from Falkirk and had already been capped by Australia when he played for Accrington in the Lancashire League in 1959. It was probably during that summer, when he visited his grandparents in Falkirk, that he played a Sunday friendly for a local side against Bill Jardine's team.

He would go on to captain Australia many times, and

later take on the national coaching role. Perhaps he is best remembered for his innings of 311 in 1964 at Old Trafford to bat England out of the game and to help retain the Ashes for his country. At the time, he was only the second Australian to score a triple century, after Don Bradman.

The letter was an exciting find. It also prompts the question as to why Simpson gave Bill Jardine his baggy green cap. We've frequently referred to Bill as a legend of the Scottish game and back in the '50s, he was involved in almost everything relating to local cricket, and no doubt he would have pulled out his kazoo to give the assembled cricketers some twelve-bar blues after the match.

It was great to find the Bobby Simpson connection, but it was equally pleasing to read of Bill Jardine's gesture, acknowledging Alex Black's first game for Motherwell. Not for the first time was Bill found to be years ahead of his time.

All Rounder

There may have been some who wondered whether a female should be playing a 'man's game' but they wouldn't dare say so to Alex's face. Her determination mirrored a famous line from another woman of the '80s – "This lady is not for turning!" – and she never did. In any case, she justified her inclusion by playing her part in a successful 2nd XI.

Alex was a team player both on and off the park. She played the game, she scored the book and, perhaps most importantly, she helped to coach the junior teams. As junior convenors, she and Marion Robertson organised training and games for so many kids at Home Park during the '90s.

Del Boy, in his own inimitable way, would have called it just about right: she was 'the crème de la menthe'. It didn't matter if you weren't familiar with Derek Trotter's malapropisms, we knew what he meant. She was one of a kind.

It needs courage to break down barriers, and to forge your own history. Alex did that, and so much more. Alex the First! Motherwell royalty!

A Decade Of Difference

A feature of our history to date has been our ability to finish a decade on a high. No matter what had gone before, there always seemed to be a message of optimism as we looked forward in anticipation of better times ahead. But not this time. In the '90s, we did it in reverse.

Let's start with the good times!

Alastair Black was captain in 1990 and, although runs were in short supply, we still had Barkat's fast bowling. Jim Donnelly's arrival strengthened our attack further and, with Grant Robertson picking up his usual share of wickets, our opponents rarely got away from us.

The batsmen all chipped in. Mike Saunders, Grant Alexander and Grant Robertson scored 50s and Steven McGill, Steve Young and Alastair Jackson were consistent scorers. The 1st XI had seven league victories, but it was only good enough for fifth place. The 2nd XI reached the McInnes Cup final for the third year in a row, but failed to make it a hat-trick of wins.

All of which was eclipsed by a wonderfully bizarre event played out in the rain!

100 Years at Home Park

It was a grey day over Home Park. Passing strangers, innocently walking their dogs or out for a romantic stroll through the woods, stopped and stared.

They adopted quizzical expressions as they took in the scene being played out on the cricket field. The most ridiculous facial hair, overgrown moustaches and sideburns, and hats of all sorts and sizes, toppers and bowlers and boaters, met their astonished gaze. And as for the two men in white coats, maybe they had come to take the white flanneled fools back to the nearest asylum.

Had they been transported back to Victorian Britain? Well, yes! Sort of … for a day, anyway.

For this was the 100th anniversary of the very first cricket match played at Home Park in 1890, on the grounds of the Duke of Hamilton's Dalzell estate. Motherwell Cricket Club decided to celebrate the occasion by playing a Gentlemen v Players match, just like they would have done a century before.

But there was a flaw in the Gentlemen v Players idea – where would you find 11 gentlemen around Motherwell? We had to import them from posher places, like Glasgow High, Hillhead and … Woodhall?

Certainly, the programme printed for the special day listed guest players like Baron Von Kampman, Chief Petty Officer McLean and Viscount Little, playing under the captaincy of Lord Simpson of Calderbank.

As for the Players XI, recruited from the Motherwell ranks, the occupational roles fitted the Players much better than did the titles of their Gentlemen opponents. There was a chimney sweep's boy, an innkeeper and bar steward, an urchin, a peasant, a juggler and performing clown. There were others, but political correctness obviously wasn't a thing in 1890 (or 1990 for that matter!). That was then, this is now.

Suffice to say that all the cricketers entered into the spirit of the occasion, posed for the inevitable photograph, and took the field – but not for long! Barkatullah Khan rattled through a couple of rapid overs, fended off by McKinnell of Khartoum, when the heavens opened.

And that was it. An excellent tea, some refreshments and a lot of chat as gentlemen and players mingled in the bar. And, of course, we are left with this very fine photograph.

(Motherwell unless stated)
Back Row: Bill Louden (umpire), Brian Kampman (East Kilbride), Alan Black, Jim Bill, John McLean (Hillhead), Tommy Halpin (Prestwick), Gavin Shaw, Alistair Jackson, Jim Donnelly, Derek Pettigrew (Prestwick), Andy Little (Glasgow High), Bill Jardine (legend), Barkatullah Khan (Pakistan B and Motherwell), Ronnie Morrison (umpire)
Middle Row: Grant Robertson, Danny Donnelly, Andy Simpson (East Kilbride), Cammie Little (Glasgow High), Ian McKinnell (Prestwick), Peter Forbes (scorer)
Front Row: Mike Saunders, David Anderson, Alastair Black, Steve Young, Alex Simpson (Woodhall), Graham Robertson

A Chance Missed

The following season, Barkatullah was replaced as professional by the run machine that was Feroz Mehdi.

There was also an influx of Woodhall players following their team's sad demise after 100 years of cricket at Calderbank. We inherited many good cricketers, and the combined resources looked good enough to win the league.

Motherwell Football Club had just won the Scottish Cup in 1991 for the first time in ages, and there was a feel-good atmosphere in the town. An omen? Was this our time?

Our new professional did his bit, scoring several centuries, but the merging of the Motherwell and Woodhall teams was more problematic than it should have been. The clubs had been fierce local rivals for 100 years, and it was difficult to manage the overnight conversion to teammates. The result was a talented team that was less than the sum of the parts.

So we didn't win the league, finishing mid-table after 7 drawn matches. Feroz helped us to post decent scores, but we missed the wicket-taking abilities of Barkatullah.

The season was by no means a disaster. We reached the semi-final of the Western Cup, and beat Irvine by 10 wickets, and two partnership records were set.

Feroz (109) and Andy Simpson (52) established a new record for the 1st wicket of 164 against North Kelvinside; and at Penicuik, Feroz (115) and Gavin Shaw (56no) put on 170 for the 2nd wicket.

Just to show we could score runs without Feroz, the Sunday XI scored 268 for 5 against Symington Tinto. Hugh McGinley top scored with an unbeaten 90 with Steven McGill scoring 55 and David Anderson 45.

Steven McGill had a great season with the bat, scoring four half-centuries, with his undefeated 75 saving the day at Hughenden. Campbell McIvor and Grant Robertson also contributed 50s, but there was a general feeling in the camp that we had under-performed.

Some of the Woodhall guys moved on, but there were a couple of new arrivals, Imtiaz and Boota, who would become regulars for Motherwell for years to come.

The next few years saw us bouncing around in mid-table. Feroz continued to rack up the centuries and formed a successful opening partnership with Roger Newton. Roger fully merited his elevation to the top team after scoring 111 against Irvine and 94 against Ardrossan.

Steven McGill maintained his great form with the bat with more half centuries, and Boota's left arm deliveries took a bundle of wickets, particularly in cup ties.

There were some memorable matches along the way. Grant Robertson (78) and Steven McGill (60) piled on the runs in a comfortable victory at Prestwick; Roger Newton and Feroz posted an undefeated 144 to defeat Hillhead by 10 wickets; Jim Bill turned back the years with 6 wickets against Vale of Leven; Steve Young (40 not out) and Grant Alexander (28) defended for almost the entire innings against Asif Mujtaba's left arm spin to frustrate East Kilbride and earn a draw.

But the greatest achievement was recorded by the 2nd XI in 1994 under the captaincy of Graham Robertson.

Home Park's Last Hurrah

Graham had at his disposal players who, let's say, had enjoyed their fifteen minutes of fame. Speary Shaw, Hughie McGinley, Jack Kelly and Graham himself all had good first-team experience, and weren't quite ready for the knacker's yard.

There were fresh faces in the line-up with Sajid Ashraf, Tommy Nicholson and Neil Mitchell still in their teens, and batting solidity in the shape of Murray Learmonth, Andy Rankine, Jim Lees and Paul Harding. Stuart MacKenzie was a great addition to the team and took his fair share of wickets opening the bowling.

Ash Hussein loved his second-team cricket, always committed to putting in a shift for the team, whether opening the batting or being placed down the order to stabilise an innings. Last, but certainly not least, the incomparable Willie Miller, the father of the team, whose grit and determination was as good a reason as any as to why he was selected to play most weeks.

It was a good blend of youth and experience, but mostly experience. In a year of many highlights, we pick out a few that stick in the memory …

Irvine: our only loss. Motherwell were all out for 99. In a tight finish, Irvine squeezed home with eight wickets down to secure the win.

Glasgow Accies: Accies batted first and scored a reasonable 127 for 9. The 2nds responded with a fine 128 for 3 with Hughie McGinley scoring 82 not out to win the game, a wonderful batting performance.

Ardrossan: Motherwell put on a decent total of 138 for 9, with Murray Learmonth top-scoring with 38 while Jack Kelly chipped in with 23. Ardrossan were bowled out for 62 with Graham Robertson taking 4 wickets for 6 runs, Hughie McGinley 3 for 12 and Stuart MacKenzie 2 for 17.

Weirs: Motherwell secured a closely fought 2-wicket victory after Weirs finished their innings at 114 all out. Andy Rankine was man of the match, taking 5 wickets for only 3 runs while

Murray Learmonth (28), Hughie McGinley (27) and Sajid Ashraf (23) polished off the runs.

Vale of Leven: This wasn't a league game but deserves special mention. Jim Lees scored an undefeated 100 in a total of 167 for 3, well supported by Murray Learmonth's 36 in a Motherwell victory.

Glasgow Accies: Back to league business and Accies stumbled to 61 all out with Sajid Ashraf and Jim Bill taking 4 wickets each. Motherwell responded with a quick-fire 64 for 3 for a comfortable win.

Irvine again: This was the crunch game against our nearest challengers, the team who had inflicted our only defeat. With the Motherwell score at 26 for 6 chasing 93 to win, victory seemed a long way off.

Jack Kelly joined Sajid Ashraf at the crease. Sajid was batting beautifully and Jack was, well, doing his thing – dogged determination. But Jack's plan was working – the longer the game went on, the more frustrated the Irvine bowlers became.

The main threat was Jack's running between the wickets, which was at times dreadful. Skipper Robertson decided to intervene and ordered Speary Shaw and Hughie McGinley to relieve the on-field umpires – not because they were doing anything wrong, but to get a message to Jack to calm down before he ran Sajid out.

The skipper's orders were received and understood and, run by run, the total crept up and the target was now within reach. Then it happened, with some style too: a beautiful cover drive by Sajid for four to win the game.

Sajid (29) and Jack (25, runs, not age!) had achieved the improbable, putting on a seventh wicket partnership of 68 for victory … a fantastic performance by both. The bowling performances of Graham Robertson (6 wickets for 19 runs) and Hughie McGinley (3 for 17) were largely forgotten in the excitement of it all.

After the game, Willie Miller, who had earlier been heard castigating the batsmen, grabbed Jack Kelly and gave him the biggest cuddle, announcing he wanted to have Jack's babies. Class! But not a thought you want to hold onto for too long.

Hillhead: The winning post was in sight. The final game against Hillhead was played at Victoria Park and Sajid's 41 propelled Motherwell to a score of 107 all out, a decent total given the weather conditions. When Hillhead batted, it became clear that the Motherwell total was beyond their grasp, but we still had to capture 10 wickets for the win we needed.

Motherwell struck early with Hughie McGinley taking four wickets but, as Hillhead hunkered down for a draw, momentum stalled. With two wickets still to take and overs running out, a draw looked the most likely outcome.

Nothing was happening. Hillhead weren't interested in scoring runs and we didn't look like breaking through. The league was becoming a distant dream when, out of the blue, Speary Shaw took a fantastic catch at leg slip to dismiss veteran Malcolm McLean and, soon after, Willie Miller pouched a catch at gully to secure the final wicket and win the title.

It had been a great team effort all summer. Everyone played their part on the field, but equally important was the camaraderie between the players off it. This played a huge part in the team's success that season.

After the game, the victory songs got underway. In the bar at Hughenden, the league vice-president Malcolm McLean presented Graham Robertson with the league trophy.

An hour or so later, the boys took the trophy back to Home

Park, where the festivities continued, as did the singing. This would be the last trophy won by a Motherwell Cricket XI before leaving their spiritual home.

And here's the team photograph of the happy chaps who all contributed to make 1994 a year to remember!

Back Row: Sajid Ashraf, Jim Lees, Stuart MacKenzie, Murray Learmonth, Neil Mitchell, Willie Miller, Gavin Shaw, Paul Harding
Front Row: Ash Hussein, Jack Kelly, Graham Robertson (captain), Hughie McGinley, Tommy Nicholson
(*Absent*: Jim Bill and Andy Rankine)

Ten Out Of Ten

A year later, things went from the sublime to the – frankly – ridiculous! It was an exciting year, 1995, very tense. So many of our matches went right to the wire.

A 4-run victory against Weirs was followed by a narrow win over Prestwick and an equally narrow defeat to Irvine.

Hillhead finished 5 runs short of our total in a drawn match and the return match with Prestwick ended in a tie, 127 each.

A young Gordon Kells made an impact with the bat, his 57 against Weirs being a highlight. Grant Robertson had a fine season with his 63 against Hillhead and made a number of other useful contributions with bat and ball. And, of course Feroz Mehdi continued to clock up more runs.

But the most incredible performance was played out at Albert Park in the south side of Glasgow where Weirs were hosting Motherwell. We had batted first and recovered from a bad start to post 171 after our allotted 50 overs. Steve Young top scored with a fine 83, with Gordon Kells adding useful runs towards the end of the innings.

Weirs were a good side but, on that mid-July day, they were second best. Boota had bowled beautifully with his left arm swing bowling without any luck, while 19-year-old Sadiq Patel wreaked carnage at the other end with his pace and aggression.

He ran through the top order and, before long, the game was dead and buried – Weirs were 9 wickets down and over 100 runs behind. Motherwell's victory was nailed on, the points heading back to Home Park, but this last wicket mattered. This was a once in a lifetime opportunity.

All 9 wickets had fallen to Sadiq's pace. He had bowled fast and straight, evidenced by the fact that 4 of his wickets were clean bowled and another 4 were leg before wicket, only one caught. One more wicket for the full set. But he was knackered.

He had bowled 15 overs on the spin, way too many for a fast bowler, and yet you couldn't prise the ball from his grasp. He had to go on.

At the other end, Boota had given way to Mehdi, who trundled away, slow-medium deliveries just outside off stump *trying not to take a wicket*! The Weirs number 11 was quite happy to leave them alone. Maiden after maiden.

Captain Steven McGill threw the ball to Sadiq one more time. The fielders were gathered round the bat – 4 slips, 2 gullies, short leg, leg slip, silly mid off – the batsman barely had room to breathe!

Umpire Bobby Adams was about to drop the fourth stone over the over into his left-hand pocket when there was an almighty appeal from the entire Motherwell team; arms were raised and 11 pairs of expectant eyes were turned towards the umpire. The batsman, probably a Greenwood (Weirs always had Greenwoods), had got an inside edge onto the pad and, as the ball looped skywards over the cluster of fielders, Gordon Kells' right arm shot up to take the catch.

Up went the umpire's finger – Weirs were all out for 57, and Motherwell had won. But most importantly, the bowler Sadiq Patel had just taken his 10th wicket of the match for 22 runs. He was almost on his knees, but he had done it – the full house.

Remarkably, this was exactly the same bowling analysis, 10 for 22, as the last Motherwell player to take 10 wickets in an innings – Archie Black in 1947.

It was quite an achievement, never before seen in Glasgow and District League cricket, and recognised next day by the Sunday Standard, who confirmed Sadiq Patel as the winner of their Scottish Cricketer of the Week award.

Comings and Goings

Also in '95, Feroz Mehdi disappeared, flying home to Pakistan mid-season. He had been the most stylish and naturally gifted batsman of the professional era, and scored far more centuries for Motherwell than any other player, professional or amateur, in the club's history. The list of his nineteen 100s shows just how prolific he was:

- 153 not out v Glasgow Accies (1991)
- 115 not out v Penicuik (1991)
- 105 not out v Lanark (1991)
- 109 not out v North Kelvinside (1991)
- 108 v Penicuik (1992)
- 108 v Symington Tinto (1992)
- 111 v Giffnock North (1992)
- 108 v Stirling County (1992)
- 129 not out v Hillhead (1992)
- 118 v Prestwick (1993)
- 130 not out v St Modans (1993)
- 104 v Ardrossan (1994)
- 105 v Prestwick (1994)
- 109 v Hyndland (1994)
- 109 v North Kelvinside (1994)
- 151 not out v Glasgow Accies (1994)
- 114 v East Kilbride (1994)
- 127 v Prestwick (1995)
- 108 not out v Irvine (1995)

Sadly, during Feroz's four years with the club, Motherwell's 1st XI didn't win anything. We comfortably retained our 1st Division status, and the 2nds had success, but all of the professional's efforts with the top team went unrewarded. We came close, regularly qualifying for the Scottish Cup, but no league title, no cup wins.

We managed to secure Baldev for the rest of the 1995 season. He was a great character and scored a couple of hundreds before the end of the season in high-scoring draws.

Like a stuck record, we again finished in the top half of the 1st division without threatening to win the title. It felt like time for a change and, with stricter regulation around work permits, we elected to employ an English professional in 1996.

Andy Cottam had a good record in county cricket, a left arm spinner who could bat a bit. With John Gillies returning to captain the team, hopes were high – well, they always are!

Although Andy had some success with the ball, we had a string of disappointing results and, when he was called away on county duty in mid-season, it allowed us to re-think our options. With a league record of played 7, lost 7, we had to get it right this time.

And we did. We spoke to Baldev, and he lined up a young player called Sanjay Raul, who had toured with the India B team. His batting was a thing of beauty, and his off-spin bowling wasn't bad either. With Sanjay's help, we turned the corner, won a few games and avoided relegation with something to spare.

Imtiaz, John Gillies, Gordon Kells and Alex Cunningham scored 50s, with Grant Robertson and Sanjay picking up 5 wicket hauls. Towards the end of the season, we posted a record score for the club – 296 for 8 against Penicuik. Predictably, Sanjay scored a century supported by Andy Rankine's unbeaten 45.

Sanjay was retained for 1997 and he had a brilliant season, and Motherwell returned to the top half of the league. This is one of the last photographs taken at Home Park.

Back row: Peter Forbes (scorer), Grant Alexander, Gordon Kells, Andy Rankine, Jim Lees, Imtiaz Ali
Front row: Graham Robertson, Steve Young, Steven McGill (captain), Scott Kyle, Sanjay Raul (professional)
(*Absent*: Grant Robertson)

Andy Rankine scored a swashbuckling 108, Gordon Kells an equally aggressive 50 and there were decent bowling returns from Boota, Steve Young and Grant Robertson, but it was Sanjay doing the business week after week.

At times, he seemed almost impossible to get out. He had scored seven centuries against good teams – Irvine, Penicuik, Dumfries (twice), Helensburgh, Weirs and Glasgow Accies. Yet, it didn't feel right.

Sanjay would bat for most of the innings and dominated the strike. Consequently, scorecards became very lop-sided with little contribution from our local players. Even when we won, it was difficult to take any great satisfaction out of the victory.

If this makes Sanjay Raul sound like a bad person, nothing

could be farther from the truth. He was a really nice guy, did a lot of coaching with the younger lads and was very popular around the Club. But he was too good!

We made the brave and principled decision to dispense with a professional for the rest of the '90s and, sure enough, we struggled.

The Lion Cubs

There was something to celebrate though. We had another good clutch of young junior cricketers, some with familiar names. Neil Robertson and David Bill, sons of our erstwhile opening bowlers, were two of the juniors who brought a much-needed smile to our faces.

David made an appearance for the 1st team in 1998 as a 12-year-old, and bowled his leg-spin to good effect. After impressing with both bat and ball, he gained a place in the Scotland Under-13 squad – a first Scottish international honour for our club.

To develop his cricket career, David joined Uddingston, and gained further international recognition right through to the Scottish Under-19s. It is fitting that David has returned to play for Motherwell as we celebrate our 150th anniversary.

Neil Robertson played for Motherwell for a number of years until 2008, when he too joined Uddingston. As a youth, he played regularly for the senior teams, turning out for 1st, 2nd and Sunday XIs, picking up wickets with his medium-fast bowling and scoring some useful runs as well.

The fact that Neil's career spanned three Motherwell grounds – Home Park, Palace Grounds and Dalziel Park – illustrates the difficulties facing the club.

Troubled Times

Indeed! Enough of the positive stuff – these were dark days.

As the clock ticked down to the new millennium, there was little to celebrate at Motherwell Cricket Club. Our mood reflected the depression in the town in a post-Ravenscraig world.

It was pretty grim. Home Park had become a playground for vandals. We would find football games being played on the square, motorbikes being driven across the ground, and the pavilion surroundings frequently littered with broken glass, the remnants of night-time drinking sessions.

There were attempts to break into the clubhouse, and we were now getting phone calls in the early hours, having to leave our beds in the middle of the night to turn off the alarm and secure the place. It was an exacting time and impossible to police.

The endless problems led to some players hanging up their boots, some of whom had been playing since the '70s. They were getting on in years, their cricketing careers approaching an end, and to be honest, it wasn't much fun anymore.

Without a professional, we were clinging onto our 1st division status by our fingernails. The arrival of Paul Whittaker, a visitor from New Zealand, was timely. A decent cricketer, he helped us to record a couple of victories which kept us in the league. Imtiaz and Boota stepped up and two of the Robertson clan (not Grant, but Graham and young Neil) had five-fors.

On 2nd May 1999, we got the call to say the pavilion was on fire, and it was front page news …

FIRE BLOW FOR CRICKET CLUB

It was totally destroyed, a write-off. For a while, we tried to continue playing at the ground, which had been home to Motherwell Cricket Club for over 100 years. The charred remains stood gloomily beside the car park, where players struggled to change into their whites in their cars, and teas were served from car boots.

It was time to say a tearful goodbye. There was a great deal of sympathy from other cricket clubs, and our opponents allowed games to be played at their grounds. This could only be a temporary measure and, of course, it meant that all our games were away fixtures.

In hindsight, avoiding relegation in 1999 was a great achievement given our circumstances. Scott Kyle and Alex Cunningham had decent scores, and Sajid Ashraf and Grant Robertson both had 5-wicket hauls as two victories kept us in the 1st division by the skin of our teeth.

We were homeless, and more players understandably decided the time was right to call it a day. The gods had spoken. A decade that had started so promisingly finished with our club staring into the abyss – a riches to rags story.

Was this the end for Motherwell Cricket Club? Absolutely not – we are made of stronger stuff. A mere flesh wound, as the black knight may have declared.

It needed all the resilience we could muster, some pig-headed individuals who wouldn't give in, some optimism, some new players, and a plan as to how we could keep cricket alive in Motherwell in the 2000s.

New Millennium, New Challenges

Well, we just about survived the 20th century – 100 years of ups and downs. Lots of great times, but it didn't end well – we were effectively homeless, with grave doubts over our future. Apart from that …

We'd been here before. Just when you think that the sun might be setting on Motherwell Cricket Club, we emerge from the darkness and live to fight another day. 1999 had been our *annus horibilis*. Perhaps the advent of a new millennium would bring a change in our fortunes.

And it did, eventually! The noughties, more than any other decade in the history of Motherwell Cricket Club, saw the greatest changes in the club's circumstances. The transition was difficult, and at times painful.

The Field of Play

Having acknowledged that any attempt to re-build a pavilion at Home Park would merely prolong the agony, and doubtless result in more fire-raising, we set out to find a new home.

Initially, we played at the Palace Grounds in the shadow of Hamilton mausoleum, and it served us well. But there was no grass wicket, with games being played on an artificial surface. As the Glasgow and District League had introduced rules that discouraged play on artificial wickets, the search continued for a new ground.

The club had always enjoyed good relations with Dalziel Rugby Club, some of whose players already had connections with Motherwell Cricket Club, as playing members or social members. They made us aware of the potential to join them at Dalziel Park and talks began around the practicalities of laying a square between two rugby pitches. A minor problem was the removal of several floodlights encased in concrete situated exactly where the new square was to be laid.

Thankfully, the cricket club had finances available to fund the project. Supported by insurance monies from the fire loss and from the Catherine Black bequest, the floodlights were re-planted at the far side of the park. The project was completed in 2002, and the square was allowed to rest for 12 months, ready for play in 2003. After three years of nomadic existence, we had a new ground.

A Changing of the Guard

Back in the early '70s, the arrival of the 'young lions' had helped to pull Motherwell out of a hole when many of the great players of the '60s retired or left the area. Now, history repeated itself. The self same 'young lions' and others of their generation grew old together, their cricketing days coming to an end.

The ageing process and 20-odd years of cricket had taken its toll – there were bad backs, fading eyesight, shoulder and knee problems. Throwing the ball in from the boundary had to be done in relays. Consequently, most of the players who had been regular fixtures on 1st XI and 2nd XI team sheets for 20 years or more were gone, leaving a chasm that was difficult to fill.

Grant Robertson and Steve Young continued to turn out and, for years to come, would share the roles of president and captain. They also kicked off a junior cricket initiative, which would pay dividends in years to come.

Imtiaz played a key role in supplying new players, good enough to keep the Motherwell teams competitive. Joe Grieg and Alex Cunningham, who had joined from Woodhall some years before, were still to the fore and the next generation of cricketers like Scott Kyle, Gordon Kells and Andy Rankine performed admirably.

Having dispensed with the employment of a professional in '98 and '99, we swallowed our principles and performed a u-turn – we needed help. Shahid Javid joined in 2000 and, after a while, his brother Arif joined him to play as an overseas amateur.

We also had a couple of overseas visitors – New Zealander Andrew Chipchase and South African Craig Lynch. Each played for a season and made their mark.

After all the comings and goings, we managed to cobble together a decent team. With David Baird holding things together with the 2nd XI, another crisis was averted. Well, not averted, but delayed!

Boom and Bust

The early years of the noughties turned out to be more exciting than we had dared hope for. There were many notable achievements along the way and, bizarrely, it was during a slide from the 1st to the 3rd division that several records were broken.

Run-scoring was taken to a new level. In 2000, when still in the first division, a club record was broken when we posted 291 for 7 against a good Kilmarnock side with a West Indian pro.

Arif scored 92 with good contributions from Shahid, Young and Tariq. And Tariq would go on to score two centuries that year as runs continued to flow, but it was only good enough for a mid-table finish.

Another record of sorts happened the following year, but not a good one. Only one team was to be relegated and, although Motherwell finished second bottom, we were well clear. But Glasgow Accies dropped down from the National Leagues, Weirs lost the play-off to replace them and, all of a sudden, there were too many teams in Division One.

Motherwell had to make way and, for the first time in over 20 years, we were relegated. Having played most of our league games away from home (the move to Dalziel Park was a couple of years away), we felt a bit cheated.

Steve Young handed the captaincy over to Grant Robertson, but the summer of 2002 was dominated by rain – only 9 games survived the weather – and our cricket didn't brighten our days much either. Mid-table in the 2nd division was below expectations but, with new professional Saleem on board, 2003 saw a significant improvement.

And we had a new home. We had moved from Dalzell to Dalziel – they sounded the same, but were to be found at opposite ends of the town. We had left Home Park in Dalzell Estate and had now arrived at Dalziel Park, the former Cleland Estate.

The first games to be played at Dalziel Park were a bit of an anti-climax. April showers led to a 2nd XI match being rained off, and a 1st XI game was washed out after the first innings. Motherwell didn't get a chance to bat but, for the record, the first wicket taken by a Motherwell player at Dalziel Park was … caught Imtiaz, bowled Boota,

Records began to tumble. Imtiaz and Shehzad put on a record first wicket partnership of 194 to beat Titwood by 10 wickets (Shehzad 110, Imtiaz 67, the rest extras).

Shehzad continued his fine form with 143 not out against Galloway, the highest score by an amateur since 1948, and against Meikleriggs, Saleem and Imtiaz helped Motherwell reach 300 for the first time ever. Yet it was only good enough for third place in the league, marginally behind Titwood and St Michaels.

If we thought that was tight, 2004 was heart-breaking. With Imran Nazir as our new professional, we had our best league performance on record (played 12, won 11, drew 1, lost 0) to finish on 95%, undefeated, the invincibles!

Imran, pictured, hit the ground running as he scored three tons in his first three matches in 2004 – 133 not out, 126 not out and an astonishing 192, the highest individual score in the long history of the club, a record that still stands. Unsurprisingly, in that game, Motherwell posted their highest team score of 320 for 7.

There was time for another mammoth opening partnership of 167 registered by Shehzad and Imtiaz, yet we didn't get promotion! What!?!

St Michaels, whom we had beaten, had experienced better weather in Dumfries, managed to get two more games played, and won 13 of their 14 matches to finish with 95.14%. Despite all our heroics, we had failed to get back into Division One, and that just about finished us off.

Grant Robertson, pictured at Dalziel Park with Imtiaz, brought the curtain down on an epic career after 35 years of bowling and with 1300 wickets to his name. His shoulder was in a bad way and, although he embarked upon a new role as wicketkeeper, his cricketing days were numbered.

Likewise, Imtiaz's bad knee brought a halt to his cricketing days. Shehzad was snapped up by Poloc, and at a stroke, our opening batsmen were gone as well. Other connections introduced by Imtiaz were also gone, leaving us short on playing numbers as well as talent.

Our professional, Imran Nazir, was a fine player who could almost win games on his own, but who were we kidding? What was the point?

For Motherwell Cricket Club to continue, we had to develop our own cricketers, so Imran was also on his way. The era of the Motherwell professional was over.

Hanging On In There...

Gordon Kells had taken over the captaincy from Grant Robertson during the 2005 season and in 2006, with Steve Young back at the helm, it was all about survival and managing to fulfill our fixtures. We had voted for short-term pain, hoping for long-term gain.

The club was at its lowest ebb in 2006, getting teams on the park was a struggle and further relegation was inevitable. One game summed up our season – an away match at Meikleriggs, Paisley. One of the cars carrying four Motherwell batsmen was delayed by a motorway accident and, by the time they reached the ground an hour after the game had started, the other seven players had already been bowled out for 39.

But at least the juniors were doing well.

The under-16s and under-11s were playing against the best teams in the west of Scotland and holding their own. Steve Young and Ronnie Edmond ran the teams and took great pleasure in watching the Motherwell kids win games against Poloc, Drumpellier, Glasgow Accies *et al,* and excelling at junior cricket festivals.

With the lack of numbers plaguing senior selection, the solution was obvious, though somewhat premature – promote the under-16s into the 1st and 2nd teams. They weren't ready for it, but it was a great learning experience and they played well. Adeel was first to break through, Peter Keay and Hoseifa followed, then Fraser McGlashan, Saaf, Josh Conway, Yasir and Andrew Duggan. They were all playing senior cricket by their mid-teens.

Predictably, we were relegated but, importantly, the club managed to fulfil their fixtures and Motherwell Cricket Club survived.

Khurram Aziz and Joe Greig shared the captaincy duties the following year as we embarked upon our first campaign in the third division. Joe had developed his game well over the years – he played some decent innings with the bat – but his greatest asset was his steady bowling, punctuated by the odd delivery launched from behind the umpire!

New Faces

And then the cavalry arrived! Students from Chennai attending Glasgow Caledonian University somehow found their way to Dalziel Park. First came Guna and Vishwa, then Raj and

Krishna, all of whom had much longer Indian names, which couldn't fit on the scoresheet, but they could play cricket. Immediately, they brought some much-needed stability to the Motherwell teams.

The new arrivals made a huge difference, and our slump was arrested. We could look forward once again. Guna, a wicket-keeper/batsman, was the stand-out performer for the next few seasons, scoring several 50s and reaching a century against Scotindians.

John Frame and Bharti bowled well and Gordon Kells and Nadeem made good all-round contributions. But the most pleasing factor was the success of the under-16 junior players drafted into the first team. Far from making up the numbers, they were helping to win matches.

In a victory against Prestwick, Hoseifa and Keay top-scored with the bat and captured most of the wickets; even in defeat against Glasgow University Staff, McGlashan, Hoseifa and Keay were the team's top scorers and helped to post a competitive total.

In terms of league finishes, these were topsy-turvy years. The 2nd XI were promoted in 2007 only to drop back down the following year, and the 1st XI repeated the trick by getting promotion in 2008, then relegated in 2009. But they were also exciting years – we were competing well in most matches, enthused about the arrival of new blood and, of course, the progress of the juniors.

The decade came to a close with very different Motherwell teams to the ones that started the new millennium. They were now much younger, and the club had more of an international feel about it. Although we were playing two divisions lower, we were able to compete comfortably in the third tier and, with more players joining the club, there was greater optimism about the place than for some time.

But there was time for one more retiral. Steve Young, 40 years after his 1st team debut, played his last 1st XI match at the end of the 2009 season. He was still chipping in with the bat and at Prestwick that year, he had taken 4 catches at gully. But perhaps his most important contribution was the way he shepherded the club through some very tricky times in the mid-2000s.

Reaching Our Sesquicentennial

Since our establishment in Victorian times, we have survived vandalism and arson and world wars, even competing with football in a football town. It was never going to be plain sailing and, sure enough, as we approached our big anniversary, another obstacle was thrown on our path.

A pandemic! Along with everything else, cricket was put on hold in 2020 and, for the first season since our formation, a whole summer went by without any games being played. Thankfully, our members survived Covid-19 and were able to take the field in 2021.

So we made it. We reached our 150th year, and Motherwell Cricket Club is still alive. As we bring our history up to date, that final stretch was full of excitement, with more records being broken along the way.

Raising the Bar

We left behind the peaks and troughs of the early 2000s, and our team retained a core of quality players throughout the next decade and beyond. Krishna, Raj, Khurram and Kishore have all been with us for 12 years or more and are still taking the field as we celebrate our 150th year.

Of course, we experienced some relegations and promotions along the way. But the bad times didn't last long – we responded well to adversity – and the good times were very good, with some astonishing scoring exploits. Where do we start?

Back in 2004, Imran Nazir had dominated the Glenpark attack to post a personal tally of 192 runs as he eclipsed Feroz Mehdi's highest score by a Motherwell batsman. Both these excellent players were professionals, doing what they were paid to do. What about the home-grown talent who play cricket for fun?

21-year-old Peter Keay set the record for an amateur in 2012 by clobbering thirteen 6s in an incredible knock of 170 against Inverclyde.

His was the main contribution in a Motherwell total of 345 for 7, also a record for the club at the time. Duncan Macsween's 34 and Khurram's 56 provided good support but, for the most part, their job was to give Peter as much of the strike as possible. He was on fire.

Here's Peter (centre, front row) with his team mates on his record-breaking day. Sadly, illness and work commitments meant that he didn't play much cricket after this epic innings, but his name is still there in the record books.

Departing the Scene

Motherwell bounced back from their 2009 relegation to come straight back up to division 2 the following year, where the young side performed well, winning most games, and were very unlucky to miss out on promotion to the top league. We finished 2nd on three occasions!

During this period, our club hit the headlines once again, but not in a good way. An ill-tempered local derby against Hamilton Palace resulted in Motherwell walking off the pitch. Neither side emerged with any credit, both were punished by the league and we moved on.

Some leading players also moved on during this period: Joe Greig, club captain for 4 years, retired; Duncan Macsween, opening bat who inherited the captaincy from Peter Keay; opening bowler Alex Fraser; all-rounder Vishwa; and Nadeem, a talented cricketer who had two centuries to his name.

Hoseifa Khan, another graduate from the juniors, deserves special mention. He left for university, but not before he made an impact with bat and ball. He opened the batting and scored consistently well, including a century, and his leg-spin bowling saw him feature among the wicket-takers game after game.

The loss of key players were bound to have an impact. Motherwell found themselves competing at the wrong end of the table and, after a couple of close shaves, the trap door opened in 2017. But their reaction was nothing less than spectacular!

2018: A Batsman's Paradise

You have to do a double take when you skim through our club statistics for 2018. Especially when you get to the game against Dumfries side, Kingholm, when Motherwell put 432 runs on the board! Seriously! And here's the scorecard to prove it.

Innings of Motherwell

+ K Selvaraj	Bowled	b J Woodhouse	72
* J Narayanasamy	Caught A McNay	b K Moore	1
R Palanismy	Caught C Bowie	b J Woodhouse	102
A Pichaimuthu	Not Out		139
D Chinnasamy	Bowled	b M Moss	12
R Jayaraman	LBW	b M Moss	30
Kh Fawad	Not Out		11
A Thirugnana Sambandam	DNB		
K Ranjan	DNB		
S Sudharshan Balasubramaniam	DNB		
S Kumar	DNB		
Extras		6b 8lb 43w 8nb	65
TOTAL	for 5 wkts (40 ovs)		**432**

Note the number of overs: 40. This means that the batsmen were clattering along at almost 11 an over all afternoon.

It's the largest ever score by a Motherwell team, and only the second time that two Motherwell centurions featured in the same match – Alaguraja Pichaimuthu (Raj) with 139 not out, and Radhakrishnan Palanisamy (Krishna) with 102. The first time happened just 6 weeks before, which gives us an immediate impression of the runfest that was 2018.

Here is a photograph of the Motherwell team taken later in our record-breaking season. Those pictured at Dalziel Park are...

Standing: Radhakrishnan Palanisamy, Ayyappan, Madhuappan, Vijay Kumar, Jaganathan Nayaranasamy, Sriram
Seated: Ramani, Kamud Ranjan, Alaguraja Pichaimuthu, Kishore Selvaraj, Khurram Fawad

Kingholm weren't a bad side – it included Sandy McNay who, although past his prime, had dished out a few heavy defeats on Motherwell teams over the years (payback time, Sandy!). In any case, the concentration and single-mindedness of Motherwell's batsmen to maintain such a run rate, while only losing 5 wickets, is admirable.

Was this a one-off? A look at the rest of the league programme through that 2018 season points to a batting unit in top form …

*28 April – **Kingholm** 77 (H Adnan 3-7); **Motherwell** 78 for 6*

*12 May – **Whiteinch** 135 (S Khan 3-17, K Fawad 3-40); **Motherwell** 136 for 4 (Pichaimuthu 46 not out)*

*19 May – **Motherwell** 345 for 3 (Pichaimuthu 125 not out, Nayaranasamy 115 not out); **Glenpark** 215 (Fawad 3-26)*

*26 May – **Motherwell** 333 for 6 (Palanisamy 79, Fawad 61 not out, Pichaimuthu 56); **Tryst** 108 (Ranjan 3-25)*

*2 June – **Motherwell 294** (Fawad 62 not out); **Marress** 143 (S Kumar 3-23)*

*23 June – **Motherwell 176; GHK** 139*

*30 June – **Motherwell 432 for 5** (Pichaimuthu 139 not out, Palanisamy 102, Selveraj 82); **Kingholm** 154 (Fawad 3-15)*

*7 July – **East Renfrewshire** 193 for 7; **Motherwell 194 for 6** (Selveraj 42)*

*14 July – **Motherwell 280** (Palanisamy 67, Pichaimuthu 64); **Whiteinch** 152 (Palanismy 3-56)*

*21 July – **Glenpark** 132; **Motherwell 134 for 4** (Pichaimuthu 41)*

*28 July – **Motherwell 159 for 8** (Palanisamy 64); **Tryst** 160 for 2*

*4 Aug – **Marress** 82; **Motherwell 86 for 4***

*11 Aug – **Motherwell 181** (Palanisamy 64); **Cavaliers** 96 (Fawad 3-9)*

*25 Aug – **Motherwell 183** (Palanisamy 44); **GHK** 104 (Fawad 3-29, Ranjan 3-22)*

*1 Sept – **Motherwell 328 for 8** (Pichaimuthu 89, Selveraj 68); **Cavaliers** 184 (Srinivasan 4-53)*

So it wasn't just the 432 against Kingholm. We scored 345 against Glenpark, 333 against Tryst, 328 against Cavaliers, 294 against Marress and 280 against Whiteinch. Almost every bowling attack in the league suffered against the might of Motherwell's batsmen.

It was a magnificent season for Motherwell Cricket Club. What makes it even more remarkable is that the team had struggled for players for a couple of seasons before. But we stuck at it, and were joined by some new faces who helped us through to 2018. Dinesh and Ramani were good additions to the squad.

It's reminiscent of times past in our 150-year history, when we've kept going through the difficult times, to find the good times just round the corner.

Of course, we ran away with the league in 2018, having won all but one of our league matches, but didn't get promoted as we did not meet the new league qualifications for 2nd division teams. You can imagine the reaction of the other 3rd division teams when they learned they'd be facing us again in 2019.

Regardless, it was a record year for the club and, although we still had to fulfill some conditions, promotion was granted the following year after another fine season. We competed well in the second division, finishing in the top half of the league for several seasons, before league reconstruction led to a place in Western Premiership 3, where we currently reside.

Ever-Present Stars

At any club, players come and players go, and that's been the case at Motherwell throughout our history. But some stick with us year after year, and step up to the plate when needed. In recent times …

Alaguraja Pichaimuthu (Raj) has been scoring runs for the club since he arrived in 2007. He was top scorer in eight of those seasons, reaching 50 on many occasions. As well as his two centuries in 2018, he scored 108 and 127 against Vale of Leven, and 112 against Gourock.

His five centuries put Raj a the top of the list of amateur century-makers in the club's history, sitting alongside the legendary R K Hinshalwood Snr, who played in the 1920s and '30s. And, like 'Old Bob', Raj takes wickets as well.

Radhakrishnan Palinasamy (Krishna) underwent a remarkable transformation. When he joined along with Raj, he was a good bowler but his batting was restricted to some cameos towards the end of the innings. He remains a fine medium-pacer, but now finds himself as a regular top-order batsman.

It was Joe Greig who gave Krishna the opportunity to take on the role of pinch-hitter, and he's still there. The improvement in Krishna's batting has enabled him to score three centuries – against Inverclyde, Kingholm and Hamilton Crescent.

Khurram Fawad announced his arrival in 2010 by taking 8 wickets against Glenpark and since then, it's remarkable how many scorecards show Khurram picking up 3 or 4 wickets.

Leading the team for many of these years, he often dropped himself down the order and came to the crease when a captain's innings was required. It worked frequently, most notably in 2022, when Khurram and Hari Brikson found themselves at the wicket with the score at 70 for 6 chasing GHK Strathclyde's 203. They got there with Khurram finishing undefeated on 66.

Beyond this triumvirate are others who have made substantial contributions during these years.

Selveraj (Kishore) has batted well and kept wicket for most of these years, his 136 against Ardencapel being one of the highest scores by a Motherwell player. Nayaranasamy (Jagan) also registered a fine undefeated 115 against Glenpark and since the start of the '20s, the aforementioned Hari Brikson and Silvapisha (Sibi) have made a positive impact.

A Modern Approach

It seems like a very different game to the one we played not so long ago. And it is.

On an international scale, with the advent of T20 cricket, it's not unusual to score at 10 runs per over. Even the strokes, from scoops to reverse sweeps, would have been unthinkable just 20 years ago.

The scores in limited overs cricket have soared. Granted, the number of Extras are much higher, with any delivery outside leg stump being called a wide, but the extraordinary scores posted by Motherwell (and other teams, of course) in recent years reflect how the game has changed at grass roots level as well.

Recent years have seen our record books revised on a number of occasions. Since the turn of the century, we have witnessed the highest ever scores by individuals (both professional and amateur) and the highest team total has been repeatedly broken.

Back in the early days of Motherwell Cricket Club in the late 19th century, anything around 60 or 70 would pretty much give you a comfortable victory. Just fifty years ago, 150 would be good innings. As recently as the 1990s, a score of 200 runs would almost always win the day, and 250 would put you out of sight.

In our centenary brochure, special mention was made of an opening stand of 101 in 10 overs by David Brady and Baxter Rae in an evening match in 1960 against Fauldhouse, and readers stared wide-eyed in wonder at such rapid scoring. Motherwell's cricketers of 2018 kept this run-rate going for 40 overs!

You do wonder how the game will develop over the next 50 years.

Here's the current 1st XI as we celebrate 150-odd years of Motherwell Cricket Club …

Back row: Steve Young (Hon President), Dinesh Chinnasamy, Jaganathan Narayanasamy, Ayyappan Thirugnana Sambandam, Sajith Sajeev, Helly Brikson, Sibin Simon Silvapicha.

Front Row: David Bill, Khurram Fawad, Alaguraja Pichaimuthu, Kishore Raj Selvaraj, Radhakrishnan Palanismy

Our Future

From a humble beginning in a farmer's field 150 years ago, we come to the end of our club's history ... except it's not the end. It's our story so far; we're just pausing to take stock before pressing on to the next landmark. Hopefully someone will put pen to paper in the 2070s to mark our 200th year.

We're by no means the oldest club in Scotland. Kelso (1821), Rossie Priory (1828) and Grange (1832) were just some of the teams playing the game long before us. That said, maintaining a cricket club in Motherwell, uninterrupted for 150 years, is no small achievement. We're proud of that.

As our current generation of cricketers extend our history and create their own story, Motherwell's 'young lions' are approaching a personal milestone. The prospective septuagenarians can look back over their 50-year association with the club with an overwhelming sense of achievement.

We remember everyone we've shared a dressing room with, opponents we've faced on the field, the cricketers who are keeping our story alive and friends we've lost along the way. We raise a glass.

As the great actor and film director Orson Welles said, " if you want a happy ending, that depends on where you stop the story".

And our story continues. Now it's all about moving forward, choosing the next path and being the best we can be. Some may quote the Dalziel High School motto *Summa Petenda* (Aim for the highest) while others may prefer the Wishaw High version *Qui Non Proficit Deficit* (He who doesn't advance falls behind). But maybe that great luminary Buzz Lightyear said it best …. "To Infinity and beyond".

Presidents and Captains (1971–2023)

Year	President	Club Captain	Year	President	Club Captain
1971	J K F Grieve	R G Kerr	1998	G Robertson	S McGill
1972	J K F Grieve	R G Kerr	1999	G Robertson	S McGill
1973	J K F Grieve	A J Johnston	2000	G Robertson	S M Young
1974	J K F Grieve	A J Johnston	2001	G Robertson	S M Young
1975	J K F Grieve	A J Johnston	2002	G Robertson	G Robertson
1976	J K F Grieve	A J Johnston	2003	G Robertson	G Robertson
1977	T Barrie	D Burke	2004	G Robertson	G Robertson
1978	T Barrie	A J Johnston	2005	G Robertson	G Robertson / G Kells
1979	R A Morrison	S M Young	2006	S M Young	S M Young
1980	R A Morrison	S M Young	2007	S M Young	K Aziz / J Greig
1981	R A Morrison	S M Young	2008	S M Young	J Greig
1982	A Hamilton	S M Young	2009	S M Young	J Greig
1983	A Hamilton	A J Johnston	2010	S M Young	J Greig
1984	J Shaw	A J Johnston	2011	S M Young	P Keay
1985	J Shaw	G Robertson	2012	S M Young	P Keay / D Macsween
1986	J Shaw	G Robertson	2013	S M Young	D Macsween
1987	J Shaw	G Robertson	2014	S M Young	K Fawad
1988	J Shaw	G Robertson	2015	S M Young	K Fawad
1989	J Shaw	G Robertson	2016	J Kelly	K Fawad
1990	S M Young	A M Black	2017	J Kelly	A Pichaimuthu / K Fawad
1991	S M Young	G Robertson	2018	J Kelly	R Palanisamy / K Fawad
1992	S M Young	G Robertson	2019	J Kelly	K Fawad
1993	S M Young	G Robertson	2020	J Kelly	(No cricket played)
1994	G Robertson	G Robertson	2021	J Kelly	K Fawad
1995	G Robertson	S McGill	2022	J Kelly	K Fawad
1996	G Robertson	J Gillies	2023	J Kelly	A Pichaimuthu
1997	G Robertson	S McGill			

The Young Lions: more than you need to know

The tale has been told of the hiatus in the early 1970s when our great league-winning teams of the '60s seemed to evaporate into thin air, and how a group of promising junior cricketers known as the 'Young Lions' helped to fill the void. Some of these kids went on to serve the club for the next 30 years and more.

Their on-field contributions have been well documented but, off the field, they pretty much ran the club from the 1980s through to the present day. Presidents, captains, treasurers, secretaries, bar convenors, match secretaries, junior convenors, social convenors – their names dominate the senior positions in the club.

They took great enjoyment out of their playing days, and 'gave back' – the circle of life.

And like Motherwell Cricket Club, they are still around. They got together again after all these years to share their memories. It's time we learned more about their stories …

Steve Young … Grant Robertson … Jim Bill … Gavin Shaw … Jack Kelly … and Graham Robertson.

A Man For All Seasons

Once Motherwell Cricket Club gets its claws into you, it's difficult to escape. Many of us turned up to a coaching session as kids and, 50-odd years later, we're still around, doing our bit for the club. Lifers! Here's how it can happen …

Serendipity

A young boy was walking through Dalzell estate with his dad and they stopped to watch the cricket, a 2nd XI friendly match. One of the Motherwell players injured himself and had to leave the field. The captain scanned the watching crowd (well, the boy and his dad were the crowd!) and asked if the boy would help out as a sub fielder.

The boy ran from fine leg to fine leg for the rest of the innings, threw the ball into the wicketkeeper a couple of times, and happily accepted the invitation to come down to junior practice the following week.

Some time later, the boy was one of a number of kids engaging in what served as junior practice, the bowlers bowling as fast as they could, the batsmen trying to hit the ball as hard as they could.

The 1st XI captain, Archie Syme, wandered towards them and, seemingly at random, asked the boy and his pal to play at Lanark the following evening – they'd had a couple of late call-offs. "OK," said both boys, a duet.

Move forward 24 hours, and it's around 8.40pm on a damp Lanark night with Motherwell struggling at 47 for 9, chasing 51 for victory. The boy is last man in, standing at the crease, petrified. The first ball fizzes past him; he didn't see it. Second ball, the umpire shouts, "No Ball."

The boy had never heard such a call before, nearly jumped out of his skin, and swung the bat more in fright than anything resembling a batting technique. He looked up to see the ball scampering through the outfield for four. The scoreboard read 51 for 9, game won.

As the boy wanders off the field, he's congratulated on hitting such a fine shot through the covers. The boy's puzzled. For the life of him, he can't understand what hitting a ball through a cover has to do with playing cricket! Anyway, he's just delighted to win his first game playing for Motherwell.

The 15-year-old lad was Steve Young or, as the Motherwell Times would label him, 'young Stevie Young'. It had a ring to it, and the reporter liked it so much that Steve was well into his twenties before he outgrew the handle.

He would go on to play for the 1st XI for 40 years, serving as captain for many of them and president for many more. All because he found himself in the right place at the right time, twice! Serendipity squared, initiating a life-long relationship with Motherwell Cricket Club. It was meant to be.

All Rounder

Steve could bat a bit. Early in his senior career, he earned a few headlines... for hitting Fauldhouse's West Indian Test spinner

Charran Singh for six, and for a couple of impressive cameo innings in prestige matches at Raeburn Place against Grange, and at Gala and Stenhousemuir.

But he obviously didn't like the limelight, so he kept the bigger scores for special occasions and settled for contributing a useful 20 most weeks.

In fact, the useful 20 became something of a habit – frequently you would find a 27 or 29 against Young in the scorebook. This irritated Steve because if you scored 30 or more, you got your name in the listing of cricket results in the Glasgow Herald on a Monday. In the same way as a batsman goes through the nervous 90s before reaching a century, for Steve it was the twitchy 20s.

He never did score a century, coming close a couple of times. Steve claims that his innings of 87, when he and Steven McGill put on 144 for the 5th wicket at Hillhead, was deserving of 100. The game was played in constant drizzle with puddles forming on the outfield, and consequently the ball wasn't running to the boundary. The fact that most of his shots were of the aerial variety rather than cultured groundstrokes would tend to counter Steve's rationale. Regardless, it was a fine knock, but despite his protestations, the scorebook says 87.

His away-swing bowling was effective. By the end of the 1970 season, the 15-year-old lad was taking wickets for the 1st XI and, two years later in the Western Cup final, he bowled right through unchanged.

The emergence of Grant Robertson and Jim Bill as a potent opening attack meant fewer overs for Steve, although he was always useful for a few wickets as a change bowler. In later life, he changed his bowling style to slow-medium in-swing – it allowed him to prolong his bowling stints and brought him more wickets as well.

There was one thing about his bowling that troubled him. Steve had a good slower ball, taking pace off the ball to deceive the batsman, but it wasn't as successful as it should have been. It was a mystery, until wicketkeeper Allan Johnston pointed out that in his delivery stride Steve's face burst out into a cheeky smile, which tended to give the game away.

He was often selected to play for a Glasgow League Select XI, usually captained by Woodhall's Alex Simpson. In 1980, the Select team played Prestwick to celebrate their 25th anniversary. Alex asked Steve to open the bowling, but he had to be taken off after capturing 5 wickets in his first few overs (including the pro, Grant Stanley), which threatened to curtail Prestwick's celebrations.

Despite Steve's runs and wickets, perhaps his most memorable moments were in the field, diving around like a frustrated goalkeeper taking catches at gully or at short leg. Short leg was a scary place to be, but that's where he ended up (no helmet or box – was it a macho thing?).

He soon developed quick reflexes and an understanding of when to hit the deck to avoid getting wiped out by a slog across the line.

You're placed there for a reason – to catch the ball when the batsman fends off a rising delivery – and such an event was captured by the Motherwell Times' photographer in a home match against Anchor … caught Young, bowled Bill.

And when Steve took a towering catch running in from the boundary to dismiss West of Scotland's last man and help secure the Western Cup in 1986, he couldn't have been happier.

Carluke: A Parallel Universe

To give this story a bit of balance, we must address an aspect of Steve's cricketing life that caused more than a few words to be exchanged. The exchange of words was in fact pointless, as it had no effect. It happened every week, every summer, almost without fail.

It was the early 1990s, the skipper Grant Robertson. He would post the team sheet on the notice board every Monday night. For home games, the postscript never changed – 'Meet at the clubhouse at 12.30 prompt'. Maybe it should have been made clear that we were talking British Summer Time to ensure that clocks had been moved forward an hour but, for most people, it meant... well, just that – meet at 12.30 prompt.

The problem was that it seemed impossible for Steve to get from Carluke to Home Park by 12.30. For the normal person, Carluke was 20 minutes away... for Steve, or for anyone sitting in Steve's car, it took at least 50 minutes!

Week after week, an irate Grant would wait for the latest excuse – Carluke must have the greatest number of roadworks anywhere on the planet, and did they have a gala day procession every weekend in the town?

Captain Grant had a theory of a parallel universe existing on an invisible plain somewhere between Carluke and Motherwell. The laws of physics in South Lanarkshire were fundamentally different from those in North Lanarkshire – Keanu Reeves wouldn't have looked out of place plying his trade in *The Matrix*.

In Carluke's parallel universe, it was feasible that Steve turned up at Home Park in good time to cut the wicket, mark it and roll it, then head into the kitchen, fill the tea urn and give the work surfaces a clean. He'd then welcome his Motherwell colleagues with the news that all the chores had been done.

The harsh reality was somewhat different. Steve's car would come to a sudden halt in the clubhouse carpark, the Carluke contingent casually disembarking. There stood Grant, incandescent with anger (again)."Where have you lot been for the past half hour?"

And so it remained for all time coming. Was it all a dream? Do parallel universes really exist?

The Correspondent

Towards the end of his playing days, it was Steve who would provide the Motherwell Times and Wishaw Press with the cricket report from Motherwell. It helped to keep the club in the public eye, and Steve decided to take the opportunity to keep himself in the public eye as well. To show that he was still an active cricketer, albeit an ageing one, he would ensure that his own name was mentioned every week.

The great thing about being an all-rounder was that, if you failed with the bat, you might pick up some wickets or take a catch or two, anything to justify a mention in the local papers. This worked well for many years but, as he grew older and his powers were on the wane, we would read … 'After the early dismissal of Young …' quite frequently.

Or, when he had done nothing at all in a game at Titwood … 'While Shehzad and Imtiaz were winning the game with a marvellous unbroken partnership of 193, Young sat in the pavilion, padded up for 36 overs, not required.'

There was one match where the team was so poor that Steve's report read … 'The only positive feature of Motherwell's performance on Saturday was that the teas were fairly good.' No-one got a mention that week.

More seriously, in relation to the hiring of professionals, there was all the correspondence with overseas agencies trying to sort out work permits in time for the start of the season. In so doing, Steve engaged with such legends of the game as Ali Bacher in South Africa and Zaheer Abbas in Pakistan to obtain all the paperwork necessary to support the application process.

TO WHOM IT MAY CONCERN:

This is to certify that Mr. S. Feroz Mehdi, P-38952, is a permanent employee of the Pakistan International Airlines, and has been playing First Class Cricket for the last ten years.

ZAHEER ABBASS
MANAGER CRICKET

An Obsession

There were other duties that fell to Steve as club president for many years. Organising fund-raising initiatives and sponsorship was an annual challenge, as was the task of finding speakers for the Annual Cricket Dinner.

Some wonderful nights are remembered at the old Garrion Hotel and later at the Davie Cooper suite at Fir Park. We were entertained by hilarious speeches from the likes of Stewart Coull and Jim Robertson, by talks from sporting heroes like John Beattie and Wilson Humphries, and the unforgettable J K Scobie's poetry reading, an unlikely but brilliant success.

These were great days, both on and off the park, but then the fun stopped. The second clubhouse burned down. A lot of players left but a few of the old stagers were determined to keep things going. We needed new blood, so a junior section was re-established and a good squad of kids formed a decent side. Steve led the coaching of the kids from under-12s through to under-18s, attending every junior game, providing transport for the away fixtures.

When senior playing resources grew perilously thin, he promoted his under-16 junior side to form an unlikely 1st XI and managed to fulfil the league fixtures. Games were lost and Motherwell were relegated, but it gave the young cricketers great experience and kept the club alive until a new influx of players came along.

With his playing days behind him, Steve continued to act as club president (now Hon. President), chairing AGMs and doing his bit to help the club where he could.

Its survival and prosperity has become something of an obsession, and when the 150th anniversary presented an opportunity to research the history of the club and effectively re-write the narrative, it was a no-brainer.

A man for all seasons? Well, from the 1969 season and every season since, and hopefully a few more seasons yet to come.

The Enforcer

It all started in the mid-1960s in the east end of Glasgow – the stomping ground, Bridgeton and Ruchazie, not the poshest parts of Glasgow. Grant Robertson was 11 years old.

A game of football was nearing its end, Grant was tackled rather robustly and was sent crashing to the ground. He took umbrage at the challenge and had a word in the player's ear. A heated argument developed, and let's say there was only going to be one winner!

Coming from Glasgow's east end would shape Grant's character in years to come. No quarter asked, none given, and that was just how it was in those days. You learned to look after yourself, showing no weakness, standing your ground.

Wind the clock forward a few years – the scene moves a dozen miles or so to Motherwell and the sport changes from football to cricket. Grant was a bit older, but the same aggressive tendencies bubbled close to the surface. His combative traits made him a fierce competitor, an enforcer.

Every club has players who fall into this category, and you're glad to have them around if the going gets tough. At Motherwell, Grant had the talent (lots of it) to go along with it, and a single-minded determination to win, and win fairly, playing by the rules.

Never intimidated, he wouldn't tolerate unsportsman-like behaviour and would protect his teammates whenever the need arose. You could identify other Motherwell players of that era with similar characteristics, like David Brady, Allan Johnston and Bobby Steel, and later Joe Greig and Steven McGill, but Grant Robertson stands out as one who led from the front.

Marathon Effort

Grant earned the nickname 'Grunt' for the effort put into every ball he bowled. He took over 1,300 1st XI wickets during his career, an achievement that may never be equalled. His success in the early days was forged in an era when there were no bowling restrictions. The Motherwell captain would plan his bowling strategy but find it impossible to put them into practice.

As senior bowler, Grant was given choice of ends. Poor Jim Bill, his opening partner, would always find himself bowling uphill or into a stiff wind. After seven or eight overs from his opening bowlers, the captain would look for a change of pace or introduce some spin, just to shake it up a bit, keep the batsmen guessing. But not if the ball was in Grant's hands.

"Just one more over, I've worked the batsman out." The captain would concede the point and give Grant another twirl. Next thing he knows, Grant has concluded a 25 overs stint, bowling unchanged. Prising the ball out of his grasp was impossible but, to be honest, it was usually the best option. Time and again, wickets would fall, or the opposition would struggle to post a challenging target.

Asif Mujtaba, who batted number 3 in the Pakistan Test team, opened for East Kilbride and would regularly make massive scores in the Glasgow and District League. Against Motherwell, on a good track, Grant and Jim Bill didn't let him get away and he eventually reached his 100 in the 50th over. He told the boys that it was one of his most hard-fought centuries in Scotland.

These marathon stints helped Grant to take multiple wickets throughout the season. And when he was appointed captain, more overs were clocked up and more wickets were notched on the Robertson bedpost.

Batting Heroics

With the bat in hand, he was known for some good knocks, but remembered for his mighty sixes and fours despatched all around the ground. He managed to score 90 runs against Kelvinside Accies, and a couple of other big scores against Prestwick and Glasgow Accies but, unfortunately, the illusive 100 escaped him.

There was a lot of respect for Grant. Within the club, he won Player of the Year on several occasions. Trophies are great things – you can give someone an award without having to tell them how good they are. That was the Motherwell way.

There was respect from other teams as well, most noticeably from many of the professionals who graced our game. The opposition knew that with Grant in Motherwell's team, a fierce challenge lay ahead, with both teams fighting tooth and nail for every wicket and every run.

Arguments occurred, and at times things became heated … but that was fine – once the game had finished, tensions disappeared (well, most of the time), and it was off to the bar for a few beers and a laugh, but always as friends.

Monday Nights

Grant's other love was rugby, and Motherwell Cricket Club has always enjoyed close relations with Dalziel Rugby Club. He played for and captained the 'Dazzlers', Dalziel's 3rd XV, and to develop the connection, introduced legendary prop, big Keith, as our fitness coach.

For a while (well, it lasted about 3 weeks), players could be seen jogging up and down 'hamburger hill' adjacent to the cricket ground but soon players found themselves busy with other stuff on a Monday night. Despite this, the club did manage to encourage a few rugby players to play cricket, with Willie Miller being one that went on to play for many years.

Some of the best times at Motherwell were the fielding practice sessions on Monday evenings.

The club bought a catching cradle, shaped like the hull of a small boat, only more rounded. The arc of waiting slip fielders would always have to be on the alert as the cricket ball flew off the cradle at unpredictable angles and at variable speed. It needed someone to throw the ball and, *quelle surprise*, Grant was always happy to fire the ball into the cradle at frightening pace. If we ignore the staved fingers and the bruised hands (remarkably nothing was broken), it was great fun!

Towards the end of the night, Grant stood with his bat in front of the pavilion, and launched the ball high into the darkening evening skies towards a group of fielders standing down at the far end of the ground. Each fielder had to take three towering catches before they were allowed to retire. Several would head back to the dressing rooms with reddened hands to go with their red faces as catching practice came to an end.

In the News

Grant found himself in the national press after an altercation at North Kelvinside. The game had been an ill-tempered affair and, on leaving the pitch, a spectator picked up a metal brush used to sweep the wicket and skelped Grant on the head with it.

The headline read 'Well Star Hit By Brush'. It was to be found in the news pages of the Daily Star, nestling amongst other sensationalist headlines. Outwith the listings of weekend cricket results in the Glasgow Herald's sports pages, Motherwell Cricket Club didn't feature in the press very often. How did we feel about it?

There was a degree of angst in some circles about the club featuring in a negative tabloid story, but most of the debate amongst the players was over the term 'star'. No-one bothered too much about poor Grant getting stitches inserted in his head wound, it was just that they had never thought of Grant as a star. But there it was in the papers, so it must be true!

The more they thought about it, the more the idea took hold. They considered all these wickets Grant had taken, and his big hitting with the bat that could change the course of a match. And it was no great shock that it was Grant who was assaulted rather than anyone else. It had to be conceded that the Daily Star might have got it right.

Of course, no-one would actually give Grant a pat on the back or tell him about his star status straight to his face – this was Lanarkshire after all – but they thought it.

In Charge

As sure as night followed day, Grant took over the 1st XI captaincy duties and, after several years in the role, assumed the title of President, again for a number of years.

Junior coaching was big on Grant's agenda, but finding volunteers to coach the kids from within the playing membership wasn't easy. The solution was to be found at home – wife Marion and her friend Alex Black (sister of Alan and Alistair Black) took on the task of organising junior sessions.

The junior section grew to over 30 boys and girls and, through innovative sponsorship, provided every kid with a club polo top. It was a great success. Here's Grant with the Juniors together with the shirt sponsor, Gordon Currie, father of Motherwell player Calum.

The mid- to late-90s were difficult years for the club, with repeated break-ins at the pavilion and intruder alarms going off in the early hours. Grant did more than his fair share of attending to the problems, and had the unfortunate experience of witnessing the Home Park clubhouse in flames in 1999.

Happenstance

But let's take things right back to the start: why cricket? Well, it's all down to a happy accident. When the Robertson family moved to Motherwell in 1967, they bought a house about 100 yards from the cricket pitch. It's probable that, had the family remained in Ruchazie or chosen a house in another corner of the steel town, the cricketing world would have been robbed of the brothers Robertson.

But fate took a hand – Grant and Graham found Home Park just down the road and as a result, for 40-odd years, cricket grounds in the west of Scotland were feistier places to play.

Many sportsmen have a very different personality off the field of play, using their sport to channel their inner aggression. Grant? No, he's exactly the same off the field... and, without that inner self-belief and steely determination, he just wouldn't be the same character. Long live 'The Enforcer'!

A Man of Many Colours

The Young Lions had strange introductions into the world of cricket, each following their own particular path. Our parents hadn't played the game, and none of us had gone to public school or attended any cricket coaching sessions. We all played a bit of football, but somehow got hooked on cricket. What was it that attracted us to the game?

Of all the boys who arrived at Home Park in the late 1960s, perhaps Jim Bill's story is the most unlikely.

Living a Lie

The year was 1963, probably June, the place a council housing estate in Pather, not the poshest part of Wishaw. Nine-year-old Jim Bill lay on the couch under a blanket, feigning illness.

But his Mum didn't know that; she was worried. It seemed to be happening all too often as soon as spring gave way to summer and, bizarrely, always towards the end of the week. The lad bounced back quickly from his malady (the beef tea and Kaoline poultices seemed to do the trick), only to suffer a relapse a couple of weeks later. What was going on?

Well … the BBC televised test match cricket in these days, always starting on a Thursday, and the kid was glued to the telly. To avoid going to school, Jim would come down with his imaginary ailment on the Wednesday night – there was no way he could possibly miss the first couple of days' play. It was the West Indies on tour, and he could rhyme off their test team – players like Gary Sobers, Basil Butcher, Rohan Kanhai and the fearsome fast bowlers, Wes Hall and Charlie Griffiths.

The poor lad couldn't tell anyone about his secret – well, no-one who would understand. Football was the religion in the house, and he couldn't speak to his pals. Watching cricket? He had seen some kids get a kicking for less. So the bouts of illness had to continue.

His mother, bless her, never made the correlation between her son's illness, his primary school absence record and the start of a test match. Her boy pulled through, that was all that mattered.

It was a strange situation. Young Jim didn't know how his love affair with cricket started. He couldn't recall how he had become addicted to the game. On winter nights, he would take his transistor radio to bed (another secret) and lie awake half the night listening to test match commentary being broadcast from the other side of the world. John Edrich, Ted Dexter, Colin Cowdrey, Ken Barrington, Fred Trueman, Derek Underwood – heroes all.

Eventually, Jim 'came out' to his pals, and over time bullied them into playing the game in the confined space that represented his back garden. It wasn't quite Lords but it had a splendid ambiance, with wickets drawn on the coal bunker and the garden shed. His poor mates had to conform to Jim's rules – it was a 5-day test match!

Closer To Paradise

The Bill family moved to Flemington and, at the same time, Jim started senior education at Wishaw High School. His first year History teacher was a gentleman named Maurice Bonner. He was a member of Motherwell Cricket Club, and informed Jim that the club was located only 300 yards from his new family home. Joy of joys.

To this day, Jim remembers with great clarity wandering through the estate and, on reaching the end of the lane, the cricket ground of Home Park coming into view. It was a green oasis surrounded by verdant woodland, fields and an ancient fairytale castle complete with turrets. The setting in the midst of industrial Motherwell was surreal, more like rural Devon.

This ground was to become his second home for many years and, with its quaint tranquility and beauty, it gave him many years of unbridled enjoyment playing the game of cricket. In the early days of the old wooden pavilion, the cricket ground was almost a secret world, hidden away through an enchanted forest, where he learned the arts of the great game.

He bought his first bat, a Slazenger poly-armoured affair, which was his pride and joy, and was soon playing in the 2nd XI, where the world of adult conversation, alcohol and general debauchery were soon baked into him, helping that tricky transition into young adulthood. It must have been a good education – all these traits have stuck with him to this day!

His performances merited elevation to the 1st XI at the same time as a smattering of other young lions. Times were changing for the club, with many of the stalwarts of the '60s and early '70s hanging up their boots or moving away from the area. The new kids were in town.

When a bunch of Motherwell juniors travelled to Glasgow to watch Scotland play the touring New Zealanders, Jim joined the queue of kids bowling in the nets at the Kiwi batsmen during their warm-up. He fizzed an away-swinger past the outside edge of Dick Motz' bat, and got a nod in return – a bit like a Paul Hollywood handshake. How could you not love this game?

And that's how it all started.

Fashion Icon

The boys who played cricket together also socialised together, indulging in as much apres-cricket as they could find in the days when pubs shut at 10pm. More than once, the rest of the lads had cause to comment on Jim's choice of wardrobe – he had a peculiar dress sense, his purple-check jacket and lime green flares being particularly memorable.

It was something that helped Jim to stand out from the crowd for years to come. He was the height of fashion … well, so he thought. The 'Jim Bill shirt' became an expression adopted into general parlance, although the dictionary writers would decree that it was impossible to define.

Common denominator: they were beyond colourful, jazzy and loud, some like the modern-day Aloha or Hawaiian shirt. They would make regular appearances in the clubhouse after games or when he attended social events. There was no stopping him. But there was one shirt … and even now, when you think back, it still makes you screw up your eyes.

It was Grant Robertson's 40th birthday party. As the evening was in full tilt, Jim calls a halt to proceedings. He makes a short speech on Grant reaching the milestone, and then proceeds to perform a sort of striptease, from the top. The jacket removed, he peels off his jumper – you can see the relief on his face, the sweat must have been pouring out of him for hours. The shirt, hitherto hidden from sight, makes its first appearance of the night.

An audible gasp from the crowd; the uninitiated are left speechless. The most garish 'Jim Bill shirt' is now on display. You needed a pair of Ray-Bans to avoid the glare. Flowers, birds, leaves, beaches – it was like a patchwork quilt, akin to your grannie's curtains in the 1960s. A grotesque sight! Everyone was in fits of laughter. The place was in an uproar. It was the talk of the party for weeks afterwards.

Jim's 'Jim Bill shirt' became synonymous with any items of clothing worn by teammates that, let's say, weren't the height of fashion. To this day, the Robertsons still use the term – to most people's bewilderment. "What does that mean?" they ask. Where do you start?

Uphill Battles

For many years, Jim opened the bowling for the 1st XI, manfully toiling up the hill whilst Grant Robertson was allowed to roll down the hill. They were right up there with the best opening partnerships in the club's history, and would appear almost every week in the papers with several wickets apiece.

Jim took 7 wickets twice but was on the losing side on both occasions – it didn't happen again as it was decided we should take him off after 6 wickets. The curse was broken!

With the bat, it was strange. There were times in his career when Jim looked every inch the accomplished batter, and at other times, he didn't. There were spells when he contributed many valuable innings, his on-drive being a highlight, but then he'd slide down the order. In one such period, his last wicket stand of 78 with Graham Robertson established a 10th wicket record.

His finest hour was the Western Cup final of 1986. Jim had been bowling well throughout the tournament and was entrusted with the new ball in the final. He not only took 5 wickets, but restricted West of Scotland to 29 off his 10 overs – not bad for any T20 match, but even more impressive to turn it on in the final.

If we were to pinpoint one heroic moment in Jim's cricket career, some may vote for his leg glance at Hyndland in '75 to clinch promotion back to Division One. But there's another candidate etched in the memory of all who played. It wasn't for his bowling or for his batting, but for a slick piece of fielding. It was as brilliant as it was unexpected!

We were playing Poloc in a Western Cup match at Shawholm in 1981. It was a horrible damp evening on a wet wicket, and Motherwell could only post a total of 50. Yet Poloc found runs hard to come by against excellent bowling and fielding, and it came down to the last ball with the last pair of batsmen at the wicket.

The batsman struck Jim's delivery straight back down the wicket and set off for the run that would tie the match. Jim skilfully picked the ball up on his follow-through, pivoted and shied the ball at the stumps at the non-striker's end.

If he missed, the ball would have run away for overthrows, allowing the Poloc batsmen to run two and win the game. But he didn't miss. With all eyes glued to the scene, the ball (seemingly in slow motion) hit the stumps. Jim had run out the last batsman and Motherwell won by a single run.

The great Omar Henry, Poloc professional at the time, stuck his head into our dressing room after the game to congratulate us on our bowling and fielding. The result was inconsequential as we were knocked out in the next round, but it was wonderful moment.

One Singer, One Song

The clubhouse bar opened in '79 and, until the fire of '99, Jim's bar management ensured it was well stocked, that the till balanced, the bar staff were managed and the financials were reported to the committee. The consistent profitability of the bar, in conjunction with donations from the Catherine Black bequest, ensured that Motherwell Cricket Club survived some difficult times.

But Jim's association with the clubhouse bar wasn't only through his stocktaking role. He excelled at being a customer too – well, the same could be said for all of us! But there was one particular area where Jim stood out from the rest of us.

There was no need for a karaoke machine. All it took was a beer or two and a couple of Bacardis, and Jim was up and running – he needed little prompting. You knew the night had 'started proper' when Jim had lit up his first cigar, followed by his go-to opening number …

"Cauld winter was howlin' o'er moor and o'er mountain…" : Jim's version of 'The Road and the Miles to Dundee' was a mélange of Andy Stewart, Kenneth McKellar and Harry Lauder, but unmistakably Jim Bill. And once he started, well… it was difficult to get him off the floor.

Whether it was New Year, a Cricket Dinner, a Burns supper, any social event or just any Saturday night, Jim was in his element. The only difference was the size of cigar – special occasions deserved to be celebrated properly.

Not bad for a sickly wee boy frae Pather!

Give Us 'Little Jimmy Brown'

Sartorially dressed, his hair smartly coiffured, his martini shaken not stirred … "The name's Shaw, Gavin Shaw." No! Stop! That could never be!

His parka was never too stylish, his hair had a mind of its own, his tipple of choice was a schooner of Croft Original and, most of all, he was never Gavin! To the world, to the universe, he was Speary. One of a kind, and we wouldn't want it any other way.

First impressions

It's 1968… the Ashy Park, North Lodge.

It was never a free kick but the referee gave it anyway, twenty-five yards out to the right of the box. The goalie, a tender 16-year-old, positions the wall – "right a bit, stop, left, right, don't move" – and takes a step back and now stands just left of the wall.

The referee blows his whistle, the striker fires a thunderbolt of a shot, which is heading straight into the top right corner. Like a swallow in mid-flight, the goalie leaps to his right, but instead of using his right hand to attempt to save the ball, he miraculously throws his left arm over his right arm and flicks it over the bar. What a save!

The goalie should be pleased with his acrobatics, a contender for save of the season, as his teammates begin to show their appreciation. He's having none of it – he immediately launches into a tirade of abuse; even the referee gets it.

It was the first time we had come across big Speary, a sportsman of some talent, but even at that early age, you could sense that temperament could be an issue …

The Crabbit Keeper

If you happened to be fielding in the slips or gully when Speary was keeping wicket, it was never dull. His constant commentary on the quality of the bowling, the weaknesses of the batsman and the placing of fielders gave endless entertainment to all around him. Here's how it was …

Speary squats behind the stumps, positioning himself just outside the batsman's off stump. A clap of his wicket-keeping gauntlets serves as encouragement to the bowler and signals that he's ready.

The ball spears down the leg side, missed by the batsman, causing Speary to shuffle substantially to his left to take the ball. "Off stump!" he grunts, muttering to himself.

If the first ball was wide of leg stump, the second ball is even wider, swinging well out of the batsman's reach. The keeper takes off to his left, diving ungracefully but effectively, and it nestles in his left gauntlet. Speary brushes himself down. "Off stump!" comes the earnest call, a little more loudly this time, said with feeling.

The third ball obeys the wicketkeeper's demands but pitches half way down the track, allowing the batsman plenty of time to get onto the back foot and pull the ball to the square leg boundary. "Pitch the ball up!" comes the cry from behind the stumps and, almost as an afterthought, a reminder of the proposed target … "Off stump!"

The fourth ball is a carbon copy of the third and is met with the same shot but, with a fielder posted on the boundary, the batsman has to settle for a single. The throw comes in, not over the bails but at knee height. Speary refuses to bend down for it, letting the ball crash into his pads. He stares at the fielder, reminding some of the famous French mime artist Marcel Marceau, possessing a unique ability to communicate without words, hands placed on hips.

The fifth ball tails down the leg side, evading the bat and escaping the desperate clutches of the keeper. It scampers away to the boundary for 4 byes which, of course, counts against the wicketkeeper rather than the bowler.

This time Speary says nothing, his face says it all, and instead, the bowler is offering up his apologies. "I know, pitch it up." Without saying a word, Speary's body language reminds him where the off stump is positioned. He squats behind the stumps and mutters away quietly, but we all know what he's thinking.

Last ball of the over, and the bowler knows what is expected of him. The extra effort only succeeds in pitching the ball even shorter, climbing sharply. The batsman tries to evade the ball, but it brushes his glove on its way through to the keeper.

Having snaffled the catch to dismiss the opener, Speary sets off to congratulate the bowler. "See, ah tell't ye."

In truth, Speary Shaw was a fine wicketkeeper with a penchant for diving catches down the leg side. And, as can be imagined, the fielders were never allowed to lose concentration when he was behind the stumps.

Gritty Batsman

Speary was a ubiquitous batsman. He could bat anywhere in the order and, regardless of whether he was number 1 or number

11, he exhibited the same doggedness and the same strokes. No prizes for style, but it was effective.

Whether playing for the 1st or 2nd XI, Speary would often hold the innings together and, if you looked through historical scorecards of the '70s, '80s and '90s for closely fought games, it's remarkable how often Speary would be there, not out, at the end. His epic last wicket stand with Morton Mitchell against Thornliebank turned an almost certain defeat into a most unlikely victory.

Now and again, he would hit the headlines. One such occasion was when Speary batted with Feroz Mehdi at Penicuik in the early'90s, his finest hour. It was a beautiful Sunday afternoon, a strong opponent and a lovely cricket ground. The pair put on 159 runs, a record 2nd wicket stand for Motherwell, Feroz notching an inevitable 100 and Speary scoring a fine 62.

Wonderful stuff … and nobody ever remembers that we managed to lose the game!

Working Lunch

Many at the club didn't know how the outfield was kept short. They saw Davie Anderson tending to the square on practice nights, and maybe took their turn on roller duty, then they'd turn up on a Saturday and the place looked great. The match was played with scarcely a thought as to how the whole thing came together. It just happened, as if by magic.

We can now exclusively reveal that the magic fairy was none other than Speary. He worked at Motherwell's civic centre, and would nip down during his lunch hour. To be fair, there were others who did their bit … well, except Stevie Young, who didn't know how to work the mowers … but anyway, it was Speary's lunchtime circuits round the outfield that kept the ground under control.

Mr President

One position was easy to fill at the AGM – that of Match Secretary. Speary started as assistant to Bill Jardine, then took over the senior role. And he did the job, and did it well, for as long as anyone can remember.

The job didn't finish with the arrangement of fixtures. If it was raining on match day (which it often was), Speary would be the point of contact for both home and away matches – "Game's off" or "Game's on" or "Game's still on, but any more rain and …" – and pass on the news before the Motherwell team or the opposition embarked upon their journey.

So for every Saturday or Sunday or midweek match, Speary would effectively be 'on call'.

Having served on the Motherwell committee for many years, Speary then stood for election onto the Glasgow & District League committee. At last our club had a voice on league matters, and that became louder when Speary was elected president 3 years later. He remains the only Motherwell man to hold the position. It must have been in the genes – his father, Jack Shaw (or Lord Jack) had been Motherwell Cricket Club president for a number of years.

There was one game at Home Park when his title was rather useful. It was a 2nd XI game at Home Park, a close affair with Motherwell in the field, having batted first. The scores were tied when young Sajid bowled a ball just outside off stump and, to everyone's astonishment, the opposition umpire signalled a wide. There was uproar on the field but Motherwell had to accept it. Game over.

Afterwards Speary went into the opposition dressing room to see what they wanted to drink, and couldn't help mentioning the unfortunate ending to an otherwise enjoyable game. It was met with a stern response: "If you think this is bad, just wait till you come down to our place."

Speary put on a serious face and stood tall. "My colleagues on the League Committee will be very interested to hear that their President has had to listen to such remarks." The atmosphere changed immediately – they were suddenly all apologetic and tried to say it was only banter.

It made it all the sweeter when, later in the season, Motherwell played the return fixture and won another close encounter. As fate would have it, Sajid scored the winning run after another last wicket stand. No controversy, no bad feeling, just an enjoyable game of cricket. Especially for Speary and the Motherwell team!

Team Player

There were good times to be had after matches at Home Park, and the scary wicketkeeper man was always at the centre of it.

But a strange thing happened – once his cricket whites and gauntlets had been packed away into his kit bag for a week's rest, Speary assumed a new personality. It was like Superman (or Bananaman) in reverse; Hyde and Jekyll if you like – once the uniform was off, he was perfectly normal!

Both sets of players would head for the bar and pick through the bones of the day's play. The beers were going down well and Speary was the life and soul of the party. It was time for a song and, after Jim Bill had warmed up the audience, it was Speary's turn. He had a few in his repertoire, but he knew what his public wanted.

> *"There is a village hidden deep in the valley, among the pine trees half forlorn…"*

Speary's version of 'The Three Bells' (the Jimmy Brown song) was the official anthem of Motherwell Cricket Club. He

launched into the first verse and the entire clubhouse responded by joining in the chorus.

His transmogrification was complete.

> *Speary was an essential cog in Motherwell's cricketing wheel, both on and off the field. He wore his heart on his sleeve, his commitment was unconditional and it's impossible to think of the Club without him.*

A Permanent Fixture

It was the early '70s and we were blessed with an unlikely Christmas Number 1 – '*Ernie, The Fastest Milkman In The West*'. Benny Hill was one of the nation's favourite TV personalities of the age, and his creation *Ernie* was the talk of the town.

But Motherwell Cricket Club didn't need Ernie or any of his milk carts. We had Jack Kelly.

At the time, he was the quickest thing on two legs at the club, and our Jack was the talk of Home Park. He had joined the Club in 1967, spotted while playing cricket for Wishaw High. The school had awarded Jack a 'blue' for cricket, an honour that escaped such luminaries as Grant Robertson and Jim Bill.

He was not yet 18 but had made a name for himself as a cover fielder, the love child of Colin Bland and Jonty Rhodes, if that had been humanly possible. He was quick, agile, thin as a pin and nothing got past him. It wasn't long before he was playing for the 1st XI, picked for his fielding prowess.

We can spot Jack in the middle of the back row (appearing shorter than he actually was) in a 2nd XI photo of 1973. The squad looks to have had a distinct blend of youth and experience.

Standing: P Forbes (scorer), R Hardie, S Solly, D Anderson, I Wilson, J Kelly, M Bonnar, D McAllister, H Forbes, R Browning, Mr R Tyrrell
Seated: G Shaw, J Welsh, J Bill, J Prentice

The photograph also reminds us of something else, by no means unique to Motherwell but valued nevertheless. Whether you're old or young, tall or short, slim or more rounded, happy or sad, there is a place for everyone at Motherwell Cricket Club!

These days, Jack's sylph-like figure is just a memory and his speed across the ground is measured in minutes rather than seconds, but what does that matter? And there's one other thing that sets him apart from the rest ... he is still actively involved in the running of the club.

Always Reliable, Sometimes

The majority of Jack's lengthy playing career was with the 2nd XI, usually at the top of the order. How do we best describe his batting? Flamboyant, no; stylish, no; focussed, gritty and determined, definitely. Most of the runs would come from deflections either side of the wicket, and the poor souls who were fielding at square leg or backward point for the opposition would be in for a busy day.

Jack probably holds the club record for playing under every 2nd team captain from his arrival in the late '60s to his last games around 2010. There were many useful knocks along the way, and he was always one of the first names on the captain's team-sheet.

The innings that defines him is worthy of repetition. It was 1994 and the 2nds were up there competing for the Glasgow and District Reserve League. His unbroken seventh wicket partnership of 68 with Sajid Ashraf that day was a cliffhanger. The way Jack managed the situation and helped his young partner across the finishing line was epic. Calm and composed, no; effective, most definitely.

Driving Us Round The Bend

It wasn't just on the field that Jack was relied upon. In his early days, there was no doubt about his selection for the team … because he had a car. He was able to pick up the Carluke contingent, stop off at Wishaw for another, and ferry them to Home Park or to the civic centre, our meeting place for Away fixtures.

That's where the problem started – the Away games. Jack had played at all the grounds in the west of Scotland but had only a vague memory of how to get there, and this was long before the days of satellite navigation. He would set off with some confidence (and usually a map) but his passengers knew that the journey would be anything but straightforward.

There would be lengthy discussion at the Civic about who was going in which car. No-one ever said out loud that they didn't want to travel in Jack's car but the way they sidled over to one of the other cars, subtly lifting the car boot and shoving in their kit bag, said it all. It was like a game of musical chairs – those left standing at the end of this pantomime knew they would be in for an adventure that afternoon.

While the toss would be taking place on a cricket field in Ayrshire, Jack's car would be lost somewhere near an East Kilbride roundabout. He would stop the car, get out and casually ask some unsuspecting passer-by if they knew where Ardrossan's cricket ground was.

Meanwhile, the Motherwell captain would be explaining to his counterpart that they only had seven men, that one of their cars was running a bit late. They definitely left Motherwell with a full team but somehow, despite repeated visits to the ground, one of our drivers still managed to get lost.

The opposition captain would nod his head knowingly. "Jack Kelly driving today?"

Once he got onto the park, Jack assumed his Billy Whizz persona in the covers, and that was fine. But his driving was much the same, veering round sharp bends at speed with only a vague idea of where he was going. His car had no smooth surfaces left on it; it was full of dents. It was rumoured that he purchased them with the dents already in them, so common were the occurrences.

The Quiz Champion

Jack had a hidden secret: he was a serial quiz winner. Whether it was general knowledge or sport – but especially sport – he somehow managed to be at the top of the leaderboard at the end of most quiz nights. He won numerous contests and proudly held the title of Clydesdale Brain of Sport.

He formed a quiz team called Home Park, made of

Motherwell cricketers who lived in Carluke. There would be Gavin Shaw, Stevie Young, Gavin White and Ash Hussein, and they performed admirably, reaching the semi-finals and finals regularly.

Their first final took place at Carluke Community Centre which, to their horror, was unlicensed! The whole idea of a quiz night was to go to a pub and have a few pints while Jack answered all the questions. But the event had been hyped up in the local papers and here they were, totally sober, on a stage with a couple of hundred people watching them.

Not only that, but the organisers had wheeled in a celebrity quizmaster from TV and the quiz was being piped through to Radio Law Hospital, where patients could listen to the event live. "Please speak clearly into the microphone," instructed the quizmaster.

"First question to Home Park," he continued. "In which car did James Hunt win the 1980 Formula One drivers' championship?" Jack and his Home Park team smiled a confident smile, but were horrified when their number one blurted out "Ferrari". They all knew the answer was McLaren. As one, they reverted to their normal pub quiz behaviour: "For f…'s sake."

Cue waving of quizmaster hands, aghast audience expressions and, one imagines, a few cases of heart failure in Law Hospital. Sadly, it wasn't to be their night.

But Jack's team did win the competition the following year, collecting a crystal trophy that was to be Jack's pride and joy, fighting for space on his crowded mantelpiece. As the team was made up of cricketers, you would think that they'd be quite good at catching things, and that the trophy would be in safe hands. But, no. After the presentation took place and a few drinks were consumed, they dropped the prize, causing the crystal to shatter on impact.

The One And Only

Jack has been involved in the running of the club seemingly forever. The fact that he was a qualified accountant marked him out as a stand-out candidate for treasurer, and the fact that he ran his own business meant that we'd probably get his services free. Consequently he has held the post in some shape or form for around 40 years.

His work for Motherwell Cricket Club should not be underestimated. After the 1999 pavilion fire and the difficult years after we left Home Park, the infrastructure of the club started to unravel. Committee meetings became less regular and convenorships went unfilled, but the business side of the club still had to be run.

One man stepped up, and that's how it came to pass that Jack Kelly became Treasurer, Secretary and President all rolled into one. Thank goodness for Jack.

The Entertainer ...

It was the late 1960s when Graham Robertson found Home Park, wandering through Dalzell estate with his big brother Grant. Around the same time, another pair of brothers were playing the famous, or infamous, Glasgow Empire – Mike and Bernie Winters.

Mike and Bernie were English, a bad start for a comedy duo at the Empire. Mike took the stage first and rattled through a couple of jokes, which were met with stony silence. It was not going well. Bernie then joined his brother and was about to deliver his opening gag when a comment came from the audience ... "Aw naw, there's two o' them!" And that's just how it felt with the Robertsons.

Yet, it turned into a love affair. Years later, when asked why Motherwell Cricket Club was so important to him, Graham bizarrely but appropriately turned to the American comedienne Lucille Ball for inspiration ... *"I'd rather regret the things I've done, than regret the things I haven't done."*

Graham's version chimed with many of us at the club ... *"If I hadn't played cricket for Motherwell, and met friends I still have to this day, it would have been one of the greatest regrets of my life."*

A False Start

"Get off the cricket pitch with that golf club!" cried an angry voice. The man started to give chase, as Graham grabbed his 7-iron and his golf balls and made a sharp exit.

Having been brought up in Glasgow's east end, he was used to being chased, and knew when to run away. But being chased from a cricket ground was a first for the 10-year-old boy – Bridgeton and Ruchazie hadn't been big on cricket. No sounds of leather on willow there.

But this piece of parkland, situated about 100 yards from his new house, intrigued the young lad, and it wasn't long before Graham and his big brother Grant had their first shot at this new sport – and it wasn't as easy as it looked. Little did they know that they would dedicate a large part of their lives to Home Park and have a lasting affinity with the club.

The Bear

Graham soon realised that there was a lot to grasp when learning to play cricket. Senior players at the time were an influence on the kids who turned up to try their hand at the game – Davie Brady and his brother Hilton, Archie Syme, Allan Johnston, all great players in their own right, and leaders on the cricket field. But one stood out, literally, for young Graham: Johnny Welsh.

'The Bear' was Graham's biggest influence. Johnny was a colossus of a man, both physically and mentally, a great motivator and always willing to give the young boys a chance. He was a gentle giant, but you crossed him at your peril – he was as strong as an ox.

Johnny had been a fast bowler in his youth. By the late '60s, there was no way he could run up to the wicket, so he converted his talents to off-spin bowling. With a shortened run-up (well, two steps) he would pitch the ball on a length time after time, leaving the batsman little choice but to play a forward defensive, prodding the ball back to the bowler.

Fielding was a challenge for the big man. When the ball was played back to him, he would stop it with his boot, or sometimes his shin, then pick it up and bowl the next ball. It was efficiency personified, with the minimum of movement, and he rattled through his overs in jig-time.

There was invariably a quick bowler, usually Gavin White, at the other end with a long run-up, a good foil for big Johnny's off-spin. His six balls delivered, he would trot down to fine leg. He had barely reached his fielding position, when Johnny had completed his over and it was his turn again. He was knackered, never getting a rest between overs.

It was no surprise that Graham Robertson became an off-spin bowler and, as a 16-year-old, he was selected to play for the 2nd XI at Prestwick. Graham remembers little about the game but recalls drinking four half pints of lager in the clubhouse after it. At the time, Johnny said nothing, but Graham knew he was watching him. The following Monday at practice night, before a ball was bowled, Johnny took Graham aside …

"Graham, how many drinks did you have on Saturday after the game?" Before he could answer, Johnny blurted out, "FOUR! Now listen, and listen good, young man – until you're 18, don't you ever again drink alcohol after a game without asking me first."

Graham was petrified … needless to say, he never took as much as a sip of the amber liquid without asking Johnny if it was ok.

Graham the Batsman

A year later, Graham made his 1st team debut, selected to play in a mid-week Rowan Cup game away to Greenock. The home side batted first and set a total that was beyond Motherwell and, by the time young Graham strode out to the crease, last man in, it was pretty dark.

Jack Clark was Scotland's strike bowler. He was rapid and, unfortunately, he was playing for Greenock that evening. Graham reckoned he'd go easy on him – it was dark, he was only young, and the game itself was dead and buried.

How wrong he was ... the first ball whizzed by his head and he barely moved; the second, he somehow managed to hit with the bat. Beyond that, Graham recalls very little. His fellow batsman was bowled the following over, they were all out and Graham, for one, was delighted! He didn't have to face any more balls from Jack. A truly terrifying baptism!

Even Graham would agree that batting wasn't his strong point. When turning out for the 1st XI, he was the strongest man in the team, holding them all up from his number 11 spot, but he loved a last wicket partnership, just not too often! There was one of 59, but that was overtaken by his sterling effort in the company of Jim Bill when the pair put together a stand of 78 against Hyndland to win the game.

With the 2nd XI, he batted middle order and could chip in with the occasional 15 or 20. That said, there were times when the lofty height of double figures was a rare experience. He would have been better batting with the aforementioned 7-iron.

Once, when captaining the 2nd XI in a 20-over match against Cumbernauld, he decided to open the batting. He hit the first three balls of the innings for six, six and four ... next ball, he was clean bowled. The innings lasted for about three minutes and his number three wasn't fully padded up by the time he returned to the pavilion – probably the reason why he never got anywhere near the top of the order again!

Graham the Bowler

Graham turned out for the 2nd XI for a number of years, and gained a good reputation as an off-spin bowler. It was in the late '70s when the 1st XI came calling once again. Captain Allan Johnston gave Graham the opportunity to bowl at that level and, after a shaky start, he went on to have a decent record under Allan's captaincy. Later, when Steve Young and then his brother Grant took over the captaincy, Graham continued to have bowling success.

Work circumstances dictated a four-year sabbatical in the mid-'80s, but Graham was soon back in the fold. He enjoyed being selected for the 1st XI and, as the only genuine spinner in the team, he was bowling regularly. There were many successes to be proud of in the top team (especially in Scottish Cup ties), but the era of the professional was beckoning.

With Graham's slow delivery, the ball would disappear over the boundary too often for his liking. The time came when he found 2nd XI cricket much more enjoyable.

Great years lay ahead. Graham played under a few captains before becoming captain himself. He had much greater success at this level, taking more than his fair share of wickets. Against Helensburgh, he was the only player to take a wicket. That day, he took 8 wickets, with the other 2 being run outs.

Graham the Captain

The 2nd XI had a strong team and, after a few years knocking on the door, success eventually arrived when Graham captained the side to victory in the Glasgow & District Reserve league in 1994.

At the Annual Dinner that year, Graham was presented with not one but two trophies by club president, Grant. Maybe one of them was for the 'Most Garish Tie' award.

Anyway, the brothers are flanked by four past presidents – Ronnie Morrison, Jack Shaw, Steve Young and Tom Barrie, with Maurice Bonnar, David McAllister, Jim Bill and Stuart MacKenzie in the back row.

Graham took his captaincy responsibilities seriously. It wasn't just on the field; he had to make sure the rest of the day went without a hitch. There was the wicket, the pavilion, and most importantly, the teas. But, one Saturday, his teas were the source of some drama.

The day started off quite innocently with Graham preparing his egg and cress sandwiches, which sounded quite posh, especially the cress bit. 'Teas for three' was the instruction for every home game, a conundrum that some players couldn't quite work out.

It was a complex equation, and triggered a few questions. 'Teas for two' would feed all the Motherwell players and the opposition players too, but who was this mystery third person? As skipper, Graham would comply with the rule but would anyone eat his 'extra' sandwiches? Maybe the leftovers could serve as post-match supper *chez Robertson.*

Lost in a fuzz of mental calculations, Graham was delighted when his wife Linda interrupted his thoughts to let him know that she'd be coming down later in the afternoon. "Leave the egg and cress sandwiches to me," she said. He left the house with a skip and a hop, and headed for Home Park.

The game got under way, and all was going to plan with an early wicket already taken. Then, out of the blue, the barman John Johnston was screaming from the balcony – the only word to be heard was 'fire'. Players ran to the boundary, concerned that something had happened in the clubhouse.

John repeated the words again, "GRAHAM, YOUR HOUSE IS ON FIRE!" Running as quickly as he could from the field of play, Graham was followed by his team mate, Allan Black, who drove his car (always carefully, always sticking to the speed limits) to the Robertson house.

A fire engine was in attendance and smoke was belching out the front door of the house. Linda and son Grant emerged from a neighbour's house, where they had taken refuge from the carnage.

Linda had put the eggs in a pan and turned on the electric ring – the wrong electric ring, as it turned out, the one under a frying pan with the remnants of the previous night's chips. Shortly thereafter, Linda caught a whiff of smoke, and on returning to the kitchen found flames leaping from the cooker. Soon, smoke was finding its way to every corner of the house.

She phoned the fire brigade and, a few hours later, everything was under control and the Robertsons were allowed back into the house. In reality, the kitchen was needing replaced anyway and, with a generous insurance settlement … happy days.

After a chat with Linda, Graham did what every good captain should do – he returned to Home Park, albeit without his sandwiches. Egg and cress had to be scratched from the menu that day.

Linda joined him in the clubhouse after the game. The fire made for great conversation in the bar that night, and for weeks after the event, every player with a dodgy kitchen was forever asking her to make their sandwiches on a Saturday morning.

She never again volunteered to make teas for three!

Graham the Working Cricketer

Like most other clubs, you don't get away with just playing cricket, you get trapped into fulfilling other posts. As the years passed, Graham took on the roles of Secretary, Treasurer, Entertainments Convenor, and Groundsman, combining a few of them simultaneously for years.

What the committee failed to tell him beforehand was the amount of abuse you get while taking on a pile of work voluntarily. That said, Graham's time spent performing his gratuitous duties brought him a lot of satisfaction.

Beyond anything else that Graham achieved at the club, many would agree that he had a great talent for organising social events in the clubhouse. Over many years, countless events were arranged to entertain members of the club. He had no shortage of assistants with his brother Grant, Stuart MacKenzie, Hugh McGinley and Steven McGill always willing to help.

We all have fond memories of quiz nights, Players of the Year dinners, curry nights, Burns suppers, music nights, comedy nights and other events in the clubhouse. There was a huge amount of work involved in the organisation and Graham thrived on it – the singers, comedians, speakers and speeches, food, programmes, prizes, ticket sales. A magnum opus.

The social nights brought players and associate members together outwith the playing season to partake of a few beers (ok, several) and it was a huge part of the club's success. Those who attended enjoyed the 'craic', but more so, the ridicule and humiliation served up to one another on the night.

Graham the Family Cricketer

Graham likened the club to his family, and it was, quite literally!

His boys, Grant and Scott, had a strange introduction to the game. Graham had taken them down to the ground to take in a few overs before playing football in an adjacent field. As they strolled round the perimeter of the cricket pitch, the Motherwell skipper asked Graham if he would bowl the first few overs of the innings as they were a man down.

Of course, he immediately agreed – even though this wasn't on the boys' agenda. Before a football was kicked, they had to endure an hour of watching their dad play cricket, as they tried to get to grips with the terminology of the sport.

When Graham eventually rejoined the kids, he was bombarded with questions: *"Where's the duck that the man got?"* and *"Why do some players have short legs and others have long legs?"*

Going back a generation, his own mum and dad, Annie and Jimmy, were also part of that family. They had a great love for the club and were associate members for many years, enjoying countless social functions along the way.

The club had a blend of like-minded individuals who worked hard to keep it going through tough times. Were there arguments? Absolutely, but laughter prevailed above everything else, and that contributing factor is one of the reasons why former players' friendships are still as strong to this day.

The American journalist, author and educator, Jane Howard, couldn't have described it any better: *"Call it a clan, call it a network, call it a tribe, call it a family. Whatever you call it, whoever you are, you need one."*

Ours was called... Motherwell Cricket Club!

Extras

We've reached our 150, and we're looking for more.
Various milestones have been passed along the way,
sometimes confidently, sometimes nervously, but
Motherwell's cricketers are still at the crease.
Whilst we have claimed everything that has come off
our own bat, what of those other contributors on the
scoresheet, those helpful additions hiding away at the
bottom – byes, leg byes and the like – that masquerade
under the heading of Extras?
We can't count them in our total but, just like every other
run in the book, they all have a story to tell. Sometimes
pleasing, other times distasteful, like when someone has
overstepped the mark.
What follows is a miscellany of mischief, a medley of
madness and a motley collection of magical memories
which reveal the realities of playing for Motherwell
Cricket Club.

Our Greatest Ever Game?

The scoreboard told us that Motherwell were 245 for 8, Gala having been bowled out for 248. After seven hours of cricket, it all came down to the last ball of the match, Hughie McGinley on strike.

It was Motherwell's first experience of Scottish Cup cricket, the big time, playing against Gala, always one of the top Border League sides. And we had history – friendly matches in previous years had always resulted in comfortable victories for Gala, with the Motherwell bowlers being blasted all round the ground by the big-hitting Rae Nicol.

But this was 1988, and Motherwell had a decent side. We were in good form too, having scored over 200 runs the day before against Hillhead with Steven McGill hitting a fine 86 and, although we were missing some senior players for the Gala match, we now had Nadeem Yousuf in our ranks. The sun shone, the ground had rarely looked better and the scene was set for a cracking match.

Gala took first use of a good batting track, and the scoreboard was soon ticking along. Grant Robertson bowled tightly to restrict the scoring, but the innings soon gathered pace with the arrival of Nicol. It was raining 4s and 6s and, just when it looked like the game was running away from Motherwell, Nicol missed one and was clean bowled by Graham Robertson's off-spin for a rapid 80.

The runs kept coming, but 4 wickets for Yousuf and 2 each for Alastair Black and the Robertson brothers helped to dismiss Gala for 248 runs.

Ordinarily, such a total would have been beyond Motherwell, but on a good wicket and a fast outfield, the local lads set about the challenge with relish. McGill (19) and Yousuf (44) got the innings off to a good start but, when they were both dismissed, many felt the game was up.

That was until Alaister Jackson lived up to his nickname of *Whakko Jacko* by dispatching the bowling to all parts. Actually, 'all parts' would be misleading as most of his shots were directed towards mid-wicket and long on, often landing on the far side of the rope. Wonderful timing; good clean hitting.

It was an incredible knock. Jackson, with his trademark floppy sun hat, scored 103 in 105 minutes off only 91 balls. Accompanied by Alastair Black and Mike Saunders (a new arrival from the Welsh valleys), Jacko took the Motherwell total to the brink of the victory target, but after his dismissal, it came down to the final over – there were still 6 runs to be scored.

Hughie McGinley and Calum Currie were at the wicket and they scampered a couple of singles to bring the game to its cliff-hanging dénouement. One ball to be bowled, 4 runs to win, 3 to tie.

For perhaps the only time in its history, the bar in the clubhouse emptied. The verandah was mobbed, the boundaries busy as all eyes were focused on the two batsmen in the middle.

The Gala captain took an age to arrange his fielders. He could not afford to give away a boundary, or all was lost. And he hadn't had the pleasure of seeing Hughie bat before. He sized up the stocky batsman – would he try to plant the bowler back over his head, or try to find a gap in the cover field? Who would be a captain?

The bowler knew exactly where to bowl, firing the ball towards leg stump, pitched up, yorker length. Dig that one out!

McGinley, as was his wont, shuffled across his stumps to glance the ball towards the unprotected fine leg boundary. Hughie was off and running.

The ball was being pursued by several Gala fielders who managed to prevent the boundary. Callum Currie, fast as a hare, was running towards the striker's end and, by the time the ball had been returned to the wicketkeeper, he had completed the third run. The scores were tied!

By virtue of having lost fewer wickets, with only 8 men down and Gala being bowled all out, Motherwell were crowned victorious in a thrilling cup tie. Unlikely heroes, Hughie McGinley and Calum Currie had won the game off the last ball of the match.

No-one could quite believe it, a victory chase as heroic as it was unexpected. And here's the scorecard to prove it really happened.

Gala Innings

S Halls		b. Graham Robertson	33
R Murray		b. Yousuf	4
D R Nichol		b. Graham Robertson	80
N Crooks	ct. Graham Robertson	b. Grant Robertson	4
C Forsyth	ct. A R Black	b. Saunders	12
D Ormiston		b. A M Black	51
A Niven	lbw	b. A M Black	19
N Niven		b. Yousuf	18
S Ormiston		b. Yousuf	1
S Thomson	not out		3
C Lawrie		b. Grant Robertson	2
Extras			21
		Total (all out)	248

Motherwell Innings

A R Black	ct. Halls	b. Thomson	5
S McGill	st. Nichol	b. Nichol	10
N Yousuf	ct. Halls	b. Lawrie	44
A Jackson		b. S Ormiston	103
M Saunders	lbw	b. Nichol	11
Grant Robertson		b. Thomson	8
A M Black		b. Thomson	13
D J Anderson	st. Murray	b. D Ormiston	5
H McGinley	not out		11
C Currie	not out		1
Graham Robertson			
			28
		Total (for 8 Wickets)	248

Best game ever? Probably

Just another Friday ...

We enjoyed our Friday nights at the Home Park clubhouse, no matter the event. Quizzes, curry nights, awards nights, Burns suppers, musical renditions – whatever the excuse, we were up for a good time. It was only when conducting some research of the early years of Motherwell Cricket Club that we realised that this had been going on for over 100 years!

The top table is immaculate, set for the arrival of the presidential party and distinguished gentry. Lengthy tables are laid out for invited guests, tablecloths (how fancy is that?), candles and too many knives, forks and spoons to count, wine and port glasses shimmering in the candlelit room. Like Christmas dinner without the party hats. A picture of Edwardian Motherwell.

We imagine that the social functions attended by the cricketers of Motherwell a hundred or so years ago would be dignified affairs – the dress code formal, punctuality paramount and a programme of events with a distinctly serious tone, all important components of the dinners of the time.

The great and the good of the town invited to attend the

soirée would arrive in formal attire and top hats, and dinner would be a multi-course affair – eating a little of each course was key if you wanted to reach the final course comfortably. Oysters, game pies and horseradish, roast beef and rabbit, apple dumplings and gingerbread served up for consumption.

That's how we imagine it … but, in truth, evidence suggests that the dinners attended by our cricketing ancestors were as wild as anything we got up to. They would assemble in Baillie's Railway Tavern in Merry Street for the *End of Season Smoker* and enjoy Mrs Baillie's excellent fare.

Awards would be made to the best batsman, the best bowler, and the player who could throw the cricket ball farthest, a gift presented to the retiring professional, and then the party started. The local paper painted a vivid picture …

The gift was suitably acknowledged in a racy speech.
A pleasant evening was thereafter spent in song and
sentiment. Mr Cunningham presided at the piano, while
selections on the gramophone were given by Mr Haynes.
Motherwell Times, September 1902

Racy speeches, singing round the piano … and a gramophone!

Jump forward 90 years or so, and we find that little has changed … well, except for the piano and gramophone. The Railway Tavern has been ditched for the Home Park pavilion, the Club Smoker given a new badge – the Player of the Year Dinner – and Mrs Baillie's delightful fare simplified to tempt the tastebuds of the modern-day cricketer.

But in any language, in any age, it's a party! The shackles of an arduous season were off and it was time for a bit of fun.

Player Of The Year Soirée

An SAS covert operation needs pinpoint accuracy to ensure the mission goes off without a hitch, but organising the end of season Player of the Year night was a much more problematic affair.

It demanded precision and meticulous planning – the SAS would have crumpled at the thought of it ... cooking 60 dinners in a kitchen the size of a telephone box, with barely enough running hot water and 2 electric rings, and no room to swing a cat. Thankfully cat was off the menu.

The big event was traditionally held on the first Friday in September, and the *plat du jour* was steak pie, potatoes and sprouts. It never changed, as that was the depth of our culinary skills, but we still needed a planning session. Three cricketers and several rounds of Bass Special and Tennent's Lager in the Dalziel Arms sorted that out.

A few days before the jamboree, the steak pie was ordered from the local butcher, the sprouts and tatties procured from the supermarket. The excitement was building, not because we loved cooking, but because we were entrusted with the bar keys on such evenings. Our thirst could be quenched and re-quenched before the peeler got anywhere near a sprout or tattie.

Friday night would arrive. At around 6.00pm and with a spring in our step, we would make our way to the clubhouse, tucker in tow, with plastic plates, knives and forks (a classy touch!) to ease the pressure post dinner. Our bar and kitchen routines had been perfected over the years.

The clubhouse was opened, window shutters raised, bar grill opened and pool table moved and converted to a serving station to fully optimise floor space. Eventually we found our way to the kitchen.

The military operation began. The sprouts were the first

item to be prepared. We filled the tea urn with water, followed by the peeled sprouts – our chef's expertise perfected over the years, cooking time down to a T. The sprouts were brought to the boil, simmered for 10 minutes and immediately turned off. They continued to cook to perfection sitting in the hot water. Genius!

Sticking to the plan, we adjourned to the bar and sank another beer before returning to the kitchen to finish our chores.

Now before you say, "*Where did all the meticulous planning come in?*" ... cooking was the easy part. There are a lot of personalities to deal with in most clubs, and ours was no different. Much more challenging was the human resource skills required to ensure all participants enjoyed the shindig, the pinnacle of our season. It had to be a special night, a fantastic night.

The evening's entertainment had been organised, a programme printed, but with a difference ... no paid advertisements, no players' interviews, no sporting photographs – just a catalogue of ridicule and humiliation aimed at every player in the club.

'This Is Your Life' would be sprung on an unsuspecting teammate, a general knowledge quiz would take place, the Player of the Year and the treasured 'Prick of the Year' trophies awarded.

And The Winner Is ...

It was accepted by all that it was an honour to receive this last award – a Greek satyr brought back from Corfu some years earlier with an impressive appendage that had been repeatedly glued back on – given to the most deserving recipient for the most outrageous (or downright stupid) things said or done during the season.

The party would be upon us. Players and associates would begin to arrive and the night would slowly get up and running. The food was served around 8pm and went down well. The festivities were now in full tilt, with an unsuspecting player having flashbacks of a life he'd forgotten, the quiz night won by the usual suspects, before the most prestigious award was made.

It was like the Oscars. "The nominations are ...", each one recognised by tumultuous applause. The nominees stood to acknowledge their stupidity and also to accept the appreciation of the baying crowd. The winner is announced. The poor chap who thought his indiscretion had been forgotten about now found his exploits laid before the audience in the most public way. Humiliation complete.

In the Middle Ages, they built stocks in the High Street to punish minor indiscretions, allowing the public to throw rotten tomatoes at the offender's protruding head. And that's how it felt when awarded the Prick of the Year trophy. The winner found himself in a strange place, being both derided as a figure of mockery and being victorious as the recipient of the night's top award, more prestigious even than the Player of the Year title.

These nights were special. Everyone associated with the club participated fully, regardless of how much they were ridiculed on the night. Some cricket clubs had Captains boards or Presidents boards, but not Motherwell – all the talk was of the Prick of the Year!

Transporting ourselves back once again to our cricketing forefathers, Motherwell Cricket Club brought them just as much fun and enjoyment, whether on the playing field or attending social events. The only difference was that our Edwardian counterparts would go home raving about this new-fangled gramophone thing that they'd heard, whereas almost a century later, a Motherwell player would have to explain to his wife that they'd have to find room on the mantelpiece for a new ornament.

Playing cricket is much more than donning your whites and taking to the field. The social side of the game plays a huge part in bringing teammates together, and building close friendships with those who follow and support the club. Glorious days, life-long memories.

The Lowden Leg Break

Bill and Norma Lowden were part of the furniture at Home Park. They had come up from England, settled in Huntly for a while, and then found themselves living in Wishaw. Cricket was their life, and they found Motherwell Cricket Club soon after, joining us in the mid-1970s. Bill would bowl all day if you asked him to, pitching the ball on a length time after time.

"By Christ, Grant, I think you've just broken my leg."

Bill Lowden lay on the wicket, right leg askew. Instinctively he knew that that would be the end of his bowling spell for the day. Too bad, as he had been bowling well – there was enough cloud cover to allow the ball to swing, and enough in the wicket for his off cutters. Still, he thought, if you're going to break your leg, then late August was the time to do it – the season was almost over and he'd be ready for the winter nets in January.

He had just clean bowled the batsman with an absolute peach of a delivery, and was feeling rather good about himself, when an over-exuberant (some might say boisterous) Grant Robertson jumped on his back to congratulate him. Bill's leg gave way, there was a crack, and it was clear that Bill would not be able to finish his over. It was suggested that he could bowl off a shortened run-up. Bill didn't really see the funny side.

Thankfully there was someone watching from the pavilion who had done a first aid course and, while the company of assembled cricketers awaited the arrival of the ambulance, Alexandra Black (Alex) raced to the scene with a couple of old cricket bats and a roll of tape. "We need to get his leg straight," said Alex, as she set about creating a splint.

"But that's my old Gray Nicholls," said Speary Shaw, keen to preserve his old weapon. He had hopes that the bat would one day form the centrepiece of a museum collection, perhaps alongside his box. This box (abdominal protector, to give it its proper name) had done the rounds, protecting the manhood of many a young lion, but it was fair to say that it was not ageing gracefully. Perhaps the museum curator would have second thoughts. Speary was reassured that he would get his bat back – the blood would wash off.

Alex had made her patient comfortable, but the perpetrator of the crime seemed none too apologetic. Grant reminded Bill that he was holding up the cricket match – did he not realise that we could have a problem with bad light if he lay there in the middle of the wicket for much longer? To everyone's relief, the sirens of the ambulance were heard in the distance and it appeared on the scene without delay.

The ambulance drove down through the car park and entered the field of play down towards where Bill lay. On reflection, this was understandable, but didn't the ambulance man know that he could have damaged the cricket ground? David Anderson was most horrified – it was he who looked after the square and prepared the wickets with great care, and he was now seen standing in front of the ambulance in a scene reminiscent of Tiananmen Square.

Thankfully, no damage was done – the ground on this warm August day was firm enough – and the paramedics got to work on the prostrate bowler. Alex was congratulated by the paramedic for her double-batted splint, and Bill was stretchered into the back of the ambulance.

His teammates gathered round to wish him well …

"Bill, remember practice Monday night, 6.30 sharp." And "Can I eat your sandwiches at the tea interval, Bill?" And, most cruelly, "Bill, is that you trying to sneak away without paying your match fee?"

All this time, the opposition batsmen hung around waiting for the game to re-start and, to be honest, were a good deal more sympathetic to the bowler's plight than any of the Motherwell players. Indeed, they had been more shocked by the black humour on show than anything else. Well, they hadn't grown up in deepest Lanarkshire, had they?

Bill Lowden managed to raise a smile. He knew that, in Motherwell, comments such as these were as close as you'd get to expressions of affection. In that moment, he knew that he was accepted as one of the boys.

A Day in Calderbank

*Jim Bill considers the delightful settings for the game
of cricket around the world – one in particular – and
remembers his first visit, his first experience.*

Within the game there is much debate about the most beautiful ground in the world. Many would hold up the coastal walled stadium of Galle in Sri Lanka, or the beauty of Newlands in South Africa, set below the majestic Table Mountain.

However, as a teenager playing for Motherwell Cricket Club, I was fortunate to play at the wonderful Maggieshaugh, which was home to Woodhall Cricket Club (*pronunciation: Wid-haw*). The club was set in the ex-mining location of Calderbank, an earthy village set somewhere in North Lanarkshire. No idea where exactly – I could never find the place.

To access the ground, one had to drive through a housing scheme, eventually reaching a dead-end where cars had to be left, and the journey would be completed on foot. On leaving the car, you would be harangued by a pack of wild dogs and a group of boys who were prepared to look after the car for 50p.

The trek continued downwards over a path barely visible

amongst grassy mounds, being careful to avoid the babbling sewer that meandered down the hill. Michael Palin would not have ventured any farther.

On my first visit, I was fortunate to secure the services of a guide – a large man walking down the path towards the ground. He was already dressed in his whites, and a huge pair of steel toe-capped cricket boots, laces tied together, were swinging around his shoulders and neck. On enquiring later, I was told that this was old man Forrester, who had been pressed into action due to some call-offs. This man had been a legend at the club for many a year.

'Old man' wasn't just a term of endearment at Woodhall, but a necessity. Generations of families played the game, and young Forrester wasn't a bad player either! But, as well as sharing the same surname, they all seemed to have the same first names too, like the Cunninghams – there was old Alex, young Alex and … Alex.

The actual ground had two particular features, one being a large black sewage pipe that ran at a fair height across the breadth of the ground, and behind the cricket pitch, there was a canal, which might not have been the Costa Clyde, but seemed a welcome source of fun for the youngsters.

The games at Maggieshaugh were always feisty, with the younger Woodhall players always pumped up. They operated as a pack, a bit like the aforementioned dogs. They were vociferous and unrelenting in their aggression, but were always held in check from going too far by the late and great Alex Simpson, who gave so much to the game. Alex was a top keeper, motivator and administrator in West of Scotland Cricket, and he kept Woodhall Cricket Club going until it celebrated its centenary in the late-'80s.

After the game, leaving the small dilapidated pavilion behind, one would make the journey back up the hill to the car, hoping your tyres were still inflated. We rarely won at Woodhall but, as you climbed into the car, there was a distinct sense of relief that you had escaped unscathed.

But it all changed at the Winning Post, the pub that served the scheme. The convivial atmosphere, as both teams sank a few pints, was in stark contrast to relations on the cricket field. Were these the same guys that wore the Woodhall colours?

So Galle, Newlands? For character and characters, the unique cricket ground that was Maggieshaugh gets my vote.

The Long And Winding Road

Car journeys can hold unforgettable memories, some good, some bad. Trips taken can remind us of joyous moments shared with friends, memories that last a lifetime. Even journeys that filled you with dread can sometimes bring happiness, and put a smile on your face every time you're reminded of them.

Those who played cricket for Motherwell will remember car journeys for many different reasons – maybe the excitement of the game to come, or the emotions associated with victory or defeat on the way home, but the one constant was laughter, and a knowledge you were amongst like-minded individuals.

There were designated drivers for away matches and it mattered whose car you travelled in. If one of the drivers announced that he had to be home sharpish, straight after the match – well, that didn't sound like much apres-cricket fun. And the company mattered as well – a good mix of personalities and good conversation along the way. It all sorted itself out nicely, the miles flew past and, next thing, you were there.

It was on the way home that things started to go a bit *off-*

piste and now, some 40 years later, the truth can be told about some famous trips, within reason. So buckle in and enjoy the ride ...

The Fancy Dress Party

They left the Swan Hotel after knocking back a pint or two. It had been another glorious day out at St Michaels, Dumfries, a fine game. They squeezed into the Vauxhall Viva – Grant Robertson, his brother Graham, Stevie Young and Jim Bill.

Everything was going to plan until Grant noticed the petrol gauge was either broken or the car was very shortly going to run out of petrol. Unfortunately the latter prevailed, and the car came to a stuttering halt on the hard shoulder of the M74, about 5 miles south of Motherwell. It was around 10.45pm, the light was fading fast, as was the heat of the day.

With the nearest services located approximately 6 miles north, their options were limited. With little choice, the travelling party decided to walk to the services. It was getting chilly so someone came up with the idea of delving into their cricket bags for extra clothing to keep them warm. An umpire's coat also made an appearance.

So off they marched, walking tight to the hard shoulder in the direction of Motherwell. Shortly into the hike they noticed blue flashing lights rapidly approaching from the rear, where the car had been abandoned. As dread set in, a police car pulled up directly behind them. Grant didn't seem too fazed – he had been drinking shandies, but it was still a tricky situation. The passengers had been less abstemious, and their fancy dress attire didn't help proceedings.

One of the officers quickly departed the police car and looked in utter disbelief at the sight before him. Was this some form of ghostly apparition standing before him? As he moved closer, his torch lit up the party of white-clothed walkers against pitch black fields around Lesmahagow.

The closer he got, his anxieties turned to bewilderment. "What the …?" In front of him stood three grown men wearing long-sleeved cricket jerseys, one wearing cricket gloves and a floppy white hat, and another wearing an umpire's coat.

"What's going on lads? Fancy dress party?"

Grant began to explain their predicament, thinking the boys in blue would never believe him. To everyone's amazement, the officer took Grant at his word, and said that he did notice the stranded Vauxhall Viva some 500 yards down the motorway. After a quick check as to the ownership of the car, his information all tied up, and the party began to relax.

Grant was taken into the police car, destined for Hamilton service station, and the rest of them were ordered to make their way back to the abandoned vehicle and to stay there. The offer was gladly accepted and the fancy dress pageant made a swift return to the car. Grant returned shortly afterwards with both policemen, petrol can in tow. The can was emptied into the tank, enough to get them to a local petrol station in Motherwell.

Both officers bid them a fond farewell, wishing them all the best for the last few games of the season. The chat on the way home was more sober; they were thanking their lucky stars that they weren't enjoying bed and breakfast at Her Majesty's pleasure … thanks to two very understanding and obliging policemen!

Room For Two … On Top!

Allan Johnston had just purchased his dream car, a two-seater Triumph Spitfire, his pride and joy, and now it was time to see how it would perform, speeding down the M74 to an away fixture at Dumfries.

Being 1st XI captain, Allan also had the enormous kit bag to contend with, which wasn't ideal given the modest size of the new brief's interior.

Allan decided to drive direct to Dumfries through Abington from Carluke as there was only enough room for one other player. He squeezed the kit bag into the car, picked up a fellow Carlukian, and put the car through its paces. The Spitfire raced through the rolling hills while the rest of the team gathered at the Civic Centre in Motherwell to plan their journey southwards.

After the game, Allan stayed for a pint, just to be hospitable, but was otherwise abstemious as he conversed with the opposition skipper. As the evening wore on, other drivers set off, taking some players with them.

When it came time to leave, Allan noticed that there was not one but three Motherwell players still sitting in the bar, and not a car amongst them. The drivers had all left for home, oblivious to the fact that Allan had just traded in his spacious 4-seater Dolomite for a 2-seater sports car. Disaster!

A plan had to be devised quickly – otherwise a day pass to play cricket was about to turn into a weekend for two in Dumfries for a couple of the Motherwell team. Allan had little choice … the soft top was wound down, the front seat passenger given a giant kit bag to sit on his knee, and two inebriated teammates were forced to sit in the boot with their legs dangling in the tiny space behind the front seats.

The car's heater was little comfort to those on the top deck, and as darkness descended, so did the temperature. Two fuzzy-headed players were sobering up a lot quicker than they had expected. The back seat duo felt like 2 cats with the proverbial nine lives, which were disappearing faster than the pints they had just consumed.

Luckily for everyone, but more importantly for Allan's new sports car, there was no rain that night and Allan managed to race up the A74 avoiding a potential encounter with the boys in blue.

They all made it home safe and sound. The two freezing cold but very sober 'back seat' passengers had difficulty explaining to their other halves why, on a mid-summer's evening, they were borderline hypothermic. The front seat passenger, who had the team's huge kit bag sitting upright on his lap the whole way, had never spent such an uncomfortable journey. As for Allan, he was a very relieved young man, and made a mental note to take a more active role in organising travel plans to away games in future.

Follow That Bus …

The match at Prestwick had finished early, and the entire team was invited to enjoy the jugs of beer and the leftovers from the ample teas laid on by the home team. Conversation flowed about the game as the teams socialised. The time flew by.

It was getting dark and Maurice Bonnar belatedly decided that it was time to head home. His passenger was Gavin White, and he would drop Gavin off in Wishaw before heading home to Glasgow.

A coastal mist made driving difficult, and shortly into the journey, Maurice found himself totally incapable of finding the road home. After driving around in circles for what seemed an age, an unintended visit to Troon and a U-turn on a road leading to Tarbolton, Maurice pulled over. The fog had really closed in, and they had only got as far as Monkton.

Exasperated and tired, his head spinning, he suggested they surrender and attempt to sleep overnight in the car. With no alternative plan forthcoming, they settled down for a less-than-comfortable night's sleep.

Suddenly headlights appeared from a distance. They hadn't seen a soul on the road for over an hour. As the light got closer, they could just about make out a Parks of Hamilton logo on the side of a passing coach.

A new plan was quickly devised, and they decided to follow the bus as it made its way back to its Lanarkshire terminus, never for one minute thinking that it might be heading in the other direction. It may have been going to Stranraer or even further afield.

After a few twists and turns on roads unfamiliar to Maurice, they determined that the bus was indeed travelling in a direction known to him. He continued to follow the bus for a few miles until he had regained his bearings and, an hour or so later, Maurice dropped Gavin off in Wishaw at some ungodly hour.

Gavin attempted to persuade him to stay overnight and complete the journey in the morning, but Maurice was having none of it. He declined the offer of bed and breakfast and proceeded to drive home.

Somewhere between Wishaw and Glasgow, the car had a fleeting encounter with a lamppost, resulting in a massive dent on the near-side wing of his car. A hefty bill, but a good story. The joys of cricket!

It's Always Prestwick ...

Davie Brady had been playing for Motherwell since the early 1950s, and had seen it all before. It was by no means his first visit to Prestwick, and he knew the form. They were the most congenial of hosts, and it was always difficult to drag the passengers out of the clubhouse. It was late on a Saturday night, after another enjoyable game of cricket, and Davie himself may have been tempted by his opponents' generous hospitality.

Davie decided it was time to head up the road. It was around 10.00pm. As the car left the ground and made its way through the town, the *craic* was as severe as ever. The driving wasn't great but Davie kept the car on the road, albeit with the car engine screaming in protest. Suddenly, just outside Prestwick, the car hit a tremendous bump right in the middle of the road, which caused it to fly through the air momentarily. Davie cursed about potholes and the generally poor state of the Ayrshire roads.

It wasn't until it was pointed out to him that he had just driven over a roundabout, scattering the council flower bed arrangements in all directions, that he realised what happened. Expecting the worse, Davie brought the car to a sudden halt, anticipating at least a flat tyre and maybe a few dents in the bodywork. Remarkably, it remained fully intact and the journey home continued as if the mishap hadn't happened.

They soon hit the dual carriageway. The noise coming from the engine hadn't abated, and it was getting louder the faster the car was going. It was a whining noise, and there was a smell of burning. Davie ignored the comments as his goal was focussed on keeping the car in a straight line. It was becoming difficult to hold conversation above the engine noise and the overpowering stench.

Davie was adamant the car was fine, but if it continued he'd get someone to check it out in the morning. The journey continued noisily, but once they had navigated the Fenwick moors, the problem became apparent.

Davie had driven the previous 15 miles or so in third gear with the handbrake partly on.

Being the experienced man he was, Davie shrugged off the adverse comments and, with his usual aplomb, summed up the situation … "Told you there was f.k all wrong with the car."

"The greatest part of a road trip isn't arriving at your
destination.
It's all the wild stuff that happens along the way."
Emma Chase

Never were truer words written!

The Motherwell Madras

Curry nights in the pavilion were legendary. Sometimes they were accompanied by a quiz or a horse-racing event, but these were mere sideshows. The curry was the attraction, not delivered from a local take-away but prepared the night before. It was all part of the fun.

"Please sir, I want some more."

It was akin to a scene from Oliver Twist. The difference? The request came not from a starving waif, but from Big Keith, a 19-stone prop forward for Dalziel Rugby Club and an associate member of the cricket club. He had sampled the food on previous occasions and knew a good curry when he tasted it.

It was Friday night in Motherwell's Home Park clubhouse. On the menu was homemade chicken curry, basmati rice and spiced onions. It never failed to impress. Our very own Asian food festival, a festival with only one curry and two options – take it or leave it. Without exception, the vote of the assembled company was … take it.

The food was served from the tiny clubhouse kitchen to around 50 enthusiasts on cold winter evenings. And it was always brilliant. But how did it happen?

Thirsty Work

The head chef was Grant Robertson, whose fast bowling and forceful batting betrayed a delicate touch when it came to the mysterious art of curry-making. He had mastered his cooking skills over the years and this was his specialty. But he needed help to prepare the feast on the evening before the big event.

The unlikely sous-chef combination was his brother Graham and Steven McGill. For clarity, the latter's nickname – 'Carrots' – had nothing to do with a love for vegetables.

Before an onion was peeled or a hint of spice hit a pot, there was one crucial bit of planning to put in place. What would Grant and the sous-chefs be drinking on the eve of the feast? Grant was rather fond of his Tennent's Lager, as was his brother, Graham – a family trait, in the genes. Carrots would vary his tipple (roughly translated … he would drink anything!).

And so it was that 24 cans of lager made their way to the Robertson kitchen. Regular hydration was essential in the melting pot of the cooking arena, the cans of Tennent's a key ingredient to ally the intricate skills required to cook a homemade curry.

The cooking ritual took place on the Thursday evening. Grant would gather all of the necessary ingredients for the curry – well, his wife Marion did. Grant, as usual, would take all the credit. Seventy chicken breasts, six pounds of uncooked basmati rice, umpteen cans of tinned tomatoes, 30 large onions, and a variety of spices too numerous to count.

Cooking night arrived and the travelling sous-chefs made their way to Grant's kitchen. He opened the fridge, big enough to accommodate all the ingredients, including the beer. First thing on the to-do list, top spot in the order of priorities … get the bar open. There was a strict routine to a night like this so, over the first beer, the culinary assistants were fully briefed of their duties, and the cooking process got underway.

The task of peeling and chopping the 30 large onions fell to Carrots and Graham, not being something a head chef would do. It was not the best job, but this would form the base of the curry, so it was important it was done right. Grant began dicing the chicken – the sous-chefs weren't allowed near the chicken. "You're not fully trained, and would dice it to the wrong size." What Grant was really saying was, "I'm in charge, and you'll both do as I say." Some things never change!

With the onions peeled and finely chopped, they were thrown into what can only be described as a cauldron. It was the biggest pot the sous-chefs had ever come across, but it was made for the job. Next, oil was added to the onions, the tinned tomatoes soon followed, and the pot was blitzed with an enormous hand blender. The base curry was coming together, but without the head chef's expertise in selecting the correct blend of spices, trouble lay ahead. The empties were beginning to pile up.

Nervous Moments

The pivotal moment arrived. Grant carefully pulled out his treasured recipe sheet marked 'For Your Eyes Only' – very 1980s. The sous chefs were told to look away … well, it just felt that way. The secret ingredients were carefully selected, blended together and added to the mixture. As the base curry boiled gently away, simmering for what seemed like an age, the hydration process continued uninterrupted.

At the precise time, the diced chicken was added to the cauldron and simmered for another hour. Once it was cooked through, the curry was complete. However, everything was now hanging in the balance – time for the taste test. Was the chicken properly cooked? Had the spices all blended? All this anxiety called for another drink.

The chefs sampled the masterpiece. The taste and consistency was of restaurant quality. The head chef couldn't hide his delight and gave a self-righteous nod of approval to his cooking skills. And a toast … to himself!

The preparation of the rice was next on the agenda. The head chef had perfected the practice over the years, and he wasn't finished yet; he had one more trick up his sleeve. No curry was complete without a starter of spicy onions.

This time the sous-chefs were invited into his magic circle – he was prepared to divulge his secrets. Onions, salt, chilli powder, mint sauce, tomato ketchup, lemon juice and sugar. Surely you don't put tomato sauce and sugar in spicy onions? Well, yes you do, and classic spicy onions are the end result.

Graham and Carrots may not have had the finesse of the head chef, but they felt valued. The feeling didn't last for long – the kitchen was a bomb site; empty chicken packets littered the worktops, as did a multitude of empty cans, plates and knives. Picture the streets during a refuse collectors' strike … well, streets where the residents really love their Tennent's lager.

The sous chefs were put to work cleaning the mess. Grant was too busy, continuing to prod and poke the cauldron of curry, thinking one more stir was going to improve the taste. With the kitchen back in an orderly state, Grant thanks Graham and Carrots for their services and serves up the remaining beer out the fridge.

The entire 24 cans have now been emptied. It has taken around three and a half hours to prepare the feast. They were faced with a cauldron of chicken curry, spicy onions and numerous batches of perfectly cooked basmati rice. It's all arranged for easy transportation to the clubhouse to be served up the following evening.

With the cooking duties at an end, the kitchen staff bid their fond farewells in the full knowledge the festivities would begin in less than 24 hours from now.

Even back then, it would have been easier and certainly less time-consuming to have ordered set-menu takeaways and opt to charge the diners for the privilege. That wasn't our style – the cooking ritual was part of the fun and the three amigos relished every moment, a preamble to the following night's entertainment. The joy they brought to everyone who attended the Friday night festivities brought a warm glow to their cheeks … or maybe that was down to another night on the bevvy.

Did our head chef ever appear in Ramsay's Kitchen Nightmares? No chance. Even the great man himself wouldn't have dared criticise our Grant!

Ronnie's Big Day

Ronald A Morrison, Latin teacher, celebrated baritone and master of the forward defensive, was a wonderful servant to Motherwell Cricket Club. Ronnie started playing in the '50s, and was still going over 30 years later. This story took place in the late '80s, towards the end of his career, around the time he took on the presidency of the club.

Ronnie sat there, in the changing room at Ayr, giggling. Yes, giggling. It's hard to imagine Ronnie being anything other than his usual upstanding self. He was now laughing uproariously.

It was so incongruous – Ronnie never lost control. He was old school, a gentleman. Emotions were well hidden, but on that particular day at Ayr's lovely old Cambusdoon ground, he'd lost it.

He would take the field in his perfectly ironed whites … no, they weren't white, they were cream, probably tailored. His place in the field was first slip, not because he ever intended to take a sharp catch off a thin edge, but because he had no intention of running after the ball in the outfield. The younger chaps could do that sort of thing.

Occasionally, very occasionally, he was allowed to bowl an over, rarely more than one over. He would be brought on to bowl to buy a wicket with his loopy leg breaks. It did work – once. One day, at Gala, his first ball pitched and turned, and found the outside edge, and the obdurate opener was back in the pavilion, caught behind.

Unfortunately, the new man at the crease took an instant liking to Ronnie's bowling and didn't allow the ball to pitch, far less turn. Ronnie's bowling analysis was one over, one wicket for nineteen runs.

But, at Ayr, Ronnie didn't bowl. He batted stylishly, straight out of the coaching manual, and contributed a few runs before being beaten by a delivery that Ronnie had decreed to be unplayable, that would have beaten the best of batsmen. Then, after a splendid tea, he stood at slip for the entire Ayr innings and managed to avoid any action whatsoever in the field.

He did, however, keep those around him entertained. As was his habit, Ronnie would practise his singing for upcoming concerts while fielding and that day, he regaled us repeatedly with a chorus of 'The De'il's Awa' Wi' Th' Exciseman', which was most appropriate as we were playing cricket in Burns country.

But there's only so much a man can take, and wicketkeeper Gavin Shaw could stand it no more, and Ronnie was asked (none too politely) to desist.

The Motherwell team had been flung together that Sunday. Late call-offs resulted in our beleaguered captain, Douglas Burke, making last minute calls to anyone who was able to make the trip to Ayr. Basically, if you owned a white shirt, you were in. The press gang would pick you up.

As a result, the convoy of cars from Lanarkshire arrived late, and the Ayr lads were not impressed. You could see them questioning why were they even playing teams like Motherwell. When Motherwell won the toss and elected to bat, their displeasure was even more apparent. Their batsmen had been looking forward to occupying the crease for the afternoon, notching up another century against inferior bowling.

But remarkably, against all expectations, Motherwell's batsmen performed pretty well. Ian Sharp and Steve Young both scored 40-odd, young Neil Leitch added useful runs and others chipped in, allowing Motherwell to post a competitive 168 runs on the scoreboard.

This was a score comfortably within Ayr's reach and their Kiwi professional, Brendan Bracewell, set about the Motherwell bowling with gusto, smashing 65 runs in the first eight overs.

But, following his dismissal, their innings fell apart. Gavin Shaw took a fine leg side catch to get rid of Scottish international Bruce Patterson; Alastair Black and Ian McDonald bowled well as wickets started to fall; and Alaister Jackson, who wasn't really a bowler at all, mopped up the tail with four wickets for one run. Motherwell's ramshackle bunch had won with runs to spare.

It was all too much for Ronnie. Between fits of laughter, by now almost hysterical, he looked round the dressing room, and got some words out. "I've been coming here since the 1950s, and we've never won. I've played in the best of Motherwell teams – Brady, Syme, Steel, Kerr and Logan … we've never beaten Ayr. Thirty years of trying …" Tears were now rolling down his face. "Brendan Bracewell, Bruce Patterson …" Ronnie's words dried up but we understood how he felt. A special moment.

He was in the twilight of his cricketing career, and had played in the great teams of the 1960s, winning several league championships, but perhaps none of these achievements gave him more pleasure than the victory for Motherwell's all-sorts over Ayr's finest.

Last Orders, Gents, The Game's About To Start

What's the job of a captain? Winning the toss, picking a batting order, changing his bowlers, placing the field – so much to do! If you win, the skipper's done a decent job; if you lose, it's all his fault! There's something else – team spirit, camaraderie. Here's the story of a captain who was loved regardless of the result.

"Skipper, I'd better stick to the soft drinks. If you win the toss, I'll be opening the bowling." The skipper, being a man of gargantuan life experience, replied, "Young man, all will be fine. Now get up to the bar and get the beers in." And so it began!

It was the mid 1980s. These were the days of Live Aid on the telly, Cabbage Patch Kids for Christmas, and of technological advances that were about to change the world. Western economies adopted laissez-faire capitalism, and the Motherwell 2nd XI adopted their own laissez-faire approach to cricket.

Away games were relished and travel to our opponents' grounds required meticulous planning, using the most complex formulae.

Team selection was paramount. The selection committee had to consider the usual suspects intent on some extra-curricular activities beyond the cricket; to work out the designated drivers; and to fill the rest of the team with skilled and energetic young players, who would bear the brunt of the bowling and fielding duties.

Those falling into the first category would set off with those in the second category, at least 90 minutes ahead of those in the third category. The reason was simple – nothing to do with traffic jams or road works, it was all about pre-match preparation: they had to work out a batting order, field placing and other important matters of the day.

The advance party would meet in a watering hole close to the opponent's ground. Suitable venues were discovered (and re-discovered the next season) en route to these away games, the favourite hostelries being found adjacent to cricket grounds in Prestwick and Alva, but many others were mentioned in despatches.

Suitably refreshed and lubricated, hunger pangs would invariably kick in, necessitating a visit to the chippy en route to the ground. Well, we couldn't play cricket on an empty stomach. These were the days before sports scientists and dieticians, so we were able apply a sufficiency of salt on the chips.

This ritual may give the wrong impression. 2nd XI cricket was all about enjoyment, allowing the youngsters full opportunity to hone their talents while the old stagers had a good day out. And that's the way it inevitably turned out, with a laugh or two along the way.

There's nothing funnier than seeing a bowler with a belly full of chips and beer breaking wind in his final delivery stride; or mid-wicket performing a juggling routine of which a circus clown would be proud; or a solitary appeal for lbw coming from deep fine leg when the ball had struck the middle of the bat;

or when mid-innings drinks were called, the race back to the pavilion to see who could reach the urinal first.

Looking back at the history of our club, it's interesting to note that our predecessors did something similar – they had beer served between innings rather than teas. So our present-day shenanigans were really just continuing the traditions set in place by Motherwell's cricketers in Victorian times.

Regardless of whether everyone approved of our pre-match preparation, it was part and parcel of playing 2nd XI cricket in the mid-1980s. Stories are still told of our 'days out' when the results of the actual games are long forgotten.

These were happy and enjoyable times, regardless of results. It engendered a fantastic team spirit, whether you drank beer or stuck to the lemonade. All glory to the 2nd team skipper.

All events in this story are based on facts gathered by the author in good faith. Any resemblance to any actual persons, living or dead, is purely coincidental... but the 2nd XI skipper might have been Jim Anderson!

A Different Ball

*Motherwell and Prestwick enjoyed many a titanic
tussle on the cricket field but, back in the late 1970s,
the rivalry extended to the football pitch. And why not?
The clubs enjoyed good relations, and we had to do
something during those long winter months between
cricket seasons.*

The challenge was issued during an apres-cricket session in the Prestwick bar. In these days, with their Aussie pro Grant Stanley, Prestwick generally had the upper hand, so it was maybe after one of those cricketing defeats that Motherwell reckoned they could turn the tables playing with a bigger ball.

The Motherwell lads might have fancied their chances, especially after a drink or two, but they had overlooked one rather obvious obstacle. In the Prestwick ranks was a South African, small in stature but hugely talented – he scored runs, took the odd wicket and captained the team.

He was also a pretty useful footballer, having played with Rangers in the '50s, known as the penalty king (scoring 65 of 68 penalty kicks) and scoring a hat trick against Celtic. Although past his prime, Johnny Hubbard was in a different class to any of the other cricketers on the football field.

It was a two-leg affair, with the first game being played at Watsonville's red ash park in Motherwell. The outcome was all too predictable, the visitors strolling to a 3-1 victory with Hubbard scoring all three – one a free kick, one direct from a corner and one, predictably, from the penalty spot. And he didn't break a sweat.

Motherwell would have to adopt a different approach in the return match, and it was a much more physical and aggressive team that took to the pitch in Prestwick. There may even have been a few 'ringers' introduced, but that seemed ok as we suspected that some of the Prestwick team had never held a cricket bat in their lives.

The referee had given both sides several warnings before the game erupted. Graham Robertson clashed with one of the Prestwick lads and, after the ensuing melee was broken up, the ref decided (inadvisedly!) that the game should be restarted by way of a drop ball. He pointed to the players nearest him to step forward – one was Graham's assailant and the other (no, don't do it, not him, anyone but him!) was Graham's brother, Grant. You didn't have to be Mystic Meg to know what would happen next.

In those days, a drop ball was contestable and was more commonly known as a bounce ball or a stoat-up. But the ball didn't get the chance to bounce or stoat or even drop before Grant took the legs from his opponent with a scything swing of his right boot.

"That's it," said the referee, "I've had enough!" He picked up the ball and stormed off the pitch.

Negotiations took place to retain the ball, and the game resumed lacking a referee. Motherwell's rough-house tactics prevailed, as they took a 3-1 lead to tie the match and, in the final minute, Jack Kelly rose salmon-like to head home the winner, completing his hat trick. Honestly, he did! Anything Johnny Hubbard can do ...

And, with that, Motherwell returned home with a 4-3 aggregate win to avenge their loss on the cricket pitch. Most importantly, despite all the aggro, our friendship with Prestwick Cricket Club prevailed ... and we'll conveniently ignore the drubbing they gave us the following year.

The Posh Boys

Motherwell, a town where hardened steelworkers and coalminers dominate its history, is not the sort of place where you'd expect to find posh boys, and yet they somehow manage to infiltrate the system. Yes, even in deepest Lanarkshire … nestling in our distinctly 'un-posh' working-class cricket club.

Here's an advertisement for a Grand Match and Promenade. There's no denying it – this is definitely posh.

MOTHERWELL CRICKET CLUB
GRAND MATCH AND PROMENADE
The Annual Match and Promenade of the Season of the above Club will take place on their field, off Milton Street, Motherwell on Saturday, the 5th June, 1875.
Brass Band in attendance
Wickets pitched at 1 o' clock pm. Promenade at 4 o' clock.
North British Daily Mail, May 1875

There are several other newspaper reports about cricket matches in Motherwell followed by promenades, which were 'attended by large numbers of the fair sex, dancing to the strains of a Brass Band'.

Music, promenades, dancing? Didn't they know where they were?

And it wasn't unique to our cricket club. Up the road at Craigneuk Glencairn, we read of an attendance of 300 who 'tripped it up in fine style on the grassy sward'. And they were even posher than Motherwell – 'the ladies presented the club with a flag and pole'.

It's difficult to believe, but this was Motherwell. And remember that many of Motherwell's cricket players of the 1870s were workers from the ironworks, who had probably just finished their Saturday morning shift.

Let's ignore for the moment the noxious fumes, the clanging of hammers from the neighbouring blacksmiths' yards and the blackened miners trudging past the cricket ground at the end of their shift – this was undoubtedly posh behaviour. The army bands, the ladies in fine frocks, the dancing.

Whatever happened to those days? Well, let's wind the clock forward 100 years or so to the 1970s.

Players from a variety of backgrounds have crossed the threshold of our wonderful club, the revolving door never standing still, but around that time, two refined gentlemen entered … and never left. They were graciously referred to as the 'posh brothers'. Brothers from a different mother, with a lifelong ambition to be 'upper class'.

They had the bearing of noble ancestry, and talked of dining with dukes. What did they do for a living? 'Something big in the city' was as much as we understood.

When they chatted in the bar, they could be overheard saying, "Do you know that there are some fellows playing cricket at this club who don't have a university education?" They hallucinated about playing cricket with the great and the good at Grange or wielding the willow at West; and stroking cover drives for four, rather than the more agricultural cross-batted shots that seemed to be all the fashion at Motherwell.

When we played away from home at Accies or High School, they cooed with delight at the home-made quiche and smoked salmon on quartered brown bread on the tea table. At Motherwell, they wondered why there was always some strange-tasting meat spread on Mothers Pride loaf, and never a vegetable in sight.

The toilet (or restroom, as they would say) at Home Park was also a cause of consternation. They were horrified at one individual who took squatter's rights, an appropriate expression as that's exactly what he did, week in, week out, for what seemed like an age.

And while the posh brothers were clapping the opposition batsmen for walking to the wicket, there would be guttural utterances from the rest of the team, especially that aggressive opening bowler and his brother – word had it that they came from a rather rough part of Glasgow. And as for that chap who was always made to bowl up the hill, the stories he told of his night-time exploits …

To the posh brothers, their team mates were rather foul-mouthed chaps, for whom the use of fruity language was the norm. What must those umpires think of us?

Still, the game would soon be over, and they could seek out the opposition in the bar to begin their bluster and self-glorification. "Surely you have a private club membership!"

The brothers reminded some of toothache – no matter what you did to ease the pain, it wouldn't go away. For others, it was Santa Clause – you put out milk and biscuits and you couldn't get rid of them.

But it was all a masquerade. These ordinary men were indulging in fantastic daydreams of what might have been, personal ideals that were never real, and a life that would never be. For underneath their thick skin, they were part of the proletariat, brought up in deepest, darkest Lanarkshire, just like everyone else at Home Park.

The values they held were never going to change, and that's what made them distinct. They didn't play for a proper posh club, they played at Motherwell, and are remembered with endearment not only for the joy they brought, but also for their uninhibited etiquette and ostentatious exploits.

Who were they? Where did they come from? It was like a reincarnation of the white-flanneled fools gamboling upon the green swards of Victorian Motherwell, their speech reminiscent of a Dickensian novel, and their circumnavigation of the modern-day cricket field a re-enactment of the promenade 100 years before.

The ghosts of cricket past!

The Jolly Boys' Secret Outing

The 1st XI routinely celebrated the end of the season at Hughenden. The last game was always away to Hillhead, with a minibus dropping them off at 12.00 noon, returning to pick them up at 11.00pm. It was always an enjoyable occasion – especially if the actual game had been rained off! However, the 2nds took things to a whole new level!

It was a dull, dreich Saturday in early September, the 2nd XI's last game of the season, away to Dumfries. A final opportunity to wield the willow before the cricketing whites were put away for the winter.

Graham Robertson had agreed to captain the side (rather, he had insisted on doing so). And there he was, inspecting the wicket with the Dumfries captain, who was making enthusiastic noises about the possibility of play.

"Give it half an hour, and it'll dry out," he said.

"I'm not so sure," retorted Graham. "It's pretty soft, we wouldn't want to damage the square."

"Nonsense," the Dumfries skipper replied. "You chaps have travelled all this way ..."

Just at that moment, the sun peeked through the heavy cloud, and Graham was starting to panic. The weather forecast had been showing an 85% chance of rain all week, and his plans had been built around a pouring wet day in Dumfries. He had no intention of playing the game. This wasn't in the script.

Graham had been looking forward to this day for a while. For both clubs, the game meant nothing as the league was done and dusted, and with a wash-out on the cards, it was a great chance to thank the guys for their efforts throughout the season with a wee day out. Well, a big day out actually.

Cricket was to play second fiddle, serving as an excuse to travel, and a 'secret' social event had been planned. Apart from Murray Learmonth, who had been co-opted to help with the plans, none of the other guys had any idea what was happening. The pressure was on.

Treasures From Far And Near

A few weeks earlier, the Robertson family had returned from a holiday in Greece with Ouzo aplenty, and duty-free brandy, whisky, gin and vodka. Graham and his wife Linda had prepared 40 small bottles filled with some unique cocktails – concoctions featuring generous measures of the spirits and various mixers, with little thought going into the alcohol content. The cocktails were certainly imaginative, though some felt that the Ouzo and Umbongo was a step too far.

The 2nds had always enjoyed a post-match drink, and Graham had confidence that the guys could handle it … most of them, anyway.

A visit to Chapman the butcher on the morning of the game produced three dozen mutton pies and sausage rolls, and a tray full of cream cakes. Class. The plan was coming together:

booze and food. And to complete the charade, Graham had also ordered a 30-seater bus from a friend in Larkhall.

The order had been given for the team to gather at the Civic Centre for 11am sharp. Puzzled expressions were exchanged as the bus arrived and, even as they stood in the Motherwell drizzle, each with their cricket bags packed for the final day of the season, the members of the team had no idea that cricket was the furthest thing from their captain's mind.

Only when trays of pies, sausage rolls and cream cakes were unloaded from Graham's car onto the bus, followed by the precious duty-free cargo and a box of straws, did it start to dawn on the 2nd XI that this would be no ordinary away fixture.

"What's all this, Robertson?" enquired a bewildered Willie Miller.

"Just a wee thank you from me to you, boys," answered Graham. But the penny hadn't dropped – they thought the glorious game would be played and drinks served afterwards. How wrong they were. Socialising rather than cricket would be the order of the day … well, that was the plan anyway.

As the bus left for Dumfries, the bar was soon opened and the food dished out. With each bottle came a straw for easy consumption and a label for identification. The food spoke for itself, literally. The drizzle developed into steady rain as they passed Lesmahagow, and the plan was coming together nicely.

"Do you think the game will go ahead? We've already had a few." Jack Kelly asked the question, shoving a cold mutton pie into his mouth, but you didn't have to be Albert Einstein to work it out. Graham's confidence in the forecast was undimmed – he had already made up his mind that the wicket was going to be too wet for play. There was no chance that the game would go ahead.

But, to his utter dismay, the nearer they got to Dumfries, the drier it became. There was even a chink of sunlight as they passed Beattock Summit. With some of the guys having downed a few, getting off the bus safely could be a challenge, never mind playing cricket.

A Prayer To The Rain Gods

And now, as he stood on the Dumfries square, captain Robertson was being urged to give it a go by his opposite number. He looked up to the sky, hoping for some divine intervention, and none came.

Graham looked back towards the pavilion and saw his players in various degrees of inebriation – some in friendly embrace, some polishing off the last of the chocolate cake, and others still sucking their cocktails through their straws. Their faces said it all – vodka martini with Irn Bru had never tasted better.

Ultimately, there was no other option but to disclose to the Dumfries captain his social plans for the day, referring to the pre-match weather forecast and how some of the guys had already started drinking on the bus down. Some of his team, watching hazily from afar, wondered why their captain was stooped on bended knee. Graham later explained that he was checking the amount of rain on the wicket!

"Ideally, it would be great if we agreed that the wicket's unplayable and that the game is called off ... please."

Graham's pleading was met with a knowing grin, a hearty laugh and a firm handshake – the fixture was officially rained off. As it happened, the gods did answer Graham's call – the two captains had to rush from the cricket field to the shelter of the pavilion as the heavens opened.

It couldn't have come together any better. When Graham broke the news, his team (well, most of them) were delighted. Happy, smiley faces. The plan had been on a knife edge at times and, had the weather brightened up, his bluff may well have been called.

They could imagine the potential headlines in the Galloway Gazette: 'Motherwell Cricketers Drunk At The Crease' or some such booze-gate sensationalism. 'The travelling party are to appear at Dumfries Sheriff Court on a date to be arranged ...' Thankfully, they were spared the embarrassment.

As they again took their seats on board, the bus driver was instructed to drop the team in Dumfries town centre so that the festivities could begin (or continue!). Of course, all of this had been pre-planned and, as the pints went down, the merrier they all got and a great day out was had by all.

The bus rounded them up around 7.30 that night, with the same number boarding the bus as had travelled down from Motherwell. An added bonus – a day on the lash and no-one posted missing. There were some casualties but none too serious, and everyone was delivered home safe and sound, back into the bosom of their families.

And this is why we love the game of cricket.

Something Smells

Baldev was the professional for Motherwell Cricket Club for only a couple of months. Yet he was one of the most popular guys to play for the club. He was a great character, one of the boys, and a fine cricketer as well. And after he moved on, he kept in touch.

When Feroz Mehdi left in 1995, mid-season, we were joined at short notice by an Indian cricketer called Baldev. He made an immediate impression by notching centuries in consecutive weeks against Helensburgh and Irvine. Although past his prime, it was evident that he still had plenty to offer.

He was well liked at the club and was instrumental in securing Sanjay Raul as Motherwell's professional in July '96. Baldev even returned to Home Park in later years and played a couple of matches as an amateur.

A couple of years later, Grant Robertson received a call out of the blue: "Any chance my wife and I can stay with you for a few days?"

"No problem, when will you be coming?"

The response … "Tonight!"

Baldev and his wife Pritti arrived later that night by bus from London. Grant picked them up at Hamilton bus station and, after a quick drink, they retired to bed. Next day, they had plans to visit Glasgow and, when they returned that evening, they had dinner and a few more drinks. Baldev liked his whisky but it had to be disguised with Coke so that Pritti didn't know!

Next day followed the same pattern. They left early to visit some local landmarks, returning early evening, but while they were away, Grant's wife Marion went into the guest bedroom to supply fresh towels and sensed a horrible smell. Grant was instructed to speak with Baldev later that night, but he was uncomfortable about the conversation, unsure how to broach the subject.

He put it off till the next night, by which time the pong was far worse, and he plucked up the courage to ask Baldev if he was aware of an aroma in the room. He said he was, but didn't like to say to Grant and Marion that their home was a bit smelly.

When it was pointed out that the noxious aroma hadn't been present prior to their arrival, Baldev immediately sprang to his feet, ran up to the bedroom and returned with half a bag of cooked peeled prawns, held at arm's length, which had been festering in their luggage, fully apologetic.

They had a good laugh … and several drinks afterwards. Both couples had been enduring the rancid smell for days, unwilling to offend each other by suggesting anything was amiss. A cultural stand-off.

And when we think of Baldev, we always picture him with a mischievous smile … and a cheeky wee half!

Professionals In Opposition

The Motherwell professionals of the '80s and '90s made quite an impact, but what about those playing for the opposition? Who was the best pro we ever played against?

Well, much depends upon the parameters of the question. In what era, in whose judgement, and what constitutes the 'best pro' – the best coach, the most successful, the most memorable?

If you go way back to the inter-war years, the Motherwell players of the time would talk about playing against Herbert Sutcliffe or Ian Peebles. And in the post-war years, they would throw Bobby Simpson's name into the hat. But these cricketing greats featured in one-off games rather than being employed as club professionals, so let's bring the question up to date … well, to the past 50 years or thereabouts.

It's an interesting debate, a debate that was had over a few beers in the company of some former players who turned out for Motherwell in the '80s and '90s, when we were playing against club professionals week in, week out. We all had our favourite memories.

Some Stand-Out Stars

John Gillies came up with Omar Henry and Salahuddin, both legendary players, but he played against them in his Uddingston days. This is Motherwell's story so, sorry John, they don't qualify for inclusion.

The easy answer would be Kim Hughes, who came to Home Park with The Bats before going on to captain Australia. He was great company after the game too, one of the boys, but again it was a one-off experience and we were looking for professionals we played against regularly.

Steve Young recalled a league match against East Kilbride, when he dismissed test player Asif Mujtaba, but the fact that the Pakistan number three bat was caught on the long off boundary having scored 170 runs had somehow slipped his mind.

Another vivid memory was Harry Tart bowling to Irvine's big-hitting South African pro, Clive Wolfson. He had just hit the most enormous 6, which landed on the dual carriageway running past the Marress ground, when he drilled a perfectly timed drive straight back at the bowler. In a cartoon, it would have gone straight through his middle and out the other side, but somehow Harry clung on to the catch to dismiss the big man.

And we all had nightmares of North Kelvinside's left arm spinner, Zaheed Ahmed. Batsmen had to be watchful for Z's lethal quicker ball, which always seemed to pitch in the blockhole. If you had any sort of backlift, it was through you before you knew it.

The discussion raged on, becoming ever more intense with every round. And you can't have this debate without including Grant Stanley at Prestwick or Grant Parmenter at Hillhead, both Aussies who gave so much to the game in Scotland.

There were other supremely talented professionals who

scored runs against us regularly but, as more beers arrived, we struggled to recall their names (must be an age thing). That in itself suggested that they weren't sufficiently memorable to qualify for the title of 'best pro'. And so it went on, more brilliant memories, until …

Grant Robertson mentioned a name that brought a smile to everyone's faces. Even though it must be over 30 years since we last clapped eyes on him, the mere mention of his name invoked feelings of terror and laughter in equal measure. Debate over.

Our Favourite Foe

Foster Lewis was the archetypal West Indian cricketer of the 1980s – rapid bowler, swashbuckling bat – yet he looked as if he couldn't care less. For full effect, you really have to read this piece with a Caribbean accent, a slow-paced drawl that was in complete contrast to how he played cricket.

He had played for Antigua, home of the great Viv Richards, before joining Dumfries side St Michaels as their overseas professional in 1985. We first came across him in a Sunday friendly match at Home Park. We didn't know anything about him, but that changed pretty quickly!

Motherwell asked St Michaels to bat first, and the cool West Indian swaggered to the wicket to open the innings. He proceeded to hit us to all parts of the ground and reached his 100 in no time at all. It's difficult to remember him running between the wickets; he just stood at the crease and no matter what we bowled at him, it seemed to find the middle of his mighty bat. The only question was whether the ball would go for 4 or 6. This photo from St Michaels' website shows Foster Lewis in a typically belligerent mood.

Having completed his century, probably the fastest 100 ever scored against Motherwell, he tucked his bat under his arm and walked with even more of a swagger back to the pavilion, saying,"I'll let someone else have a go."

St Michaels went on to post an impressive total, way too many for us, but their pro wasn't

finished. Lewis opened the bowling, but even before he bowled a ball, we knew that we were in for a hard time. He started his run up at the boundary fence and skittled our openers in quick succession.

One of our batsmen dared to ask the bowler, "Is that you at full pace?" The response was typical of Lewis, "No man, I don't even have my boots on." To his credit, he realised there was no point in continuing to bowl and passed the ball to another bowler to make a game of it.

It was a couple of years later when we played St Michaels at their picturesque ground on the banks of the Nith. By that time, Foster Lewis had made quite a name for himself, taking loads of wickets. He rattled through the Motherwell top order but Grant Robertson entered the fray with a more aggressive mindset – the best form of defence was attack.

The first ball was pitched up just outside off stump, which Grant dispatched for 6 straight over his head. The murmurs from the St Michaels slip cordon suggested that this hadn't been a wise move. Time seemed to stand still. Foster Lewis clearly didn't appreciate the shot and strolled – nay, swaggered – up to the wicket and whispered "Don't do that again" in a tone which carried more than a hint of menace. Having adjusted his field, the next ball flew past the batsman's nose. Message received.

Grant continued to frustrate the West Indian, who displayed his full repertoire of yorkers, bouncers and even beamers, and as the bowler tired, runs were easier to come by and Motherwell were able to post a decent total. The result of the match is long forgotten, but we all remember how we had taken on the mighty Foster Lewis and emerged from Dumfries with our heads held high (and still attached to our shoulders).

He wasn't the best player we'd ever come up against – others had better technique and consistently scored more runs. So perhaps it's a macho thing, hitting the ball out the ground and sending stumps cartwheeling … and all done with such a laidback attitude. It was something special.

It's difficult to say his name without a smile spreading across your face, and that's what makes him stand out as our favourite professional in opposition.

Foster Lewis, great memories.

Play Up! Play Up! And Play The Game!

For anyone who has ever played cricket, this one's for you. Think back to that very first time you ventured out to the middle, a wee boy stepping up from the juniors to play in your first senior cricket match.

His head was spinning, chest tight, legs shaking like jelly, blood pressure through the roof. "Do you think we should call an ambulance?" said a worried voice. The captain gave a wry smile, shaking his head knowingly. He had seen the signs many times before. "It's ok, he's just about to head out to face his first ball."

That's how it was for a young lad, a virgin of senior cricket, getting ready for that first knock in the 2nd XI. It was fine playing junior cricket with kids of his own age, or getting some balls lobbed up to him in practice, but this was the real thing. And from the comfort of the pavilion, it looked a scary proposition.

What was all the fuss about, you may ask? Batsmen wore protective pads and gloves, boxes, arm and elbow protectors, thigh guards, and everyone wears a helmet, right? Wrong! This was the early '70s, long before all of this stuff was considered necessary.

The vast majority of cricketers didn't benefit from protective armour. In fact, on one of the first occasions when an English test player wore a helmet on the cricket field, the crowd turned on him. "Booooooo …"

The boy sat on the pavilion steps, waiting his turn, last man in, trying to work out how to put on pads that were far too big. There was no Velcro in those days – there were rusted buckles with bent pins, some that wouldn't tighten properly on skinny teenage legs, and others broken. You sort of dragged the pads around with you when you walked or tried to run.

And those gloves! The expression about being all fingers and thumbs must have originated from one of these old pairs of batting gloves. You got the four fingers of your left hand inserted individually, then you wrapped the thumb holder round your wrist until it would stretch over your thumb. And then you repeated the procedure for your right hand, but with your left hand already gloved. It was impossible.

Then came the call: "You're in." From the club kit bag, a bat appeared, again too big, The long walk to the crease, thinking that you really should have gone to the toilet, and trying to remember what to ask the umpire – 'middle and leg', was it? Then a distant cry from the pavilion, "Did you remember to put your box on?"

Cricket has always been perceived as a gracious affair played by gentlemen with superior sportsmanship, a game for aristocrats. So you'd think some polite encouragement would await the boy's arrival at the crease. Maybe a slower delivery to get off the mark, followed by a chatter of "Well played, lad." Well, maybe not, not in Lanarkshire.

The batsman at the other end awaited his arrival and offered some friendly words of advice. "The bowler's pretty quick, so get into line, don't back away!" The boy knew that to do so would be regarded as cowardice, akin to desertion from the front line.

First ball fended off by a bony arm, next one taken on the thigh above the pad and the third in the midriff, perilously close to where the box should have been. More helpful advice from the other end: "Don't let the bowler see you're hurt," as tears began to form.

Brave face on, taking guard for the next delivery, wondering if the bowler would try to hit the stumps this time, a stage whisper comes from someone in the slip cordon … "You know you can use your bat if you want, son?" Laughter was followed by his side-kick: "Aye, just wait till you see his quicker ball."

Sledging, before it had a name.

Physical injury was one thing, but standing there anticipating a 70mph projectile hurtling in your direction, and trying to think of a witty retort to Morcambe and Wise behind the stumps, was quite another. Verbal abuse and intimidation of opposing players is as old as cricket itself – often crude, occasionally funny – but no-one thought much about sports psychology in the '70s.

The boy knew it was futile to take offence, or to react in any way, but it still preyed on his mind. He liked the story about the Aussie fast bowler Dennis Lillee welcoming an incoming batsman. "There's a piece of dog shit on your bat, mate." When the batsman glanced at the bottom of his bat, Lillee quipped, "Wrong end, mate."

Attention diverted, concentration broken, the young lad turned to see his middle stump lying flat on the ground, bowled for a duck, his team all out. He made his way back to the pavilion, a walk that seemed a lot longer than on the way out, and the opposition (including the comedy duo) waited to clap him off the field. Not for the last time in his cricketing life, he wondered, "What did I do to justify such applause?"

But that was just the half of it. After the strangest of teas, he had to field!

There was an unwritten rule that young players in the team should take up the positions close to the wicket, like short leg or silly mid-off. Such positions were still something of a mystery for a young lad, but he was shown where to stand.

The logic was that teenage reflexes would be that much sharper than those of the old stagers, who had served their apprenticeship many years before. The trouble was that batsmen, when confronted by close fielders, were intent on removing them by whatever means possible.

At least when you batted, you had some protective equipment. In the field – nothing! As the boy crouched no more than a couple of yards from the batsman, hands cupped more in prayer than for catching, more helpful advice came his way. "Don't watch the bowler running in, keep your eyes on the bat." No need to worry about that, he was watching it very closely indeed! And then … "A bit closer, son."

The game over, and a draw declared, players shook hands. Wait a minute? A draw? After five and a half hours? "But we scored more runs than them!" As they stood at a bar half an hour later, the boy learned that cricket was much more complicated than who scored more runs. Two pints later, everything seemed clear as day.

He had mentioned that he was just shy of his 18th birthday (2 years, 3 months shy, to be precise) but his protestations fell on deaf ears. Anyway, he had escaped with his life (and his bits) intact, so that was something worthy of celebration.

After the 10 o' clock closing time bell signalled the end of the day's cricket, it was time to go home, where Mum and Dad were waiting to hear how he'd got on. He'd been sent on his way before lunch with sandwiches and a packet of biscuits, and Mum telling him how cricket was a wonderful sport for boys to be playing, much safer than rugby. "That's a rough game, you could get badly injured." If only she knew!

The boy didn't really want to talk about his badly bruised body, the psychological trauma when batting or his terrifying experience at silly mid-on, when his hair had been parted by a booming on-drive. He tried a smile, but effected a rather silly grin, and stumbled up the stairs towards his bedroom, followed by his mother's voice. "Have you been drinking?"

That night, he prayed that he'd be allowed to play cricket again next week.

There's a breathless hush in the close to-night
Ten to make and the match to win
A bumping pitch and a blinding light,
An hour to play, and the last man in.
And it's not for the sake of a ribboned coat.
Or the selfish hope of a season's fame,
But his captain's hand on his shoulder smote
"Play up! Play up! And play the game!"
Henry Newbolt

Absent Friends

Reaching our 150-year milestone is quite an achievement … even if we do say so ourselves! We can pinpoint several times when our club could easily have gone the way of many others but, somehow, we have always pulled through.

It's not just Motherwell, of course – every club has faced these challenges and more. Some survive, some don't, and we can't write a potted history of our club without remembering the clubs that haven't made it. Teams we played against year after year. They are an important part of our 150 years. They might not be around today, but they have left memories we can still cherish.

Motherwell Cricket Club's most challenging times? It's easy to identify the world wars, when almost all of our players were called up to fight. But thankfully most of them returned and were pleased to see their club still there, a place to go and forget about the horrors they'd been through.

And the two pavilion fires were crippling blows, especially in 1999, when we knew that any effort to rebuild the clubhouse would result in fire number three. What to do? We seemed to be snookered, in checkmate. Yet we're still here, almost a quarter of a century after we had to leave Home Park.

Even the fluctuating popularity of cricket as a sport killed off a number of clubs. Looking way back to the early years of cricket in Motherwell, when as many as five clubs would compete for supremacy in the town, that didn't last long when football made its grand entrance. As we know, only one club survived – Motherwell Britannia, who became Motherwell Trinity for a short time before dropping the suffix to leave good old Motherwell Cricket Club.

We have been fortunate to have had some determined and resourceful people at the helm to ensure we negotiated these difficult periods in our history. Pig-headed, obsessive, never-say-die or even lucky – whatever the quality, it's been there when we needed it.

But what of our opponents, our rivals through the years, who aren't around to help us celebrate our 150th?

Going Way Back

In the early years, there were lots of teams to play against, even in the Motherwell area – Holytown, Dellburn, Craigneuk Glencairn and Dalziel Star to name but a few. The bigger games seemed to be with Airdrie and Coatbridge teams like St John and Wesley, and must have been big days out, given the transport limitations of Victorian Lanarkshire. Yet the teams still took plenty of followers with them to away matches.

Our 1906 Fixture Card is one of the oldest, and captured local cricket at its peak in terms of spectators. In these days, local rivalries with Wishaw, Bellshill and Newmains were intense, every bit as fierce as local derbies in football.

Motherwell Cricket Club. FIRST ELEVEN.

Fixtures, 1906. SECOND ELEVEN.

DATE.	AGAINST.	GROUND	RESULT
Apl. 14	Opening Match	Home	
,, 21	Bothwell	Away	
,, 28	Johnstone	Away	
May 5	Hamilton	Home	
,, 12	Newmains (L)	Home	
,, 19	Victoria (L)	Away	
,, 26	Wishaw (L)	Away	
June 1	Drumpellier Club Sen'r 11	Home	
,, 2	Bute County	Away	
,, 6	Glasgow University	Home	
,, 9	Hamilton	Away	
,, 13	Moth'll Bowlers sec XI	Home	
,, 16	Bellshill (L)	Away	
,, 20	Polloc XI	Home	
,, 23	Wesley (L)	Home	
,, 30	Newmains (L)	Away	
July 7	Victoria (L)	Home	
,, 14	Fair Holidays		
,, 21	Bothwell	Home	
,, 28	Airdrie	Away	
Aug. 4	Wishaw (L)	Home	
,, 11	Bellshill (L)	Home	
,, 18	Wesley (L)	Away	
,, 25	2nd Drumpellier	Home	
Sept. 1	Johnstone	Home	
,, 8	Airdrie	Home	

L Denotes League Matches.

DATE.	AGAINST.	GROUND	RESULT
Apl. 14	Opening Match	Home	
,, 21	Brittania	Home	
,, 28	Johnstone	Home	
May 5	Beith Woodside	Away	
,, 12	Newmains (L)	Away	
,, 19	Victoria (L)	Home	
,, 26	Boys Brigade Sp'ts		
June 9	Hamilton	Home	
,, 16	Bellshill (L)	Home	
,, 23	Wesley (L)	Away	
,, 25	Glasgow Unv'ty 'A'	Home	
,, 30	Newmains (L)	Home	
July 7	Victoria (L)	Away	
,, 14	Fair Holidays		
,, 21	Hamilton	Away	
,, 28	Airdrie	Home	
Aug. 4	Wishaw (L)	Away	
,, 11	Bellshill (L)	Away	
,, 18	Wesley (L)	Home	
,, 25			
Sept. 1	Johnstone	Away	
,, 8	Airdrie	Away	
,, 15	Wishaw (L)	Home	

L Denotes League Matches.

If football was the winter sport, cricket was the summer sport, and crowds of over 2,000 would gather round the Home Park boundary, generating a noisy atmosphere, carrying their victorious Motherwell heroes off the park shoulder-high.

Inter-War Years

The Motherwell-Newmains match continued to be the biggest game of the season for many years, with the original R K Hinshalwood starring for Newmains in the same way that his son and grandson would shine for Motherwell in years to come. It was an eagerly awaited fixture, always well reported in the newspapers.

The fixture card of 1924 shows annual games against Milngavie and Bearsden and Golfhill, and we continued playing against them for the next 50 years. And it's great to see Colonel Aikman's Ross Ramblers on the card – they brought players from the forces, and from private schools. The Motherwell lads never knew who they'd be playing against, and ended up sharing a cricket pitch with Herbert Sutcliffe and Sir Alec Douglas-Home.

1st XI. Fixtures.

DATE	OPPONENTS	GROUND	RLT.
April 12	Practice Game	Home Park	
19	Uddingston	Uddingston	
26	Kilmarnock	Kilmarnock	
May 3	Milng'e & Bearsden	Home Park	
10	Harland & Wolff	Govan	
17	Renfrew	Renfrew	
*22	Wishaw	Home Park	
24	East Stirlingshire	Home Park	
*28	Uddingston	Home Park	
31			
June *6	Drumpellier	Home Park	
7	Selkirk	Selkirk	
*10	Ferguslie	Meikleriggs	
14	Hilln'd H.S.F.P.'s	Home Park	
*18	Tannochside	Tannochside	
21	Cowlairs	Home Park	
*25	Newmains	Toll Park	
28	Helensburgh	Helensburgh	
July *3	Mr H.B. Rowan's XI	Home Park	
5	Cowlairs	Springburn	
12	Harland & Wolff	Home Park	
19	Fair Holidays		
26	Ferguslie	Home Park	
Aug. 2	Renfrew	Home Park	
9	Golfhill	Dennistoun	
16	Milng'e & Bearsden	Milngavie	
23	Newmains	Home Park	
30	Ross Ramblers	Home Park	
Sept. 6	Hilln'd H.S.F.P.'s	Glasgow	
13	Golfhill	Home Park	

*Evening Games

2nd XI. Fixtures.

DATE	OPPONENTS	GROUND	RLT.
April 19	Practice Game	Home Park	
26	Kelburne 2nd XI.	Home Park	
May 3	Milng'e & Bearsden	Milngavie	
10	Uddingston 2nd XI	Home Park	
*15	Uddingston 3rd XI	Uddingston	
17	Cambuslang	Home Park	
*22	Drumpellier 3rd XI	Drumpellier	
24	Hilln'd H.S.F.P.'s	Glasgow	
31	Garturk	Home Park	
June 7	Holiday		
*11	Stewartville	Wishaw	
14	Coatdyke	Airdrie	
*18	Drumpellier 3rd XI	Home Park	
21	Cowlairs	Springburn	
*25	Newmains	Home Park	
28	Coatdyke	Home Park	
July 5	Cowlairs	Home Park	
*9	Stewartville	Home Park	
12	Garturk	Whifflet	
*15	Uddingston 2nd XI	Uddingston	
19	Fair Holidays		
26			
Aug. 2			
9	Golfhill	Home Park	
16	Milng'e & Bearsden	Home Park	
23	Newmains	Toll Park	
30			
Sept. 6	Uddingston 3rd XI	Home Park	
13	Golfhill	Dennistoun	

*Evening Games.

By the 1930s, Carfin Hall had become a force in local cricket, fighting toe to toe with Motherwell for bragging rights in the burgh. Around the same time, in Calderbank, Woodhall's rise to prominence kick-started a rivalry that would last down through the generations. Fierce competitors on the field, and great characters off it, several of the Woodhall boys found their way to Home Park in later years. Harry Tart, the Donnelly brothers, Joe Grieg, Alex Cunningham and more all played an important part at Motherwell Cricket Club.

Post-War Cricket

The 1963 Fixture Card finds Motherwell in the midst of our most successful period, and it's easy to spot the League matches, marked with an 'x'. It's also helpful to see the results of each game scratched in pencil by the owner of the card. The 1st XI looks to have had a great season, the 2nd XI less so.

FIRST ELEVEN FIXTURES.			
Apr.27 s	Babcock and Wilcox		h
May 4 s	Milngavie and Bearsden	x	h
11 s	Helensburgh	x	h
13	Drumpellier	Rowan Cup	a
15	Clydesdale		a
18 s	Anchor	x	h
23	Uddingston	Western Cup	h
25 s	Helensburgh	x	a
June 1 s	Glasgow University		h
8 s	Prestwick	x	h
13	Lanark	Connell Cup	h
15 s	Golfhill	x	a
22 s	Kelvinside Academicals	x	a
26/27	Glasgow H.S.F.P.	x	h
29 s			
July 3	Uddingston		a
6 s	Glasgow H.S.F.P.	x	a
13 s			
20 s	Hillhead H.S.F.P.		a
27 s	Milngavie and Bearsden	x	a
Aug. 1	Partick XI (West of Scotland)		a
3 s	Drumpellier		a
10 s	Kelvinside Academicals	x	h
17 s	Golfhill	x	h
24 s	Anchor	x	a
31 s	Prestwick	x	a
Sept. 7 s			

x   Glasgow and District League
s   Saturday Match

SECOND ELEVEN FIXTURES.		
May 4 s	Milngavie and Bearsden	a
11 s	Babcock and Wilcox	a
18 s	Anchor	a
21	Uddingston Castle XI	h
25 s	Armadale	h
June 6	Stobcross	a
8 s	Prestwick	a
11	Kelvinside Academicals	a
15 s	Babcock and Wilcox	h
18	Stobcross	h
20	Uddingston Castle XI	a
22 s	Metropolitan Vickers	h
29 s	Albion Motors	a
July 4	Motherwell Burgh Staff	h
6 s	Collins	a
20 s	Hillhead H.S.F.P.	h
27 s	Milngavie and Bearsden	h
Aug.24 s	Albion Motors	h
31 s	Prestwick	h
Sept. 7 s	Collins	h

A MOTHERWELL XI - FIXTURES			
May 29	Woodhall	(W. & L.)	a
June 1 s	Metropolitan Vickers	L.	a
5	Honeywell Brown	L.	h
July 10	Strathaven	L.	h
to be arranged	Rolls Royce	L.	h

W   Wrangholm Cup
L.   Lanarkshire League

We find names that were part of the furniture for year after year – Babcock & Wilcox and Anchor, whose Blackhall ground had the most stunning Tudor-style pavilion. And Lanark too – our near neighbours who played at the racecourse.

One name from the 2nd team fixtures still brings a smile – Armadale. Their ground was never quite big enough, a factory wall standing not far behind the stumps.

There were local rules in place when the bowler ran in from the factory end, dictated by a horizontal line drawn on the wall. If you hit the ball over the line, it was a four; under the line, the ball was still in play and the batsmen kept running as the ball bounced off the wall. And you always had the jam sandwiches to look forward to at the tea interval. Proper cricket! Loved it!

Another fixture that was played almost every year since the

late 19th century was against Fauldhouse. A football manager would say, "It was never an easy place to go" – always a fiercely contested battle. Neighbouring tenements overlooked the wall that encircled the cricket ground, and some occupants took an active interest in the game.

On one occasion, when a Motherwell fielder took a towering catch, a woman who was hanging out of her tenement window was insistent that the fielder had stepped over the boundary rope to complete the catch. For the rest of the innings, in an atmosphere more akin to a football match, she gave voice to a tirade of abuse towards any Motherwell player who dared to field below her window.

And we could go on. These cards list games against teams like Thornliebank and Kilmacolm, Hillend and Old Grammarians, Ardeer and Bishopbriggs, Collins and Dunlop. We can remember their grounds, their characters and some close-fought tussles with every one of them.

Motherwell have made it, by hook or by crook, to our 150th year, and here we are wallowing in our long history. But that history would mean nothing without the memories of the games we played. Some clubs may no longer be around but we remember them well. So let's raise a glass to …

"Absent friends."

The Cherry Tree

For as long as we can remember, it was called the
'Cherry Tree'. But it wasn't a cherry tree, it was a plain
old chestnut tree, one of many within Dalzell Estate. It
stood there in all its splendour and was a landmark that
defined part of our ground's boundary.
You could climb the tree, sit in the shade of its impressive
canopy or shelter from the rain. In autumn, many waited
excitedly to gather its plentiful fruit, the conker.
And batsmen would boast about hitting a 6 into the
Cherry Tree, as if it required more skill than hitting any
other 6. In fact, as it was positioned at wide mid-wicket
for batsmen taking strike at the Muirhouse end, a slog to
cow corner usually did the trick. But it did seem special.

But it was just a tree, wasn't it?

The Cherry Tree had the pleasure of watching every cricketer who ever played at Home Park. It witnessed every ball bowled, every run scored and every game ever played.

The tree saw it all, from our early beginnings at Home Park through to the sad day when we had to leave our spiritual home.

It was our very own guardian angel looking over Motherwell Cricket Club for over a century. In this story, it even gets capital letters, like a King or Queen, or even God.

But, *spoiler alert*, the tree suffered disease not long after we entered the 21st century and had to be felled, a bit like a trusty old steed being put down. It had stood there, loud and proud, for well over 100 years … and that is something to be celebrated.

Now, where's this going? The tree is no more. Is that it? A story about a dead tree? Dead but deified. Well, read on and hopefully things will become a bit clearer!

It was only after we left in 1999 that the tree, its job done, succumbed to disease and waved goodbye to its arboreal friends in Dalzell Estate. Almost poetic!

If only we had a poet in our midst. If only we could summon the ghost of John Smellie Martin, our 1901 club captain and celebrated poet of his day. He could guide our hand as we celebrate the life of the Cherry Tree.

And here it is. A simple poem about a tree. The words are plain and uncomplicated and the poetry amateurish but, if you remember Home Park, this simple sonnet might just transport you back to a moment in time.

You may have donned the whites and played cricket, or you may have stopped to watch, or maybe you were up to something else down in Dalzell Estate. And you thought you were alone, unseen …

The Cherry Tree

The year's 1890, we came to Home Park.
Our tree's only small, just revealing its bark.
A puzzled young cricketer scratched his head,
"It's a chessie tree, son," a teammate said!
But "Cherry" not "Chessie," he heard, you see,

The Cherry Tree

So ever since then, it's 'The Cherry Tree'!

The name it stuck, for 100 years plus,
The tree raised a smile, no need to fuss,
From the place where it stood, it saw every match
Every ball bowled, every run, every catch.
From afar, it stood proud with its splendour on show,
As the years passed by, it watched our club grow.

The estate, well away from the grey of the town,
Home Park was pretty, the best ground around.
A pavilion was built in 1906,
A timber construction, rather than bricks.
Some toilets might have made more sense,
Instead we erected a racecourse fence.

The Great War began in 1914
Our ground went quiet, though an odd game was seen.
The second war started in '39,
Again we played on to slow the decline.
Our tree made a promise: again all would play
On the ground at Home Park, come what may.

Findlay was leader when war was won.
Hinshalwoods played, father and son.
Some fine players came, Crossley and Clark,
Then a bit later, Ritchie and Park.
Lots of talent, a very rich seam,
They all trialled for the national team.

We had Logan and Steel, Brady and Syme
For more than a decade, this was our time.
And Welsh and Smith, Johnston and Kerr

Our club at its strongest, all would aver.
Then came the Robertsons, Young, Shaw and Bill
The Cherry Tree bowed, admiring their skill.

The club grew and grew with faces weel kent
With Bonnar, Anderson, Sharp and Bent,
McGinley, Newton, Kelly, the Blacks
Harding and Learmonth, our tree knew the facts
Carrots and Jacko were two of the best,
The Tree was able to name all the rest.

When the old clubhouse burned, disappeared without trace,
A shiny new structure rose in its place.
Tom Barrie, as president, led from the front
He would not be defeated by fire-raising runts.
The Tree was impressed, more than just proud
To see the club opened by Ally Macleod.

The Cherry Tree's eye would be cast round our ground.
For old Willie Jardine, a legend renowned.
He appeared every week through a gap in the trees
To enjoy every game, our Tree always pleased.
He was Bill to his friends and played the kazoo
Our faithful old Tree loved his jazz, his blues.

We hosted some stars, these guys were big news,
There was Mujtaba, Sutcliffe and Aussie Kim Hughes.
In the '20s, we hosted a future prime minister,
In '99, our guests were more sinister.
Déjà vu, we had seen it before,
A clubhouse in flames … and then no more.

The Cherry Tree

On that cold April night, the flames soared high,
Players, officials with tears in their eyes,
Dressing rooms, bar and lounge all gone,
They headed back home, stifling a yawn.
To have played for so long, the end was in sight.
"No," said the tree, on that fateful spring night.

The pavilion was gone, but it wasn't the end.
Grant and Steve and their white-flanneled friends,
Continued the fight, hard work was needed,
Belief and commitment – again we succeeded.
Did we do this ourselves, or was something at work?
The Cherry Tree swayed with a smile and a smirk.

Just as we packed up to leave Home Park,
Disease took root in the Cherry Tree's bark.
It seemed like it knew that it's job was done,
The chainsaws arrived, and then it was gone.
It had guarded our door for 100 years.
Standing resplendent amongst its peers.

The tree's now gone, but let's not dismay,
It left a reminder for all those who played.
It dropped a chestnut, its seed was sown,
One day, might we see that tree fully grown?
It's the circle of life, some would say,
When times get tough, we'll find a way.

So here's to the future, let's leave the past
The years have gone by, we've all had a blast.
Please tell your kids you were part of the club,
Whether you played, or drank in the pub.
The cricket goes on, from ashes we rose,
The Cherry Tree watched, our secrets it knows.